364. 6809416 ERI

Justice in Transition

Justice in Transition
Community restorative justice in Northern Ireland

Anna Eriksson

WILLAN
PUBLISHING

Published by

Willan Publishing
Culmcott House
Mill Street, Uffculme
Cullompton, Devon
EX15 3AT, UK
Tel: +44(0)1884 840337
Fax: +44(0)1884 840251
e-mail: info@willanpublishing.co.uk
website: www.willanpublishing.co.uk

Published simultaneously in the USA and Canada by

Willan Publishing
c/o ISBS, 920 NE 58th Ave, Suite 300
Portland, Oregon 97213-3786, USA
Tel: +001(0)503 287 3093
Fax: +001(0)503 280 8832
e-mail: info@isbs.com
website: www.isbs.com

First published 2009

ISBN   978-1-84392-518-7 hardback

British Library Cataloguing-in-Publication Data

A catalogue record for this book is available from the British Library.

FSC
Mixed Sources
Product group from well-managed
forests and other controlled sources
Cert no. SGS-COC-2482
www.fsc.org
© 1996 Forest Stewardship Council

Project managed by Deer Park Productions, Tavistock, Devon
Typeset by GCS, Leighton Buzzard, Bedfordshire
Printed and bound by T.J. International Ltd, Padstow, Cornwall

Contents

Tables and figures   *vii*

Abbreviations   *viii*

Acknowledgements   *ix*

Foreword by Kieran McEvoy   *xi*

Introduction   *xiii*

1   Restorative justice: an introduction   **1**
Values and goals of restorative justice   3
Restorative justice and the contested community   11

**2   Restorative justice in transition and the case for
criminology**   **17**
Approaches to transitional justice and the argument for
grass-roots models   18
The emergence of criminology in transitional justice   21
Restorative justice on the edge: the transitional society   24

**3   Paramilitaries and vigilantes: punitive populism
as social control**   **33**
Informal justice in a historical Irish context   34
Paramilitary justice in Northern Ireland: the organised
community   36
Vigilantism: the disorganised community   48

4   **The beginning of CRJI and Alternatives: legitimising
      restorative justice in a punitive community**   **59**
      Establishing community restorative justice in Northern Ireland   59
      Paramilitaries and restorative justice: competing modes of
         informal social control   68
      Community reactions to restorative justice   70

5   **The practice of community restorative justice in
      Northern Ireland**   **80**
      Community Restorative Justice Ireland   81
      Reintegration and restorative justice   89
      Northern Ireland Alternatives   96
      Challenging cultures of violence through restorative
         justice: transforming communities in transition   105

6   **Volunteers and practitioners: leadership in a culture
      of violence**   **123**
      Volunteers in community restorative justice   124
      Restorative justice, ex-prisoners and leadership in transition   129

7   **State–community partnerships in transition: a question
      of trust**   **139**
      Bridge-building and partnerships from 'below'   141
      Bridge-building from 'above' and the regulatory state   148

8   **The road less travelled: policing and partnerships
      in transition**   **160**
      Legitimisation of former adversaries   162
      The beginning of partnerships   168

Conclusion: Rethinking restorative justice   **182**

Appendix A: Paramilitary groups in Northern Ireland   **192**
Republican organisations   192
Loyalist organisations   194

**Appendix B: Timeline for key events and government
documents relating to community restorative justice in
Northern Ireland**   **197**

References   *204*

Index   *224*

Tables and figures

Table 3.1   Paramilitary attacks 1989–2006   47

Figure 3.1   Paramilitary-style shootings and assaults in
Northern Ireland   46

Figure 5.1   Source of referrals to CRJI Belfast in 2007   82

Figure 5.2   All cases by category referred to CRJI Belfast
in 2007   83

Figure 5.3   Case statistics for CRJI Belfast in 2007   84

Figure 5.4   Reasons for unresolved cases at CRJI Belfast
in 2007   90

Figure 7.1   Outside agencies involved in CRJI cases in 2007   145

Abbreviations

AP	Atlantic Philanthropies
Alternatives	Northern Ireland Alternatives
CIRA	Continuity Irish Republican Army
CRJI	Community Restorative Justice Ireland
DUP	Democratic Unionist Party
ICC	International Criminal Court
ICTR	International Criminal Tribunal for Rwanda
ICTY	International Criminal Tribunal for Former Yugoslavia
IMC	International Monitoring Commission
LVF	Loyalist Volunteer Force
MLA	Member of the Legislative Assembly
NIA	Northern Ireland Alternatives
NIACRO	Northern Ireland Association for the Care and Resettlement of Offenders
NIHE	Northern Ireland Housing Executive
NIO	Northern Ireland Office
OIRA	Official Irish Republican Army
PIRA	Provisional Irish Republican Army – also known as the IRA
PSNI	Police Service of Northern Ireland
PUP	Progressive Unionist Party
RHC	Red Hand Commando
RIRA	Real Irish Republican Army
RUC	Royal Ulster Constabulary
SDLP	Social Democratic Labour Party
TRC	Truth and Reconciliation Commission
UDA	Ulster Defence Association
UUP	Ulster Unionist Party
UVF	Ulster Volunteer Force
YJA	Youth Justice Agency

Acknowledgements

This book started its life as a PhD thesis undertaken at Queen's University Belfast, and became a monograph after moving with me to Monash University, Melbourne. It has been an extraordinary experience. Some days were less than fun and the computer no friend of mine. However, I have had more good times than I'd ever imagined when this journey began, thanks in no small part to the people I met along the way.

Above all, a most sincere thank you to all staff and volunteers at Community Restorative Justice Ireland and Northern Ireland Alternatives, for the unprecedented access which facilitated this research. They are an extraordinary group of people who introduced me not only to the intricacies of Northern Ireland but also to their own lives, and for that I will always be immensely grateful. This is their story, and it has been an absolute privilege to be able to tell it. Any mistakes and unusual academic interpretations included in this book are very much my own.

Thanks also to all other interviewees who generously gave their time and shared their experiences with me. Their candid comments have had an important impact on the discussions in this book, and I am very appreciative of the significant work they do in this time of transition in Northern Ireland. In particular, the Police Service of Northern Ireland, the Northern Ireland Housing Executive, the Northern Ireland Probation Board, the Social Services, the Youth Justice Agency, and representatives from political parties, thank you so very much. The individuals I spoke with know who they are, and I very much hope to continue our discussions in the near future.

Kieran McEvoy, who has travelled this journey with me through good days and bad – first as the supervisor of my PhD thesis at Queen's University Belfast and later as a colleague and friend even though I have temporarily deserted the shores of Northern Ireland in moving to the other side of the world – thank you. Always.

And a sincere thank you to Professors Shad Maruna and Heather Strang who as examiners of the original thesis provided important and valuable feedback and encouragement.

And thanks to all other friends and colleagues at Queen's – who provided a supportive, challenging and exciting environment for a PhD student with a funny accent. In particular, thanks are extended to Louise Mallinder and Vicky Conway, dear friends and colleagues, who probably know more about this journey than is healthy – we will soon share a pint in the Parlour beer garden – weather permitting, that is.

Writing a PhD thesis can sometimes be a lonely and frustrating experience. Hence, a very special thank you goes to the extraordinary staff and residents at the De Paul Trust in Belfast. You know you've had a bad day when someone who has been put out of their home by paramilitaries and who is trying to put their life back together tells you, 'You look like shite' and 'Do you want a cup of tea?' Apart from making me feel worthwhile for doing a decent job, they also provided me with hope and the conviction that Northern Ireland is filled with people of resilience, courage and good humour in the face of adversity and that it will take a lot more than 30 years of violent conflict to break their spirit.

In Australia, thank you to Sanja Milivojevic, who not only suffered through early drafts of this book and provided invaluable feedback, but who also made my own transition from Belfast to Melbourne a brilliant experience and who has become a friend for life. Sydney is lucky to have you. And a very big thanks to my new colleagues at Monash University, both academic and general staff, who have provided invaluable support and encouragement during the writing of this book. And Heli Askola, my fellow Scandinavian (even though we pretend that Finland is much better than Sweden), thank you for providing frank and welcome feedback on individual chapters, and for accepting my home-cooked food by way of payment.

Last, but never least, my most heartfelt thank you to my family: Mum, Dad and Syster Yster Maria, for their encouragement, support and unwavering faith throughout this process. Thank you for keeping me sane, and for giving me a place to rest when life becomes a bit too much. This project is finally finished, and I even got a 'real' job at the end of it!

Foreword

Belfast can be an unforgiving place. As the novelist David Parks wrote, this is a place that eulogises a ship that sank and an alcoholic footballer – the Titanic and George Best to the uninitiated. Perhaps it is the harsh history of industrialisation and centuries of sustained violence, or our legendary certainties as to the rightness of those historic enmities, or the pitch black sense of humour of the city's citizenry – whatever the reasons, it is not a place that suffers academic pretensions lightly. For the years of her PhD, Anna Eriksson, a Swede, educated in Australia and Cambridge, immersed herself in the unlikely setting of community-based restorative justice projects in some of the most socio-economically deprived areas of the city. *Justice in Transition* is the book that emerged from that thesis and the results are impressive. In a thoughtful, measured and persuasive fashion, Eriksson charts the development of these programmes, the tensions between community-based and state structures concerning the 'ownership' of justice, the role that the projects have played in transforming cultures of violence, and the theoretical insights to restorative justice more broadly which the Northern Ireland experience has to offer.

The community-based projects of which Eriksson writes have enjoyed a high profile both nationally and internationally over the last decade. Numerous television documentaries, newspaper articles, magazine features, a number of 'popular' books and an increasing range of scholarly outputs have discussed the putative merits and demerits of the programs. Unlike Eriksson, many of the most critical of these efforts have been largely unencumbered by data. The fact that the projects emerged from direct dialogue with paramilitary organisations and are run by former Loyalists and Republican combatants obviously made them noteworthy. In addition, their emergence coincided with an often vicious contest concerning the legitimacy of state policing in the jurisdiction and the projects often appeared to suffer collateral damage in the ensuing political dog-fights. More broadly, the work of the projects well illustrates broader criminological concerns regarding legitimacy and capacity of state justice systems in *delivering* justice in settled societies in general and transitional societies in particular. Informed by her fieldwork, and with theoretical aplomb, Anna Eriksson has captured well the nuances and subtleties of these competing dynamics.

Eriksson charts how projects which were initially designed to supplant systems of violent informalism practiced by paramilitaries groups during the conflict, have grown in scope and ambition to a range of broader community mediation work. She argues that despite their past acts of politically motivated violence, the theory and practice of restorative justice resonated strongly with the ideology and politics of former combatants. She details the tortured evolution of the relationship between the local police and these projects which continues to develop apace. Finally she argues that the high politics involved in the development of the Belfast projects has contributed directly to the sophistication of the practice of many of those involved, the nature of their relations with local communities and their determination to engage with statutory organisations as equal partners rather than passive service providers.

I have every confidence that this book will become a key reference point in the literature on community, restorative and transitional justice and Anna fully deserves every scholarly accolade which will follow. In addition however, those highly committed, politicised and deeply cynical Belfast practitioners whom she studied will recognise a fair, objective and 'warts and all' account of their work. Anna Eriksson's book is 'a fair enough account' I suspect will be the verdict. In Belfast, in these circles in particular, that counts as effusive praise indeed.

Professor Kieran McEvoy, Director, Institute of Criminology and Criminal Justice, Queens University Belfast.

Introduction

Informal practices of dispute resolution in the Global North have waxed and waned in popularity over the last three decades. They came to prominence in the 1970s as an alternative approach to the dominant utilitarian and retributive philosophies of punishment, in part as a practical and symbolic expression of disillusionment with the effectiveness of the formal criminal justice system (Abel 1982a, b; Matthews 1988; Mani 2002). They were also a response to widespread dissatisfaction with the increased punitiveness in sentencing, the self-evident risks associated with stigmatisation of offenders, the professionalisation of justice delivery, net-widening, and the remoteness of the judiciary from the community and its needs and interests. Such factors led 'to arguments for more localised forums involving a genuine level of public participation' (see also Matthews 1988: 5; Marshall 1988; Mani 2002). Informal alternatives, it was argued, would offer more flexibility and 'produce greater community involvement in the process of settling disputes which in turn would strengthen social bonds, repair social relations and ultimately help to re-establish social cohesion' (Matthews 1988: 7). Several different terms have been associated with informal modes of dispute processing and resolution – for example, 'popular', 'community', or simply 'alternative' justice. As Munck (1988) has noted, they are all terms that effectively have the same meaning, as all refer to processes which take place outside the formal justice system and its adversarial procedures (Matthews 1998; Knox and Monaghan 2002), such as mediation, reconciliation, arbitration and reparation.

Much optimism surrounded the revival of informal justice in the 1970s and 1980s, and a similar enthusiasm was evident in relation to the restorative justice movement in the 1990s. This fervour frequently emanated from the assertion that informal and restorative measures were a return to 'natural' or 'universal' principles of justice, with their cultural and historical roots in traditional and indigenous societies around the globe (Abel 1982a, b; Zehr 1990; Van Ness 1993; Sullivan and Tifft 2001, 2006). As such, it resonated strongly with those who argued that the state had too much influence over the instruments and methods of social control, in effect excluding people from their own conflicts (Christie 1977), with a resulting loss of responsibility and accountability for their actions. Active participation in informal justice processes, it was argued, would create civic responsibility and a regeneration of 'community', through more direct and active involvement of the people affected by a dispute (Bazemore 2001).

However, informal justice has also been the subject of intense and sustained critique, eloquently summed up by Maureen Cain (1985) as 'informal justice ... [is] unnecessary, that it has failed, that it is sinister, and that it is impossible' (p. 52). Further, it has been argued that informal approaches to dispute resolution can lead to a two-tier justice system, with one option (the courts) for the rich, and another for the poor. It is also said to result in not only fewer legal and human rights protections for victims and offenders, but also different expressions of violence, such as vigilantism (Matthews 1988; Knox and Monaghan 2002; Mani 2002). Such critiques tend to focus mainly on attempts at informal justice that have failed, some of which led to large-scale violence (Abel 1982a, b; Matthews 1988). The usual riposte to such criticism is a defensive formalism (McEvoy and Mika 2002; McEvoy and Eriksson 2008), saying, in effect, that justice is best left in the hands of the state. Critics have also questioned 'the relevance and feasibility of community-based informal justice at a time when the widespread reality in most societies is observed to be fragmenting communities and crumbling values' (Mani 2002: 37).

McEvoy and Mika (2002) have taken up the challenge of such criticism and used it as a template around which to analyse community restorative justice schemes in Northern Ireland. They conclude that 'the Northern Ireland experience suggests grounds for a rejection of the cynicism of "nothing works"' (p. 534). The critique of informalism as it relates to Northern Ireland is 'crude and dated', as it fails to take into account the impact of restorative justice in mitigating against exclusionary, authoritarian or indeed state-dominated versions of informalism which have been rightly criticised elsewhere. Informalism is indeed possible. It is possible when it is based upon a genuine commitment to the values and practice of restorative justice; located in politically organized and dynamic communities; well managed and staffed by committed volunteers; and guided by locally developed standards of practice which are based upon accepted human rights principles. (p. 556)

Hence, the practice of community restorative justice in Northern Ireland can be seen to constitute a revival of the positive aspects of informal justice.[1]

The paramilitary ceasefires and the signing of the Good Friday Agreement in 1998 did not lead to an end of violence in Northern Ireland (Jarman 2004). Paramilitary 'policing' and some vigilante actions have been utilised since the beginning of the conflict, and they have proven difficult to eradicate in the transitional phase. In fact, such forms of violence increased for a period after the signing of the Good Friday Agreement (McEvoy and Mika 2001, 2002; Feenan 2002; Monaghan 2002, 2004; Jarman 2004). This pattern is common to many other transitional societies, where a decrease in political violence occurs simultaneously with an increase in ordinary violence and crime (Shirlow and Murtagh 2006). Sectarian attacks are still taking place and interface violence intensified again during 2005, leading to renewed degeneration in community relations and tensions between state and community (Brewer *et al.* 1998; Monaghan 2002, 2004; Jarman 2004). Added to this are the consequences of renewed violence by dissident paramilitary organisations in 2008. New types of violence have also entered the picture, taking the form of racist and homophobic attacks (Jarman 2004), and organised crime is now an established feature, the effects of which are experienced across community divides and social classes (Maguire 1993; Knox 2002; Jarman 2004). These different expressions of crime and disorder are arguably manifestations of an ingrained culture of violence (Steenkamp 2005), a feature of many post-conflict societies.[2]

Despite this culture of violence, as a transitional society, Northern Ireland differs quite radically from several other post-conflict countries in that many geographical areas and economic structures were largely untouched by the conflict. Moreover, as the country is a part of the European Union, the economic position of Northern Ireland is relatively strong compared to transitional societies elsewhere, allowing rapid and ambitious regeneration projects to take place. Indeed, Northern Ireland seems like a 'normal' society in many ways, and it is mainly the working-class areas most affected by the Troubles[3] that today struggle to find ways of dealing with the legacy of the conflict and moving forward.

The community-based restorative justice projects in Republican and Loyalist communities in Northern Ireland which are at the centre of the discussions in this book are arguably some of the most high-profile developments of restorative justice in the world.[4] The projects – Community Restorative Justice Ireland (CRJI) in Republican communities and Northern Ireland Alternatives ('Alternatives') in Loyalist areas – are led by ex-political prisoners and former combatants of the Provisional Irish Republican Army (IRA) and the Ulster Volunteer force (UVF), respectively, the backgrounds of whom have caused much controversy within Northern Ireland. These projects were established in 1998, with the explicit aim of providing a non-violent alternative to practices of paramilitary 'policing' and punishment violence in both communities (Auld *et al.* 1997; Winston 1997; McEvoy and Mika 2001, 2002). Such punishment violence formed part of an informal system of 'justice' that involved shootings (of arms, legs, joints, or a combination) and/or beatings (with baseball bats, iron bars, cudgels or hurley sticks), for the purpose of punishing offenders of crime and antisocial behaviour and as a means of securing internal discipline within paramilitary organisations. Measures such as warnings, curfews and exclusions from the community were also common (Bell 1996; Feenan 2002b; Hamill 2002; Monaghan 2002; Jarman 2004). The existence of such an informal system of 'justice' was not a problem confined to local communities, but signified a direct challenge to the legitimacy of the Northern Irish state, resulting in an intense politicisation of informal justice and a high-profile contest between community and state over the ownership of justice. Politicisation in this instance refers not only to the violent systems of punishment violence, but also to the community-based restorative justice alternatives that surpassed it.

Some authors have argued that punishment violence in Northern Ireland was a straightforward question of community oppression and control by hegemonic paramilitary organisations (see Silke 1998a, b; 1999; 2000a, b). This is, however, only part of the truth, the reality being much more complex. As McEvoy (2003) has persuasively argued, such informal systems of 'policing' are best viewed as:

a complex interplay between the contested legitimacy of state policing (particularly in Republican areas); a reliance upon and demand for paramilitary retribution by local communities; the organisational capacity and self-image of the paramilitary groups as 'protectors' of their communities; and the emergence of groups of alienated young antisocial men who viewed punishment violence as an occupational hazard of their lifestyles and in some instances, as a badge of honour. (p. 322)

Community restorative justice projects in Northern Ireland, which emerged as a non-violent alternative to such practices, clearly demonstrate an acute awareness of such multifaceted reasons underpinning practices of punishment violence, both during their establishment phase and their subsequent practice (Auld *et al.* 1997; Winston 1997). I have aimed to transfer such an awareness to my own analyses of the practices and potential of community restorative justice in Northern Ireland. This relates not only to informal systems of social control within the jurisdiction, but also to understandings of the leadership potential of ex-political prisoners and former combatants; the construction and role of communities in transition; deeply embedded cultures of violence; and the merging of informal and formal social control through the formation of partnerships between communities and statutory organisations, including the police. These dynamics take place within a sharply divided society where an intense politicisation of crime and justice at both state and community levels is a constant feature, reflected in a great deal of controversy surrounding restorative justice in Northern Ireland evident throughout the researching and writing of this book.[5] Importantly, the community restorative justice projects are unique in that they were established and have operated independently of the state, representing a truly grass-roots response to local problems with crime and antisocial behaviour.

The book traces the development and practice of these projects, from their commencement in 1998 to their contemporary form in 2008. The discussions focus on their day-to-day work, the leadership provided by ex-political prisoners, the possibility of challenging embedded cultures of violence in the transitional context, and the latest developments toward a formal working relationship with the criminal justice system. These partnerships represent an unprecedented development in Northern Ireland, where for the first time Republican communities and the Police Service of Northern Ireland (PSNI) are forming working partnerships in the aftermath of 35 years of violent conflict. CRJI and Alternatives occupy a key role in these changes, acting both as facilitators and transformers of social control – through the practice of community restorative justice – within the transitional context.

The arguments in this book are based on access to the different community projects between 2004 and 2008, significantly adding to previous publications which have touched on the subject of community restorative justice in Northern Ireland. The arguments and tensions outlined above have been investigated through a combination of qualitative and quantitative methods, including interviews with all practitioners of community restorative justice in Republican and Loyalist communities (the majority of whom are former political prisoners or ex-combatants), and samples of volunteers, victims, offenders and families who have participated in these projects. This style of embedded ethnography with former combatants from both Loyalist and Republican backgrounds is extremely rare and provides useful insights into the role that these people play in the post-conflict context. Moreover, quantitative data covering over 1,500 cases have been collected and analysed in their own right, including 200 cases from the last period of field research (December 2007 – January 2008) that exclusively involve projects working directly with the police. Interviews with statutory agencies and political party representatives were also conducted, including the PSNI, Northern Ireland Housing Executive (HE), the Probation Board, Social Services, Criminal Justice Inspectorate (CJI), the Youth Justice Agency (YJA), the Democratic Unionist Party (DUP), Sinn Féin, the Social Democratic Labour Party (SDLP), and the Progressive Unionist Party (PUP). The majority of groups and individuals were interviewed twice: once during the initial field research between 2004 and 2007, which formed the basis of a PhD thesis, and again in light of new developments in Northern Ireland, in December 2007 and January 2008. The aim of the combined qualitative and quantitative methods is to provide as complete a picture as possible of these projects and the dynamics surrounding them. Moreover, the empirical discussions around community restorative justice in Northern Ireland follow the sequential timeline of events as they developed on the ground, providing the underlying narrative of the book.

There have been several empirically robust evaluations of restorative justice programmes in other jurisdictions (Moore and Forsyth 1995; Daly et al. 1998; McCold and Wachtel 1998; Strang et al. 1999; Daly 2001), and recently in Northern Ireland (see Campbell et al. 2005) in relation to the formal criminal justice system. These have generally been concerned with comparative studies of recidivism rates, victim satisfaction, and procedural justice compared to formal court proceedings. However, criminological research in a transitional society is an inherently political exercise, and an analysis of restorative justice alternatives in such a context will arguably follow the same trajectory. Consequently, this book takes a critical view of the impact that the composition of a community can have on restorative practices, keeping in mind the dangers of community as a site of exclusionary practices or unequal power relationships (e.g. Etzioni 1994; Boutellier 1997 2001; Crawford 1999a; Pavlich 2001, 2004, 2005; Mulcahy 2006). The approach is one of critical analysis of the tensions around ownership of justice in transitional societies, tensions which are also highly relevant to many contemporary Western societies. Furthermore, this book seeks to theorise better the link between restorative justice and transition from conflict within a 'bottom-up' framework, as opposed to the more usual 'top-down' application of the concept through institutions such as truth and reconciliation commissions (e.g. Van Zyl 1999; Villa-Vincencio 1999, 2006; Teitel 2000; Hayner 2002; McEvoy 2007).

The transitional context presents several challenges to research, but also new opportunities. McEvoy and Mika (2002) have argued that, instead of limiting the remit of criminological evaluation to the usual benchmarks,

> the transitional nature of the Northern Ireland context presents an opportunity to go much further ... where [community-based restorative justice can be] a catalyst for transforming relationships of power through advocacy, group and community development and organization, and empowerment. (2002: 553)

Subjects that need to be taken into account are, to name a few, the transformation of the attitudes of combatants and former combatants to violence as a mechanism of social control; the views and behaviour of communities with respect to alleged antisocial elements; and the reshaping of criminal justice agencies and their structures, practices and occupational cultures (McEvoy 2003). Furthermore, equally important as these larger structural and political issues are the procedural aims of any specific restorative initiative against which its success can be judged. These include empowering key participants (victim, offender and community), repairing the harm caused by conflict, reintegrating offenders and victims, and shifting communal response to conflict from violent to non-violent approaches through community education.

Despite the plethora of publications on the subject of restorative justice, the majority focus on initiatives that are established, controlled and funded by the state (see Johnstone 2002; Bazemore and Umbreit 2003; Roche 2003; Walgrave 2003; Johnstone and Van Ness 2007), as opposed to truly community-based alternatives. There is also a substantial body of literature on informal justice, albeit rather dated (see Abel 1982a, b; Matthews 1998). There is, however, a dearth of literature that theoretically and practically links the older informal justice debates with contemporary restorative justice discourses,[6] and the Northern Irish experience can contribute to filling this gap.

Outline of this book

Restorative justice is a field under development, reflected in the debates surrounding its 'appropriate' application, the values and processes that should be core to its practice, the types of cases with which such processes should deal, and the ideal nature of the relationship between the formal criminal justice system and the more informal processes of restorative justice (Sharpe 2004). Chapter 1 explores some of these main debates within the literature, with particular attention paid to the definition, practice, and the key stakeholders of restorative justice, whereas Chapter 2 explores applications of restorative justice in the transitional context. The aim of these two chapters is to provide a theoretical backdrop to some of the key issues, and situates restorative and transitional justice within the broader criminological literature.

Chapter 3 explores the different modes of informal social control adopted within Republican and Loyalist communities in Northern Ireland. These modes include paramilitary systems of 'policing', vigilantism and restorative justice. The discussion is set within the social context of traditional working-class areas, characterised by alienation from the state (particularly in Nationalist areas), relatively high levels of crime, high unemployment, and a large proportion of young people. Moreover, these communities are denoted by sharp community borders, dividing them physically, geographically, socially and psychologically from 'the other' community.

Chapters 4, 5 and 6 discuss different aspects of the practice of community restorative justice in Northern Ireland, including the establishment process of the projects, the issues faced in their day-to-day work, the potential of challenging ingrained cultures of violence through the practice of restorative justice, and the important role played by volunteers and ex-political prisoners within the application of restorative justice in transition.

Chapters 7 and 8 examine the merging of informal and formal social control within the current transitional context. Importantly, I will outline how community restorative justice — as one mode of informal social control – is acting as a facilitator for the changes that are currently taking place. This has been particularly the case in Nationalist communities since the Republican political party Sinn Féin formally acknowledged the PSNI in early 2007.[7] The social milieu within which these developments are taking place is characterised by rapid social change, and a tangible tension between communities and the criminal justice system in Northern Ireland. I will discuss how partnerships between such former enemies are slowly emerging, as well as the obstacles, challenges and positive directions of these changes. It will be argued that community restorative justice is acting as a vital 'conduit' between community and police and that it provides the space and processes through which such difficult exchanges can be facilitated. These developments are unprecedented in this context and contain valuable lessons for partnerships around community crime prevention between the state and formerly alienated communities elsewhere.

The arguments in this book speak to broader debates within restorative justice by exploring the extent to which the framework may be applied to much more serious incidents of violence and criminality, rather than the traditional focus on its efficacy for juvenile and minor crimes. Consequently, the Conclusion argues for a broader and more courageous application of restorative justice – to communities marked by violence, exclusion and historical injustice – and for the possibility of transformative justice within the context of rapid social change. Moreover, and perhaps somewhat ambitiously, the book aims to contribute to the emerging literature on a criminological approach to peace-building,[8] within both post-conflict societies and high-crime communities elsewhere.

Notes

1 Such a view, however, is not one to which everyone subscribes. The projects have also been the subject of intense and sustained criticism from a range of different sources, much of it echoing the 'dangers of informal justice' outlined above, which will be discussed in more detail in Chapters 7 and 8.

2 For a further analysis in relation to the culture of violence and restorative justice in Northern Ireland, see Eriksson (2008).

3 The conflicting political and religious differences between Catholics and Protestants have existed for centuries, but reached their peak in the late 1960s in what is commonly referred to as 'the Troubles'. This period in Northern Ireland's history is generally seen to have continued up until 1998 when the peace agreement was signed. Contrary to common opinion, the conflict was not about religion per se, but rather about issues of self-governance, economic independence, and political representation, and was ethno-national in character (Whyte 1991; Holter *et al.* 2006). The differences between the two communities – Protestant/Unionist/Loyalist and Catholic/Nationalist/Republican – then and now, are made even more stark by the physical sectarian separation of the two groups, such that communities and their boundaries are marked by flags, painted kerbstones and murals, and in some places by what are known as 'peace walls'.

4 In Northern Ireland, restorative justice practices were also introduced as a new initiative within the formal criminal justice system in December 2003, with the use of conferencing when dealing with juvenile offenders. The programme is administered by the Youth Justice Agency (YJA). For an evaluation of this initiative, see Campbell *et al.* 2005.

5 A large body of literature wrestles with Northern Ireland's recent history, with the majority of writings falling within the areas of politics and conflict resolution (see Whyte 1991; Tonge 1998; Coulter 1999; English 2003; McGarry and O'Leary 2004). A detailed description of the background to the conflict and the period between 1969 and 1998, commonly referred to as 'the Troubles', has been sacrificed in favour of clarity and succinctness. The book focuses instead on themes that are of direct relevance to the praxis of community restorative justice.

6 For some exceptions, see Mika and McEvoy 2001; McEvoy and Mika 2002.

7 On 28 January 2007, Sinn Féin held a special party conference to permit its ruling executive to support policing and justice structures, in effect 'signing up to policing'. The motion supported at this conference read: 'Support the Police Service of Northern Ireland (PSNI) and the criminal justice system; Hold the police and criminal justice system north and south fully to account, both democratically and legally, on the basis of fairness and impartiality and objectivity; Authorise our elected representatives to participate in local policing structures in the interest of justice, the quality of life for the community and to secure policing with the community as the core function of the PSNI and actively encouraging everyone in the community to co-operate fully with the police services in tackling crime in all areas and actively supporting all the criminal justice institutions'. See Ard Fheis Motion passed by Sinn Féin Ard Fheis – 28 January 2007, at www.sinnfeinonline.com/policies (last visited on 26 November 2008).

8   In the UN Secretary-General's Agenda for Peace in 1992, peace-building was defined as 'actions to identify and support structures which will tend to strengthen and solidify peace in order to avoid a relapse into conflict'. Lederach offers a conceptual framework wherein he describes peace-building as 'a comprehensive approach to the transformation of conflict that addresses the structural issues, social dynamics of relationship building, and the development of a supportive infrastructure for peace'. Boutros-Ghali emphasises the social and economic aspects of peace-building and states that 'only sustained, co-ordinated work to deal with underlying economic, social, cultural and humanitarian problems can place an achieved peace on a durable foundation' (1992). It has also been noted that peace-building needs to be domestically rooted and 'owned' by the local population, and the role of international actors should be to facilitate peace-building, not impose or dictate its terms (Mani 2002). Moreover, John Braithwaite and colleagues have recently begun an expansive and ambitious research project, which will be conducted over a 20-year period, investigating peace-building efforts after conflict in 48 countries. More details about the project and reports published so far can be viewed at: http://peacebuilding.anu.edu.au/index.php.

Chapter 1

Restorative justice: an introduction

Restorative justice has been presented as a response to crime that promotes inclusive dialogue, acceptance of responsibility, reparation of harm, and rebuilding of relations among victims, offenders and communities (Christie 1977; Braithwaite 1989; Hayes *et al.* 1998; Walgrave 1998; Tutu 1999; Ahmed *et al.* 2001; Roche 2001; Strang and Braithwaite 2001). As one approach within the informal tradition of dispute resolution, restorative justice is most commonly used to describe non-adjudicative methods of solving conflict that give victims, offenders and the community a central role in decision making (Braithwaite 1989; Roach 2000). A fundamental tenet of the restorative justice paradigm is a shift in accountability – from offenders owing a debt to society for their criminal behaviour, to being directly accountable to their victim(s) (Corrado *et al.* 2003) – with a focus on problem solving and on repairing harm (Umbreit 1995).

Restorative justice has also been portrayed as an original and natural way of dealing with conflict (Zehr 1990; Van Ness 1993; Sullivan and Tifft 2001; Sullivan and Tifft 2006). As argued by Braithwaite (2002a), 'restorative justice has been the dominant model of criminal justice throughout most of human history for perhaps all the world's people' (p. 5). He argues elsewhere that 'restorative justice is grounded in moral intuitions of considerable resonance for most people because they have a long history, particularly in the spirituality of the world's greatest religions' (2003: 1). Daly (2002) has referred to such claims as 'extraordinary', and they have also been criticised for being somewhat romanticised and, as such, having a tendency to gloss over the negative aspects of restorative or informal justice in favour of highlighting the positives (Johnstone 2002; Roche 2003).

Restorative justice is frequently contrasted with retributive justice, where the former is portrayed as 'good' or 'superior' and the latter as 'evil' or inferior'. For example, Howard Zehr (1990) has described how retributive justice focuses on the violation of law, whereas restorative justice shifts the focus to the violation of people and relationships. While retributive justice seeks to vindicate law by determining blame and administering punishment, restorative justice seeks to vindicate victims by acknowledging their injury and by creating obligations for those responsible to make things right. Furthermore, retributive justice involves the state and the offender in a formal process of adjudication, whereas restorative justice is an informal, consensual, decision-making process involving victims, offenders and community members in a search for solutions – a distinction highlighted by several authors (see Daly 2000b; Van Ness *et al.* 2001; Roche 2003). Such dichotomies, however, do not necessarily engage with the question of what restorative justice is; rather they explain what restorative justice *is not* (Daly 2002). They have also been dubbed false and misleading (Barton 2000), as both frameworks have strengths and weaknesses. Importantly, if a retributive system is to be *replaced* with a restorative one, as some proponents argue (Walgrave 2000), one needs to be assured that the situation will not be made worse in the eagerness to do better. As asserted by Johnstone:

> We need to ask whether a shift to restorative justice would result in a whole range of deleterious consequences such as a trivialisation of evil, a loss of security, a less fair system, an undesirable extension of police power, an erosion of important procedural safeguards, unwelcome net-widening, or weakening of already weak parties. (2002: 7)

Such comments generally refer to restorative justice programmes that are firmly embedded within the formal criminal justice system.[1] One argument could be that these dangers of restorative practices may very well be minimised when a programme or initiative is located *outside* criminal justice institutions, where the power of the state is dispersed. However, the concern then shifts to one about the 'dangers of community' (Pavlich 2004) – a question which will be returned to later.

In practice, restorative justice programmes typically aim to bring together the victim and the offender for the purpose of allowing both sides to understand the context of the offence and the impact of the offence on both parties, and, usually, to establish some kind of reparation outcome, which is agreed upon through a process of consensual decision making (Braithwaite 1989; Walgrave 1995; Bazemore and Umbreit 2003). Since restorative justice covers a wide range of practices – not all in relation to criminal behaviour – definitions, values and goals vary depending on the context. Some are more inclusive than others, and it has been argued that these differences stem largely from the fact that restorative justice theory has developed through practice (Ashworth 2002).

The contentiousness surrounding the definition of restorative justice is also reflected in its application. Several models are associated with restorative justice practice, with three in particular generally claimed to encompass the core values of the paradigm: victim–offender mediation, family group conferencing, and sentencing circles. All have been extensively covered in the literature (see Morris and Maxwell 1993; Braithwaite and Mugford 1994; Umbreit 2000; Van Ness et al. 2001; Johnstone 2002; Roche 2003), and will not be explored in any detail here; what is perhaps more interesting in the context of this book is the debate in relation to restorative justice as a process- or goal-oriented practice. As will be discussed later, community restorative practices in Northern Ireland take a process view, arguing that the process is central to the work they do, with certain important values guiding that process. What form the process takes – whether conferencing, or direct or indirect mediation – is of less importance; rather, the process is based on participants' needs and as a consequence is inherently flexible in its application. Firstly, however, the following section will briefly discuss the values and goals of restorative justice, some of which differ among the various models and others which are generally seen as central for any process to be called restorative (Johnstone 2002; Roche 2003). The particular values discussed are also those which practitioners and volunteers of community restorative justice in Northern Ireland identified as central to their work during the research.

Values and goals of restorative justice

If restorative justice is to emerge as a justice paradigm, a shared vocabulary and parameters of the theory need to be established. ... Theory, research, and practice cannot proceed without a shared understanding of fundamental terms and

3

ways to operationalize those understandings. (McCold 2000: 359)

Many writers have attempted to define what they see as the key goals of restorative justice, the most commonly agreed upon being participation and consensual decision making, healing what is broken, accountability of offenders, reducing recidivism, and restoring relationships through the reintegration of both victim and offender into the community (Maxwell *et al.* 2006). Restorative justice further aims to restore emotionally and empower the key stakeholders of a crime, and can potentially increase empathy, understanding and respect for all participants (Christie 1977; Touval and Zartman 1985; Braithwaite and Mugford 1994; Van Ness and Strong 1997; Sullivan and Tifft 2001; Johnstone 2002; Weitekamp and Kerner 2002).

The core values of restorative justice, as far as they can commonly be agreed upon, tend to cluster around concepts of inclusion, reintegration, democracy, responsibility, reparation and healing (Braithwaite and Mugford 1994; Johnstone 2002; Sharpe 2004). Other fundamental principles include ensuring community protection/ safety, promoting offender responsibility, and removing the stigma of crime (Umbreit 1995). Declan Roche (2003) summarised the different opinions regarding the values of restorative justice in *Accountability in Restorative Justice,* in which he identifies four core values: personalism, participation, reparation and reintegration. I have found these values both theoretically persuasive and closely resonant with the practice of community restorative justice in Northern Ireland. In addition, it will be argued that empowerment should be a fifth and crucial value of restorative justice interventions due to the centrality it assumes within the Northern Ireland context and in other transitional societies.

Personalism

This refers to the approach of restorative justice that crime is a violation of, or injury to, people and their relationships, not a mere violation of law. This violation or injury extends beyond the victim's suffering, as it also includes the impact on offenders, the families of both victims and offenders, and the wider community. This can be contrasted to the impersonal nature of the formal criminal justice system, where the physical and emotional damage to everyone involved is suppressed. One reason why this occurs is because the sentence is not based on the needs of the stakeholders (victims, offenders and community) but on legal precedents.

Participation

Restorative justice encourages the participation of the people most directly affected by the crime – victims, offenders, and their communities – to take part jointly in the resolution of the conflict. This value is crucial to restorative justice, and is recognised in Tony Marshall's much cited definition:

> Restorative justice is a process whereby all the parties with a stake in a particular offence come together to resolve collectively how to deal with the aftermath of the offence and its implication for the future. (1996: 37)

It is also important that participation involve a collective and consensual decision-making process. Such processes promote the values of reparation and reintegration through the empowerment of participants, and can also act as a crucial informal accountability mechanism (Roche 2003). The consensual decision-making process takes several forms within the restorative justice paradigm, including family group conferencing, victim–offender mediation, and circles of support. Meetings between victims and offenders provide victims with the opportunity to detail their victimisation (Strang 2002), and the process can contribute to offenders accepting responsibility for their actions and being held accountable (Roche 2003). It can also help to restore and empower community members by dispelling the anxiety that many people feel about crime (Van Ness and Strong 2002).

Reparation

What needs to be repaired by restorative justice processes depends on the circumstances surrounding a specific crime or conflict, and on the victim's injury – whether it is physical, emotional, economic or psychological (Strang 2002). The losses experienced are not limited to tangible entities, but can extend to emotional and psychological ones such as the loss of dignity, happiness, confidence, security, self-worth and personal power (Zehr 1990; Braithwaite 2002a; Strang 2002). However, reparation should not be limited to victims. For restorative justice to have the impact that many advocate, it is crucial to acknowledge that often the offender, too, has suffered losses, which are part of the underlying causes of the offending behaviour. Thus, to heal people and truly reintegrate them into their communities, such issues need to be addressed (Sullivan and Tifft 2006).

It is important to note that 'restoration' is not included as a core value here, but has been replaced by 'reparation'. This is because many losses suffered by the parties within a conflict (such as personal, communal or armed conflict) cannot be restored, if restoration is understood according to its dictionary definition: 'to bring back to a (supposed) former state or to a normal state'. The losses are often simply too great. One should ideally work towards the goal of restoration, but if restoration does not occur, and 'only' reparation is achieved, this should not be seen as a failure, but as a reasonable and satisfactory outcome. Moreover, as was argued by several interviewees in Northern Ireland, 'restoration' in their line of work would mean restoring people to the context that resulted in the conflict in the first place. This, they argued, referred not only to the particular case at hand, but also to the broader structures which gave rise to an armed conflict lasting more than 30 years – structures which they aim to challenge and change.

Reintegration

Reintegration means the 'victim's or offender's re-entry into community life as a whole, contributing, productive person' (Van Ness and Strong 2002: 106). This can arguably be accomplished by strengthening a person's ties with the community, and requires a process whereby offenders are shamed without stigmatisation and where they acknowledge the wrongdoing, thus demonstrating their willingness to be part of the (law-abiding) community and to recognise the norms of acceptable behaviour. Reintegration is crucial for minimising reoffending, by preventing a drift into deviant subcultures that can result from stigmatisation and subsequent exclusion (Braithwaite 1989).

An important responsibility of the community is to ensure that offenders are indeed accepted and included (Roche 2003). This is fundamental to the success of any restorative justice programme (Johnstone 2002), since without effective community participation, reintegration might be only partial or not occur at all. This process can be onerous for the community, and it is important that this be recognised so that appropriate support and facilities are made available. However, this can be a challenging task, especially after long periods of violent conflict characterised by widespread victimisation. Strengthening a person's ties to the community is by no means a straightforward process, particularly considering the construction of community in many places, where exclusion and hierarchical power structures are often its central features. Thus, empowerment of participants and the wider community is essential if such negative community features are to be rejected.

Empowerment

Restorative justice processes which involve all stakeholders are arguably models of empowerment that must be clearly grounded in grass-roots commitment at the local level (Pranis 2004). Empowerment can be seen as a vital aspect of restorative justice but has largely been under-theorised, with the notable exception of Barton (2000, 2003), who provides a model of what he sees as ideal restorative justice practice. He argues that a 'good' restorative justice process that results in high levels of satisfaction among all participants is one characterised by empowerment. Conversely, low levels of empowerment in a process generally result in lower levels of satisfaction and an inability to address the causes and consequences of the issue at hand in ways that are meaningful or relevant for the participants.

Hence, it can be argued that empowerment both overrides and underpins the other values outlined above, and is the fundamental difference between justice delivery in the formal criminal justice system and restorative alternatives. Reparation, reintegration, and workable outcome agreements cannot be reached without the sufficient empowerment of *all* participants. Moreover, if the goals of reparation and reintegration are not reached at all or only partially, the restorative justice process can still be of great value by virtue of its empowering of participants.

I would argue that the five values discussed above should be central to both the processes and outcomes of restorative justice. Yet, in relation to the process/outcome debate (Bazemore and Walgrave 1999; Braithwaite and Strang 2001) alluded to earlier, it is arguably the *process* that is the most fundamental aspect of restorative justice, especially when employed in the context of transitional societies. By placing the primary emphasis on the *outcome*,[2] the transformative potential of an inclusive, participatory process can be lost. For example, the outcome of a juvenile justice conference may be a number of hours of community service to repair the harm and be accountable to the community. However, if this 'restorative' outcome has been reached by an exclusionary and retributive process, then participants are unlikely to feel satisfied with the outcome. The procedural justice argument advocated by Tyler (Tyler 1990; Sunshine and Tyler 2003) is central here, where the added consequences of a procedurally

7

just process of increased satisfaction and trust in the organisation responsible for the process are important. This is normally the police and the criminal justice system, but can also be a community-based alternative such as in Northern Ireland. Practical examples of how the process has acted in a transformative manner in Northern Ireland will be provided throughout this book.

By seeing the process as a cornerstone in any restorative intervention, many of the dangers associated with informal justice can be minimised (McEvoy and Mika 2001), with the process functioning as an informal accountability mechanism (Roche 2003). Moreover, an emphasis on process allows restorative justice to work towards other goals for which the formal criminal justice system is less suited, such as reparation of harm, reconciliation of conflicting parties and empowerment. It can also increase the participants' sense of personal efficacy and power, increase the capacity of people locked in conflict to 'recognise' the other party, and increase the confidence, capacity and inclination of members of the community to resolve their own disputes and keep their own order (Johnstone 2002).

The discussion now continues with an exploration of what are widely seen as the three key stakeholders of restorative justice: victims, offenders and communities (Christie 1977; Braithwaite 1989; Hayes *et al.* 1998; Walgrave 1998; Tutu 1999; Ahmed *et al.* 2001; Strang and Braithwaite 2001). At a glance, their involvement is uncomplicated; each crime will have an offender and victim, and both will have family and friends that make up their personal communities. All three categories, however, are highly contested (Strang 2002; Daly 2003; Pavlich 2005).

Victims in restorative justice

Gaarder and Presser (2006) have argued that the unique features of restorative justice could potentially make it more appropriate for dealing with victimisation and offending than the formal criminal justice system. In their view, restorative justice provides a forum for narrative, allowing issues of multiple victimisation (as in many domestic violence cases or in the aftermath of armed conflict) to be raised and an opportunity to address underlying correlates of offending such as a history of sexual and/or physical abuse, racism or poverty (Sudsbury 2005). As asserted by Strang (2002, 2004), these features have long been recognised as important to victims of crime, both for their healing ability and as an essential component of the restorative process as a whole. Moreover, the central involvement of victims in restorative justice processes is argued by Pranis (2004) to be critical to the task of defining harm and addressing how it can be repaired.

Victim satisfaction with the restorative process and its outcome is commonly viewed as an important measure of 'success' in evaluations of the initiative. Several extensive evaluations in Australia, New Zealand and the UK have indeed confirmed that, in general, victims are satisfied with their experiences in restorative justice processes, and more satisfied than with a comparative experience in court (Strang et al. 1999; Daly 2001; Strang 2002; Crawford and Newburn 2003; Campbell et al. 2005). Satisfaction with a restorative process is closely linked to the degree to which a participant's needs have been addressed and met. According to Strang (2002, 2004), the needs of victims in the aftermath of experiencing a criminal event include a less formal process in which their views count, active participation in their case, access to sufficient information about the proceedings and outcome of their case, respectful and fair treatment, material restoration, and, most importantly of all, emotional restoration, including an apology (Strang 2004: 96). However, considering that most restorative justice programmes are embedded within the formal criminal justice system, and that only a small percentage of criminal cases result in a court appearance (Dignan 2005), it has been questioned whether restorative justice in practice really addresses the needs of victims (Achilles and Zehr 2001; Braithwaite 2002b; Achilles 2004; Strang 2004).

Indeed, one of the criticisms of restorative justice, as noted by Pavlich (2005), is the necessary labelling of participants as 'victim' or 'offender'. As a consequence of this categorisation, the restorative process produces, by default, particular kinds of victim identities, often characterised by disempowerment. Hence, one has to be identified as a victim before being allowed to participate in a restorative process through which one can become empowered again. In essence, a person has to be labelled (as victim or offender) to allow for a process where labelling can be challenged and removed. Such a dichotomy does not take into account that many people feel uncomfortable with the victim label,[3] nor that, especially in relation to juvenile crime, the line between victim and offender is often blurred (Zehr and Mika 2003). This is true for many juvenile offenders and victims, but it is equally important when dealing with larger and more deep-running conflicts whose roots lie in political or religious beliefs (Borer 2003; Elster 2004; Govier and Verwoerd 2004), such as in Northern Ireland (Smyth 1998). In such contexts, a process which simply involves 'participants' and explicitly avoids labelling might be preferable.

Offenders in restorative justice

Offenders who participate in restorative justice processes are expected to confront the damage resulting from their behaviour, work to repair harm and avoid future offending – a process which can be very onerous (Toews and Katounas 2004). Offenders in restorative processes also have needs, such as being reintegrated into the community or being provided with assistance in addressing the underlying causes of their offending. According to Toews and Katounas (2004: 109), offenders need the opportunity to:

> Express remorse, sorrow and regret for the harm done and offer apologies to the victim.
>
> Have others, ideally including victims, accept their remorse as genuine, no matter how inadequately expressed.
>
> Tell their stories – without justifying or excusing their offending. ...
>
> Have others, including the victims, realize that they, the offenders, may have come from a world in which they themselves were victims of violence, abuse and neglect.
>
> Receive acknowledgement of their experiences with victimization and attention to their needs as crime victims.
>
> Experience personal growth and transformation and be able to demonstrate their new lives.
>
> Have opportunities to make things right and build relationships with their families and the broader community.

Such a needs-perspective on offenders is an important goal towards which restorative justice should aim. Without such a focus, it is unlikely that the underlying reasons for offending could be addressed, and this would likely affect the prospects of reducing recidivism. As will be explored throughout this book, such a perspective also reflects the approach taken by practitioners of community restorative justice in Northern Ireland, an approach which positions it further away from the retributive views of crime according to which the offenders' only obligation in justice processes is to receive proportionate punishment (Ashworth 2002; Duff 2003). One limitation of much contemporary restorative justice practice, however, is that offenders, like victims, must adhere to certain labels or scripts of 'doing' justice. Consequently, as argued by Pavlich (2005), restorative justice does not allow offenders to address their needs without first fully confronting the harm they have done. Such stringent requirements concerning how the offender 'should' respond may actually counteract reintegrative shaming by placing overly high expectations on the 'ideal' participation of an offender (Pavlich 2005).

Importantly, Hudson and Galaway (1996) have argued that one of the fundamental imperatives for effective restorative justice is that people see crime as an injury to the community to which the victim and offender both belong, and only secondarily as a violation of state law. This perspective is highly relevant to the discussions in this book, in that some behaviours which in Northern Ireland are legally categorised as crime may not be perceived as harmful within a particular community context, whereas others which fall outside the criminal definition may be perceived as very serious, with tangible consequences for people's perceptions of safety and security. A more flexible approach to harm definition (Tombs and Hilliard 2004) arguably facilitates a practice which is needs-based and holistic, in that harm affects not only the primary victims, but also has secondary (such as family and friends) and tertiary effects (the wider community).

Restorative justice and the contested community

> The concept of community has been one of the most compelling and attractive themes in modern social science, and at the same time one of the most elusive to define. (Editor's foreword in A.P. Cohen's *The Symbolic Construction of Community*, 1985: 7)

It is important to devote special attention to the construction and use of community not only because it is one of the key stakeholders in restorative justice, but also because it is a highly contested concept both within the literature and within Northern Ireland. Community has come to play a major role in crime prevention policies and rhetoric around 'partnerships', while the negative aspects of community, such as exclusionary practices and hierarchies of power, are rarely addressed in restorative justice literature. Such aspects of community are central in Northern Ireland as a sharply divided society, and since the restorative justice projects under discussion are explicitly based within and draw their legitimacy from these local communities, this is an area which will be explored in some detail.

For restorative justice, community is both subject and object, in that restorative justice is realised *in* community and, at the same time, can be transformative *of* community (Nelken 1985). In a transitional context, community involvement in restorative justice is arguably particularly important, as the transition involves the creation or rebuilding of community; that is, the restoration of an inherently social equilibrium (Llewellyn and Howse 1999). However, the community by its very nature possesses strong characteristics of exclusion with boundaries constructed through symbolism and actions, dividing 'us' from 'them' (Cohen 1985). Who is excluded and by what means depends on the historical and political social forces that shaped the community in the first place (Cunneen 2004). Within the relevant literature on informal and restorative justice (Abel 1982a, b; Crawford 1999a, b; Bauman 2001; Pavlich 2005), the concept is indeed highly contested; within informalism debates, it is viewed as a concept that is ambiguous, overused and under-defined (Matthews 1988). Similarly, within restorative justice writings, where community is frequently portrayed as a key to the entire justice equation, there is comparatively little literature that analyses the role of community beyond the superficial.[4]

Community is often mentioned as something which we have lost, an ideal towards which we should aspire. The rhetoric glorifies the 'good old days', when we knew our neighbours and could leave our doors unlocked, no one was afraid of walking home after dark, and someone was always willing to lend a helping hand (Braithwaite 2002a). The less positive reality is conveniently forgotten, where those who were 'different' (the mentally ill, those of the wrong origin, or simply the very poor) were ostracised, punished or 'asked' to leave the community. The distinction between 'us' (the right-thinking, the good and the just) and 'them' (most people who threatened the status quo and therefore were inherently dangerous and bad) was as acute then as it is today (Cohen 1987; Crawford 1999a, b; Dignan 2000; Pavlich 2004, 2005). Community members for their part are often equally cognisant of the power of community as a basis for claims-making (Pavlich 2005). For example, *our* community can be deployed in opposition to *their* community, emphasising difference from others outside the community as well as shared similarities with those inside (Cohen 1985; Crawford 1999a, 1999b) – a tangible reality in Northern Ireland as a starkly divided society.

How we define 'community' has an important bearing on what we expect it do to, what it is capable of, and what kind of resource or threat we perceive it to be. Across a range of social science disciplines, the notion of community has been defined through a multitude of meanings (Butcher *et al.* 1993). It has been described as 'interlocking social networks of neighbourhood, kinship and friendship' (Crow and Allan 1994: 178–179), and as including something shared in common among people – whether in terms of territoriality, ethnicity, religious background, or occupational or leisure pursuits (Wilmott 1987) – and is in effect socially constructed (Cohen 1985). It is viewed in some contexts as a 'feel-good' concept (Hughes 1998), and a focal point around which individual, communal and indeed national life is collectively 'imagined' (Anderson 1983, 1991). As argued by McCold and Wachtel:

> When we speak of the 'sense of community' that is missing from modern society, we are speaking about the absence of meaningful interrelationships between human beings and an absence of a sense of belonging to and common interest in something that is greater than ourselves. (2003: 295)

In some contexts, such as state-led 'community prevention' initiatives, community is almost exclusively defined as a geographical space (Crawford 1999b). In such instances, its usage is often deployed strategically by state agencies, occasionally morphing into 'a convenient political and rhetorical device used like an aerosol can, to be sprayed on to any social programme, giving it a more progressive and sympathetic cachet' (Cochrane 1986: 51, cited in Foster 2002: 173). In contrast, a non-geographical understanding of 'community' is constructed in such a way that it ensures that people can belong to several communities simultaneously, as in one's work, sport and religious communities. Such a definition has been developed by Strang (1995), who argues that the concept of community extends beyond locality (spatial or geographical descriptions), embracing a multiplicity of groups and networks to which, it is believed, we all belong. Braithwaite and Daly (1994) have also referred to this understanding as 'communities of care': networks of obligations and respect between individuals and those who care about them the most. Inherent in this view is the lack of coerced or constrained membership of any particular geographic community, and it is thus supposed to be more relevant to contemporary living in urban societies (Crawford and Clear 2003). A non-geographical perspective can be used to focus on and define what community justice *should* look like and what we should be trying to achieve. It has been argued that notions of community that focus less on locality and more on relationships among people – that is, communities of care and networks of obligation and respect – more closely mirror contemporary social life (Strang 1995). Such a conceptualisation marks a significant development in our understanding of contemporary communities (Crawford and Clear 2001).

In restorative justice, community is often seen as a resource for reconciliation of victims and offenders, and a place for monitoring and enforcing community standards of behaviour (Pranis 1998). McCold (1996) has advocated an active and inclusive role for the community and suggested that, when a crime occurs, the responsibilities of the local community are to (1) act immediately to protect victim and offender; (2) hold offenders accountable and insist on active involvement of interested parties in the resolution process; (3) provide the local resources for victims and offenders to seek their healing; (4) provide local education and serve as a model for peaceful resolution processes; and (5) seek the systemic sources of recurring conflicts and encourage amelioration of their aetiological source. Similar sentiments around the role of community have been echoed by Pavlich (2005), despite his early reservations about the easy deployment of the term. He argues that the main objective of a community's responsibility in relation to crime and antisocial behaviour is 'to restore a community's fabric by dealing effectively with victims' needs, successfully reintegrating offenders and building community strength by requiring communities to deal with criminal events through restorative processes' (p. 33).

Based on the above defined roles of this collective, it can be seen that restorative justice requires significant resources to be employed by the community, particularly as communities differ in their capabilities to assist in the reintegration of offenders, supporting victims, and providing volunteers for programmes (Bazemore 2001). Restorative justice programmes could increase the burden of expectation and involvement of local people and groups to a level they cannot sustain (Marshall 1998), or, just as likely, this responsibility might be more than people are willing to take on. As one victim described: 'It is like being hit by a car and having to go out and help the other driver when all you were doing was minding your own business' (Roche 2003: 14). As Johnstone (2002) argues, the emphasis on the role of communities suggests that the campaign for restorative justice is

> no longer confined to developing and promoting restorative alternatives to conventional models of sentencing and punishment. It entails an attempt to relocate the work of crime control and criminal justice, shifting it from state agencies to the local community. (p. 156)

How 'local' this community should be is debated by McCold (2004), who notes that restorative justice theory and practice are evolving along two paths: one that focuses on the role of the *micro-community*, and the other on the role of the *macro-community*. The micro-community includes the people most affected by a particular offence or conflict, one's 'community of care' (Braithwaite 2002b) such as family members, friends and others with whom we are emotionally connected. From the perspective of the micro-community, crime harms specific people, and 'community' is a network of relationships not dependent on geography. Macro-communities, on the other hand, are groups defined by geography, not membership (McCold 2004). Crime and conflict, within this context, are not viewed in terms of specific harms, but rather as an aggregate of harm. When the macro-community perceives such aggregates to be high, feelings of fear, insecurity and reduced guardianship can result – or decreased informal social control – over certain areas, which by extension can result in even higher levels of crime.

The primary goal of restorative justice in relation to micro-communities is to repair the harm caused by offending in relation to the direct participants of any particular conflict and the restorative process is central to such work; other outcomes, such as reducing reoffending, are side benefits (McCold 2004). In relation to macro-communities, the focus is more on outcomes as opposed to process, in particular reducing the fear of crime and insecurity with the aim of challenging punitive attitudes within the wider community. Hence, both approaches aim to challenge and ultimately change value sets within a particular place; for example, changing punitive, exclusionary, and violent practices to those that reflect the restorative justice values of inclusion, participation and reintegration. It is evident that many state-based restorative justice programmes tend to focus on the former – micro-communities – and are less well suited to managing the needs of the latter, even though 'community' is portrayed as a key stakeholder. Community-based initiatives, on the other hand, freer as they are from the constraints of the formal criminal justice system, can be better placed to address both macro- and micro-communities. A central argument in this book is that community-based restorative justice as practised in Northern Ireland not only can, but does, affect both, by placing equal emphasis on individuals and the larger community as participants of restorative processes.

However, irrespective of the role one envisions for the community within restorative justice theory and practice, it is important to recognise the contested nature of community and to avoid simplified or romanticised notions of its structures and functions. A more realistic understanding of the concept is also vital for the exploration of community-based restorative projects, particularly in the Northern Irish context where local communities have been at the centre of armed conflict. This will be further explored in the next chapter, together with a more detailed introduction to transitional justice and the role of criminology in endeavours of research, evaluation and peace-building in transitional societies. It will be argued that the principles of restorative justice resonate strongly with the needs of societies undergoing political transition, in so far as values such as justice reconstruction, peace-building and reintegration are pursued concurrently (Minow 1998; Teitel 2000; Leebaw 2001; Eisnaugle 2003).

Notes

1 Perhaps with the exception of peacemaking circles that operate alongside the formal system – sometimes independently of it, sometimes in cooperation with it (Stuart and Pranis 2006).
2 Bazemore and Walgrave advocate a definition of restorative justice that focuses on the outcome: 'restorative justice ... is every action that is primarily oriented towards doing justice by restoring the harm that has been caused by crime' (1999: 48). However, it should be noted that these authors are arguing for a 'maximalist' model of restorative justice, which they take to mean that the whole of the current formal criminal justice system should aim towards restorative justice. For that to happen, the focus necessarily needs to be on the outcome, since a process definition would mean a total restructuring of most, if not all, criminal justice institutions.
3 Many people, especially those who have been subjected to sexual or physical abuse, often seem to prefer the term 'survivor' to 'victim', a state that indicates empowerment (Leisenring 2006).
4 For a more critical perspective, see Pavlich (2001, 2004 and 2005).

Chapter 2

Restorative justice in transition and the case for criminology

As mentioned in the previous chapter, there is a plethora of publications on the subject of restorative justice. The majority, however, focus on initiatives that are established, controlled and funded by the state (see Johnstone 2002; Strang 2002; Bazemore and Umbreit 2003; Roche 2003; Johnstone and Van Ness 2007), as opposed to strictly community-based approaches. The same conclusions can be applied to efforts of justice reconstruction within transitional societies, be they restorative or not.[1] Restorative justice in transitional societies faces a number of additional difficulties to those traditionally associated with more stable jurisdictions. State-based initiatives may be regarded with some cynicism in communities where the justice system has been contorted during the conflict (as through emergency legislation) or where the police or state security forces have been guilty of human rights abuses (Roche 2002; Nowrojee 2005). Adherence to legal formalism, due process, proportionality and related benchmarks for ensuring good restorative justice practice in state-based programmes is not easily separated from such violent histories when government and politics have been so closely related (Chayes and Chayes 1998; Ruth-Heffelbower 2000). Indeed, as has been the case in Northern Ireland, restorative justice programmes led by police or other criminal justice agencies (O'Mahony *et al.* 2002; Campbell *et al.* 2005) struggle to develop partnerships with precisely those local communities most directly affected by the conflict, thus severely limiting the transformative potential of restorative justice in the areas where it is most needed.

Despite an international preference for top-down applications of justice reconstruction, there has been an increase in transitional justice initiatives 'from below', which involve civil society and local communities (Belloni 2001; Evans-Kent 2002; Van Tongeren 2005) and include measures of informal and, particularly, restorative justice (Drumbl 2000a, b, c; Roche 2002; Cartwright and Jenneker 2005; Shearing *et al.* 2006; McEvoy and McGregor 2008). Taking this notion as a starting point, this chapter engages with broader debates around the restorative justice framework and explores the extent to which it may be applied to much more serious incidents of violence and criminality, rather than the traditional focus on juvenile and minor crimes. This section also includes a discussion on community within transitional societies, and takes a critical view of the potential consequences of the construction and make-up of community for informal justice practices, keeping in mind the dangers of community as a site of exclusionary practices and unequal power relationships (e.g. Etzioni 1994; Boutellier 1997, 2001; Crawford 1999a, b; Pavlich 2001, 2004, 2005; Mulcahy 2006).

Approaches to transitional justice and the argument for grass-roots models

> A transitional society is by definition located between an illegitimate past and a future shaped by a set of ideals to which it aspires – without such aspirations being immediately realizable. (Villa-Vincencio 2006: 390)

Transitional justice has been defined as a bounded period between two regimes, from a previously oppressive, violent or dictatorial social order towards a democratic one (Teitel 2000). The central question in much of the relevant literature on the topic revolves around how fledgling democracies should engage with severe human rights abuses that earlier authoritarian regimes, their opponents, or combatants in internal conflict have committed (Crocker 1998; Minow 1998; Little 1999; Teitel 2000; Rigby 2001; Torpey 2003; Etcheson 2005; Mallinder 2008; McEvoy and McGregor 2008). Societies going through a transition have adopted a variety of approaches to deal with past abuses, approaches that range from the very personal and local to the global and structural, and which aim to achieve justice, reconciliation and/or nation-building (Teitel 1997, 2000, 2003a, b; Gready 2005; Mallinder 2008). The approach chosen should ideally be based on the specific needs of each society, its capacities, culture, history and political reality, as well as its legal system (Seigle 1998; Goldstone 1999; Little 1999; Elster 2004, 2006; Harper 2005). Within such societal transformations, the state aims to reassert its authority and legitimacy, and the institutions of justice are central to such efforts (McEvoy 2007).[2]

Transitional justice approaches can consist of both formal procedures, such as trials and truth and reconciliation commissions (Goldstone 1999), and informal ones such as mediation and reconciliation at the community level through the use of restorative or other informal justice measures (Nina 1993; Drumbl 2002; Roche 2002). These procedures can be implemented by a group or institution of accepted legitimacy (Kaminski *et al.* 2006), which can incorporate both state and civil society formations. To date, transitional justice approaches have included truth commissions; trials and prosecutions; amnesties (Mallinder 2008); non-judicial sanctions of lustration and compensation; and symbolic gestures such as commemorations and memorials (Crocker 1998; Mani 2002).

Where formal prosecutions are pursued, perpetrators of gross human rights violations have been prosecuted by an international court such as the International Criminal Court (ICC) (Schabas 2004), the International Criminal Tribunal for Rwanda (ICTR), or the International Criminal Tribunal for the Former Yugoslavia (ICTY) (Humphrey 2004; Kerr 2004). National courts have also been utilised, either independently or through cooperation with international actors in so-called hybrid tribunals that combine the efforts of local and international legal actors, and domestic and international law (Schabas 2003). Hybrid tribunals have, for example, been implemented in Sierra Leone (Evenson 2004), East Timor (Katzenstein 2003), Kosovo (Dickinson 2003) and Cambodia (Etcheson 2005).

Much transitional justice literature focuses on truth commissions, particularly South Africa's Truth and Reconciliation Commission,[3] arguably the most researched transitional justice institution in the world. Truth commissions emerged initially as an alternative to prosecution, as both national and international courts were too slow to prosecute the high number of perpetrators often present in civil war, and were unable to deal satisfactorily with the needs of victims and the wider community. Moreover, prosecutions, by their narrow legalistic focus, were unable to address wider issues such as reintegration of victims and perpetrators, truth, forgiveness and national healing. Although each truth commission has its own unique mandate, they are generally constituted to establish a historical record of abuse and to investigate the causes and consequences of these abuses by a variety of methodologies, including 'holding public hearings, conducting fact-finding missions, and taking statements from victims, witnesses, and even perpetrators' (Evenson 2004: 731).

Hence, much of the existing literature on justice in times of transition focuses upon the construction or reconstruction of more efficient and effective formal criminal justice systems that have been damaged or distorted by the conflict (McEvoy 2007). During such endeavours, top-down and state-centred approaches are often preferred to more organic, 'building from the grass-roots' approaches to the management of change (Roberts and McMillan 2003; McEvoy and McGregor 2008). In particular, the discussions centre on how supranational justice mechanisms can facilitate such developments (Siegel 1998; Goldstone 1999; Humphrey 2004; Schabas 2004), instead of the possibility of actively utilising local community structures. As will be argued throughout this book, the top-down focus in the transitional justice literature is not only an intellectual limitation but also a political obstacle to the process of conflict transformation. Often, despite the reform of state institutions, the apparent failure to achieve tangible change on the ground is viewed by local communities as a failure by the state to deliver justice, security and equality in the aftermath of conflict. I would argue that there is a need for a concurrent *bottom-up* focus on the dynamics of transition at a grass-roots, community level.

Paradoxically, a state-centred focus on governance in times of transition is at odds with much of the generic writing in non-transitional societies that has emerged, in particular since the 1990s. Such writings argue for a more nuanced understanding of the relationships among the state, the community and the individual in the governance of justice and security (e.g. Crawford 1999a, b; Hope and Sparks 2000; Garland 2001) in relation to community crime prevention, and maintain a focus on informal social controls (Bursik and Grasmick 1993; Foster 1995; Brewer *et al.* 1998; Bazemore 2001). In recent years, such a shift has also been emerging within transitional justice literature, where, even given the traditionally retributive and adversarial focus of the realm of international criminal justice, scholars have begun to suggest that justice initiatives located at the grass-roots level also must play a role in dealing with the after-effects of war (McEvoy and McGregor 2008). In a similar vein, Gready (2005) has argued that the position of law within transitional justice has been privileged while dismissing the potential of locally generated and embedded justice, and the idea that justice needs to be 'embedded within' to engage with the communities, cultures and contexts of conflict. Community restorative justice in Northern Ireland exemplifies such an approach, and the strengths and weaknesses of such an informal initiative will be explored throughout this book.

The emergence of criminology in transitional justice

Few publications focus on the important topic of crime control and prevention in societies that are going through major social change, a topic the urgency of which has been demonstrated by the situation in South Africa, Central and South America, the former Eastern Europe, and of course Afghanistan and Iraq, to mention but a few. It is my contention that a critical criminological approach can greatly contribute to the challenges faced by these societies, but has not been sufficiently engaged with to date. Importantly, such an approach to transitional justice is closely connected to the political reality of the society in question, and since crime and justice matters cannot be analysed independently of political and cultural variables (Cohen 1996), critical criminology is a useful framework within which to address the complex questions faced by transitional societies (Roberts and McMillan 2003). As argued by Roberts:

> By marginalising or entirely displacing local remedies, the international community could be failing to exploit the best prospects for national reconciliation and regeneration. Standardised supranational processes tend to obscure the unique character and circumstances of particular instances of international criminality and mass human rights violations. ... To rise to these considerable challenges, international criminal justice theorists and practitioners would do well to acquaint themselves with criminological data and methodologies of empirical investigation and comparative cultural analysis. (2003: 325)

The rigour of scholarship which characterises much criminological writing and its inherent interdisciplinary focus are often lacking in transitional justice analyses (McEvoy 2007). Therefore:

> Criminology brings a number of attributes to the table which can assist in developing a 'thicker' understanding of transitional justice. In particular, criminology provides a helpful framework

in asking practical questions about judging whether transitional justice *works* as well as more philosophical questions as to who and what it is *for*. (McEvoy 2007: 42)

In a similar vein, Roberts and McMillan (2003) have argued for a central place for criminology within post-conflict justice, stating that a criminological approach can broaden the horizons by incorporating a 'methodological pluralism' that opens up new avenues for further multidisciplinary inquiry (p. 316). Such a multidisciplinary approach is necessary when one considers the daunting challenges faced by many transitional societies (Steenkamp 2005). For example:

> Other specific factors that exacerbate the problem include rapid urbanisation, the precariousness of major city services, sustained disparities between rich and poor, a culture of violence that is the legacy of years of conflict, the swelling influence in social life of gang activities, the availability of weapons and drugs, the effects of the demobilisation of military or rebel groups, social dislocation, systemic discrimination, and the abuses and corruption of the police. In addition, the illegitimacy of public institutions and the rule by force rather than consent compound the problem, and constitute factors of resentment. (International Council on Human Rights Policy, cited in Mani 2002: 32)

As many of these issues are present in contemporary Northern Ireland, they will be addressed in the following chapters in relation to the role restorative justice can have in transforming such social situations.

The expansion of the scope of criminology within transitional justice to include mass violations of human rights is, as noted above, a fairly recent phenomenon; but, perhaps somewhat surprisingly, the more traditional areas of criminology have received even less attention in the context of transitional societies. This is despite the fact that rising crime levels, particularly violent and organised crime, are often a serious and common consequence of sweeping social transformations (Dixon and Van der Spuy 2004), and issues related to areas such as prisons, police, courts, crime prevention and reintegration are perceived as central to the reconstruction of a society after conflict (McEvoy and Newburn 2003). Criminological research in non-transitional societies has long wrestled with questions around 'crime' and has developed an advanced understanding of forces inherent in its construction. Moreover, critical perspectives on the role of the state (Garland and Sparks 2000); multi-layered discourses about 'victims', 'offenders', and 'the community' (Crawford 1999a, b; Bazemore and Schiff 2001; Hughes and Edwards 2002; Hughes 2006); and rationales for and the effectiveness of punishment (Von Hirsch *et al.* 1999; von Hirsch and Ashworth 2000) are other key areas of criminological investigation which are highly relevant to societies in transition. Importantly, there are unique opportunities in transitional societies to manage efforts of justice reconstruction that deal with these key areas outside organised state structures, through which meaningful civil society participation can thus be promoted (McEvoy 2007; McEvoy and McGregor 2008).

Some criminologists have sought to bridge the gaps between community, national and international peacemaking efforts through the framework of restorative justice (see Braithwaite 2002a). Such examples are, however, rare, and while considerable attention has been paid to the relationship between criminal justice agencies and local communities in transition, usually the management of criminal justice reform has been *system-* rather than *community-*focused. I would argue that the experiences of community restorative justice in Northern Ireland can act as a corrective to such system-focused and top-down initiatives in the transitional context, by outlining how communities themselves can provide leadership in efforts of peacemaking 'from below'.

The transitional context presents several challenges to research, but also new opportunities. Rather than limiting the remit of evaluation to the usual benchmarks concerning recidivism rates and levels of satisfaction among participants, the transitional nature of the Northern Ireland context presents an opportunity to go much further, where community-based restorative justice can be a catalyst for transforming relationships of power through advocacy, group and community development and organisation, and empowerment (McEvoy 2003). Issues that need to be taken into account include, for example, the transformation of the attitudes of combatants and former combatants to violence as a mechanism of social control, the views and behaviours of communities with respect to alleged antisocial elements, and the restructuring of criminal justice agencies, their practices, and occupational cultures.

Furthermore, as important as these larger structural and political issues are the procedural aims of any specific restorative intervention, such as empowering key participants (victim, offender and community), repairing the harm caused by the offence, reintegrating offenders and victims, and shifting communal response to conflict from violent to non-violent modes. The following sections will briefly discuss these issues in relation to practices in transitional societies such as Rwanda and South Africa, and provide a broad and internationally comparative framework for the arguments to follow regarding the situation in Northern Ireland.

Restorative justice on the edge: the transitional society

> The acid test for restorative justice within such contexts is whether it can succeed where retribution has failed – whether it can reduce recidivism and facilitate the emergence of a more just social order. (Villa-Vincencio 2006: 389)

This section will focus on how restorative justice principles and practices have been implemented in transitional societies. It is argued that the principles of restorative justice resonate strongly with the needs of a society in the midst of political transition, whereby values such as justice reconstruction, peace-building, and reintegration often need to be pursued concurrently (Minow 1998; Teitel 2000; Leebaw 2001; Eisnaugle 2003). Some key themes that emerge from this discussion – such as grass-roots governance, ownership of justice, conflict around the interface between informal and formal social control, the roles of ex-combatants, possible partnership between state and community, and the role of community in such endeavours – are of particular importance for Northern Ireland and will be explored in more detail throughout this book.

Restorative justice has recently been implemented as part of conflict resolution interventions in relation to broader political conflicts (Auld *et al.* 1997; Winston 1997; McEvoy and Mika 2001). For example, South Africa has utilised different initiatives of restorative justice to deal with the legacy of the apartheid regime (Hayner 1994, 2001; Villa-Vincencio 1999; Skelton 2002; Llewellyn 2007), and in relation to community-based Peace Committees (Shearing 2001; Roche 2002; Cartwright *et al.* 2004; Cartwright and Jenneker 2005; Froestad and Shearing 2007). In Peru, grass-roots programmes have operated to help reintegrate rebels from a former communist guerrilla organisation which had killed close to 70,000 people during a widespread rebellion. In Rwanda, the *gacaca* system has been implemented to deal with the aftermath of the genocide which took place there in 1994, and it arguably reflects many of the key values and processes of restorative justice (Waldorf 2006). These new and extended uses of restorative justice in transitional societies indicate a shift in thinking regarding the possible applications of restorative justice, even though many disagree on the appropriateness of such developments. Nonetheless, this is arguably the direction we must take if we wish to address effectively issues of social and political injustice (Napoleon 2004).

Among the countries that have looked towards restorative justice processes to address the aftermath of political injustice and as a means of positive social change, South Africa was arguably the first in relation to the Truth and Reconciliation Commission (TRC), which McCold (2004) has referred to as an aggregate process of restorative justice. The TRC was tasked to uncover the fate of the victims of gross violations of human rights that occurred between 1 March 1960 and 10 May 1994, and there is an extensive literature covering its establishment, workings and outcomes (see van Zyl 1999; Hamber 2002; Eisnaugle 2003). However, the TRC has received much criticism since the completion of its work; in particular of its emphasis on top-down processes, which for local communities raised important questions regarding leadership, trust and victim involvement. It has been argued that there was 'pressure' on victims to participate in the process, which negated its supposedly voluntary aspect, and an expectation that victims would forgive (Wilson 2001). Moreover, some of the cases selected for the TRC were of little relevance to local communities. As Leebaw (2001) has argued, 'by confusing symbolic national healing with actual individual and community healing, the TRC then overlooked key complexities of all three levels' (p. 280).

A more explicit grass-roots approach to conflict resolution and the governance of security at a local level in South Africa was the so-called Community Peace Programme in the Western Cape Province, initiated by Clifford Shearing and colleagues in 1997 (Shearing 2001; Roche 2002; Cartwright et al. 2004; Cartwright and Jenneker 2005; Froestad and Shearing 2007). This was an experiment in building a model which, drawing upon local skills, knowledge and capacities, could help local communities to help themselves, especially in relation to areas of safety and security. After the end of apartheid, there was – and still is – 'a serious "governance deficit" in poor communities, not only in relation to security but also in matters such as health and the provision of services such as garbage removal, water and electricity' (Cartwright et al. 2004: 5–6). One major difference between the South African version of grass-roots justice initiatives and that of Northern Ireland is that the former developed in partnership with the state and relevant statutory agencies, a dynamic which the latter projects struggled long to develop.

Another example of a grass-roots approach to transitional justice is provided by Theidon (2006), who considers justice at the local level – which she refers to as embedded justice – in the context of Peru. Starting in 1980, the communist guerrilla group Shining Path waged a rebellion in which almost 70,000 people were killed. In the transitional period, grass-roots procedures were used by communities to reintegrate rebels into village life. Based on folk and religious beliefs, the methods combined repentance with physical punishment. Some of the ex-collaborators were turned over to the military, but those who were forgiven received full village citizenship, land to make a living, and support from the other villagers. Theidon (2006) further argues that nationally imposed institutions may not only be less effective but can also sometimes interfere with local norms and reconciliation procedures.

In Rwanda, the adaptation of the *gacaca* system of tribal justice to address the legacy of genocide can arguably be viewed as being located within a restorative justice framework (Drumbl 2002; Roberts 2003). The genocide in Rwanda, which took place between April and July 1994, resulted in from 800,000 to 1 million deaths. The number of victims and perpetrators was overwhelming: 130,000 people were arrested and placed in prisons marked by severe overcrowding and appalling conditions. At the same time, there was an almost total destruction of the personnel and infrastructure of the criminal justice system (Drumbl 2002; Uvin and Mironko 2003; Gready 2005). The transitional justice structures in Rwanda are a mixture of the International Criminal Tribunal for Rwanda (ICTR), national courts, and the community-based *gacaca* courts, the last of which can be viewed as a third tier of efforts towards justice reconstruction.

In 2001, the *gacaca* courts set up a three-year deliberation regarding the inefficiency and slowness of formal prosecutions. The discussions also centred on how justice could be linked to social reconstruction and reconciliation (Gready 2005; Nowrojee 2005; Waldorf 2006). *Gacaca* procedures are participatory, inclusive and indigenous to Rwanda, and 'the provision for community justice service as an alternative component of certain sentences introduces a form of restorative justice, which aims to assist in the reintegration of offenders back into their communities' (Gready 2005: 12). There are several features of *gacaca*, especially in its initial design, which can be seen as restorative and which contributed to reconciliation and community empowerment in the wake of genocide (Drumbl 2002; Waldorf 2006), and, in general, supporters of restorative justice have lauded the *gacaca* courts for promoting a restorative justice model rooted in local, customary practice (Drumbl 2002; Uvin and Mironko 2003). As noted by Gready (2005), '[t]he *gacaca* process will clearly speed up trials and free up resources. However, it is also potentially culturally embedded, participatory, and restorative. In short, it is a revolution in transitional justice' (p. 13). *Gacaca* courts' jurisdiction excludes the most serious categories of crime, such as planning or leading the genocide, torture, rape or other sexual crimes. These are prosecuted by national criminal courts. The *gacaca* courts can, however, adjudicate in cases involving 'simple' murder, bodily injury and property damage (Gready 2005).

The *gacaca* system is not without its critics. It has been argued that the system is a failing experiment of restorative justice, as it has become more retributive in nature, with public confessions not leading to reintegration. The *gacaca* courts are also firmly located within state structures which essentially position them as a top-down project, trying to revive grass-roots responses. Participation has become less voluntary and more coercive. Moreover, the Rwandan government has prohibited *gacaca* from seeking accountability for war crimes committed by the state forces against Hutu civilians (Waldorf 2006), making 'justice' unavailable for large groups of people.

Generally, the attractiveness of transitional models of justice, such as the *gacaca* courts in Rwanda and the Peace Committees in South Africa, is that they are perceived as being able to deal with *individual* as well as social reconciliation (Pankhurst 1999). They tend to be portrayed as old approaches to justice which are revived and given new meaning, and are often referred to as 'traditional' or 'cultural'. However, one should be careful not therefore to view them through rose-tinted glasses. It is erroneous to assume that just because they exist outside the control of the state they embody superior qualities of morality or concern for the greater good (Pankhurst 1999). The limitations of the formal criminal justice system to respond adequately to the requirements of justice in a transitional society need to be recognised, and initiatives need to be adopted in a culturally and politically appropriate manner (Cunneen 2002; Nowrojee 2005). However, restorative justice, narrowly defined, carries a weakness in that it generally responds to the *consequences* of structural violence and injustice, not to their *causes*. This has also been noted by others (Blagg 2001; Cunneen 2002, 2003; Dyck 2006), who argue that restorative justice has frequently failed to address the structural and underlying dimensions of conflict, ignoring issues of class, race and gender. Instead, it focuses too much on the interpersonal dimensions, which are often the final consequence of broader inequalities, which in turn are historically, politically, socially and economically constructed.

Despite such limitations, it is a central tenet of this book that restorative justice has much to offer in the wider context of conflict resolution in transitional societies, when focusing on the dimensions of restoration relevant to victims, offenders and communities (Neuffer 2002; Nowrojee 2005; Villa-Vincencio 2006). The inherent flexibility of restorative processes makes them capable of being highly sensitive to the political, social and cultural context, and hence suitable for a wide range of conflicts. Within the transitional context, restorative processes can empower individuals, strengthen communities and address legitimacy deficits (Llewellyn and Howse 1999; Roche 2002; Froestad and Shearing 2007). They have the potential to deal with the relationship between traditionally excluded communities and the state through procedural justice measures. Moreover, restorative justice in transitional societies can, through a bottom-up approach, challenge ingrained cultures of violence and facilitate bridge-building between communities and the state by engaging in crime management and prevention at the local level. Community participation in decision-making processes regarding the rebuilding of a society adds transparency, accountability and legitimacy, and, importantly, minimises the risk of renewed conflict (Candio and Bleiker 2001; Roche 2003).

This section has provided a necessarily brief overview of some of the attempts to implement restorative justice at a grass-roots level in the aftermath of violent conflict within the broader international arena. The discussion now moves on to focus more explicitly on Northern Ireland and the community-based restorative justice projects in operation there. However, before exploring the projects in depth, it is useful to engage in a further exploration of the role of community in both transitional societies more generally, and Northern Ireland particularly. The role of community as a site for informal justice initiatives is by no means an uncontroversial area, as indicated in the previous chapter. In Northern Ireland, community is not only a site where restorative justice takes place, but is also highly contested, divided, politicised, and for a long time constructed as the 'sea in which the paramilitary fish swims' (Sluka 1989). Consequently, a critical approach to the role and construction of community, particularly in societies where the relationship between communities and the state has been severely damaged, is a necessary undertaking.

Community in the transitional society

Central to discussions around the position of community in transitional societies and elsewhere is the role of informal social control. A presumption exists that strong informal social control is inherently beneficial, resulting in a situation where crime is reduced and safety and security enhanced. However, in transitional societies, the existence of strong informal social control networks is often a contributing factor to armed conflict. For example, in Northern Ireland, strong, organised communities gave rise to the Provisional IRA, the Ulster Defence Association (UDA), and several other paramilitary organisations. Hence, strong communities are often feared by the state during periods of transition, and attempts to reassert formal social control via the criminal justice system are one of the state's key goals in such scenarios, while concurrently attempting to weaken existing community structures. This argument will be substantially developed in the following chapters, but it is important to note here that much of the existing criminological thinking – not to mention official policies in the UK, much of Europe and Australia – emphasises the importance of actively involving communities in crime prevention and control, thereby increasing collective efficacy and social capital as both the means and ends of such endeavours. Such arguments do not fit neatly within the transitional context; instead, the situation is often reversed.

In the generic criminological literature, a frequently rehearsed argument is Wilson and Kelling's (1982) 'broken windows' thesis, which basically postulates that more community equals less crime. The authors argue that communities have a crucial role in preventing moral decline and promoting regeneration of neighbourhood life, which in turn lead to the prevention of crime. More recent writings on this theory focus on a systematic model of community attachment to explain the relationship between exogenous variables and informal social control (Sampson 1987; Sampson and Groves 1989; Bursik and Grasmick 1993). As Crawford (2001) has argued, 'communities are identified, therefore, as a powerful site of social order and control' (p. 151). There is hence 'a direct causal relationship between a lack of informal social control – in other words a lack of "community" – and the existence of high levels of crime' (Crawford 2001: 152). In such a view, community is unquestioned as a benevolent entity, echoing the utopian notions and the concept of community as an inherently 'good thing' mentioned earlier (Hughes 1998; Bauman 2001).

The standard criminological approaches to community, however, fail to take into account that neighbourhoods can have high levels of informal social control – possessing a strong 'sense of community' – and yet be characterised by high levels of crime and violence (Hope and Foster 1992; Foster 1995). The research by Foster (1995) and Hope and Foster (1992) resonate more closely with the Northern Irish experience than the more simplistic assertion of 'more community equals less crime'. Throughout the conflict in Northern Ireland, when one could perhaps have expected crime rates to be high due to a general discourse of 'lawlessness' and state opposition, crime rates remained low in comparison to other industrialised nations (Morison and Geary 1993; Geary et al. 2000; O'Mahony et al. 2000; McEvoy and Ellison 2003). It has been argued that conflict with outgroups, such as the police, military or the 'other' community, helped reinforce the solidarity of the ingroup, resulting in a strong sense of community within these areas (Brewer et al. 1998). This community was characterised by powerful agents of informal social control, such as the Provisional IRA, who were keen to fortify feelings of togetherness and single identity (Shirlow and Murtagh 2006), leading to lower levels of offending against one's own community and instead a focus on protection from the enemy located outside community structures.

The idea of community as a geographical place that is constructed through a strong rhetoric of symbolism (Cohen 1985), and around feelings of safety, identity and belonging, is a diminishing reality in many developed societies. The situation in a post-conflict society, however, is arguably reversed, where 'community' can form an important base for identity and claims-making in a rapidly changing environment – effectively a counter-weight to tendencies of anomie. This has important implications for the application of criminology within transitional societies. The geographically defined community, signified by strong social bonds and interconnectivity and an almost tangible imaginary construction, is an empirical reality in Northern Ireland, particularly in working-class areas that were affected by much of the violence throughout the conflict. This particular construction of community created a unique environment in which community-based informal justice initiatives had a chance to flourish.

The existence of strong communities within a divided society also elicits powerful notions of exclusion. Such a construction of community boundaries – between 'us' and 'them' – is starkly evident in Northern Ireland. It is important to note, however, that the conflict was too often portrayed in an overly simplistic fashion as a binary one between two warring communities refereed by a 'neutral' and ultimately benevolent British state (e.g. O'Leary and MacGarry 1995; Ruane and Todd 1996). However, it is indisputable that the notion of community can have strongly negative connotations in the jurisdiction. In Northern Ireland, categories such as the Catholic/ Protestant, Nationalist/Unionist or Republican/Loyalist[4] community are deployed in an exclusionary and sectarian fashion. The lived reality for many working-class urban communities in particular is highly segregated. Local community identity in these areas is symbolised in the construction of community borders by means of painted kerbstones, flags, murals and so-called peace walls as part of an ingrained communal segregation (Shirlow and Murtagh 2006).[5] As Crawford and Clear (2001) have noted:

> The ideal of unrestricted entry to, and exit from, communities needs to be reconciled with the existence of relations of dominance, exclusion, and differential power. The reality is that many stable communities tend to resist innovations, creativity, and experimentation, as well as informal social control, and the way these processes play out lacks inclusive qualities and offender-sensitive styles. They can be coercive and tolerant of bigotry and discriminatory behaviour. Weaker parties within such communities often experience them not as a home of connectedness and mutuality but as a mainspring of inequalities that sustain and reinforce relations of dependence. They are often hostile to minorities, dissenters, and outsiders. (p. 137)

When considering utilising restorative justice initiatives to address communal conflict, such features must be acknowledged, and it is within such communal contexts that informal justice takes place in Northern Ireland – a reality which forms the backdrop to the discussions to follow.

Transitional societies can be signified by strong community and weak state structures in contrast to many 'ordinary' societies. It is this dynamic that leaves space for informal justice alternatives, both violent and non-violent. Northern Ireland has had its fair share of the former in the guise of paramilitary organisations and vigilantism, while the newer developments of restorative justice exemplify the latter. The question today, then, is not so much about how communities can build capacity and empower themselves,[6] but rather how these communities can *keep* these strong informal networks alive while simultaneously changing the *values* held by such informal networks. Thus, the challenge is this: how do we move from violence as a means of informal social control to non-violence while keeping old and encouraging new social networks to develop? Community restorative justice initiatives in Republican and Loyalist communities play a central role in such personal and communal transformations, as will be explored in detail in later chapters. First, however, the next chapter will provide an overview of practices of informal justice in Ireland and Northern Ireland prior to the establishment of the current restorative justice projects, practices which provide both a precedent and a *raison d'être* for the contemporary community restorative justice projects.

Notes

1 For a recent exception, see McEvoy and McGregor (2008).
2 See generally Cherif Bassiouni (ed.) (2002).
3 For an in-depth discussion on a range of other truth commissions, see Hayner 1994.
4 Nationalists are generally Catholics (but not necessarily) and support the unification of Ireland by political means. 'Republican' is the term used for Nationalists who also aim for the unification of Ireland but support violent means – the armed struggle. These loosely defined groups tend to identify themselves as Irish. Unionists are generally Protestant (but not necessarily) and support the maintenance of the union with Britain by political means; Loyalists have the same aim but support violent means for doing so. They also tend to claim a nationality as British. The membership of these real or 'imagined' groups varies, however, and this brief description is of a generalist nature.
5 The number of the so-called peace walls has actually increased since 1998. In the ceasefire year of 1994, there were a reported 15 such walls in Belfast; in 2000 there were 27; and in 2003 they had increased to 37. The best known wall is the one dividing west Belfast into the Falls and the Shankill. The highest number of walls, however, is to be found in north Belfast, indicating higher levels of segregation between communities that are geographically smaller, and where feeling of being under threat from the 'Other' are still prominent (Jarman 2004; Shirlow and Murtagh 2006).
6 Even though this is an issue, particularly in Loyalist areas.

Chapter 3

Paramilitaries and vigilantes: punitive populism as social control

This chapter provides an in-depth discussion of the informal justice practices which preceded the current community restorative justice projects in Northern Ireland. It particularly explores the intricacies of paramilitary punishment violence, practices for which community restorative justice was explicitly established as an alternative. Earlier practices of informal justice in Ireland also form part of the discussion, partly because they demonstrate the long tradition of informal justice on the island and because current restorative justice practices in Republican communities in the north initially drew legitimacy from such precedents. The discussion then moves on to focus on more contemporary practices of informal justice in Northern Ireland – apart from the recent community restorative justice developments – which can be divided into two overarching categories: paramilitarism and vigilantism. These are analysed as two different categories of community action, where the first is viewed as an expression of the 'organised community', and the second as indicative of the 'disorganised community'. Discussions of informal justice in Northern Ireland often refer to it as vigilantism, and little regard is given to the source of such violence, be it paramilitary organisations or 'ordinary' community members. However, the distinction is important since they require different means by which their practices can be challenged and changed within the transitional context.

The 'organised community' is defined by a well-developed organisational structure and loosely permanent membership, where people are allocated specific tasks and guided by written and/or unwritten rules and regulations, enforced through groups such as the Provisional IRA and the UVF. Practices of punishment violence belong firmly within this category and will be analysed here. The 'disorganised' community, on the other hand, is defined by a lack of structure, floating membership, and ad hoc reactions to law and norm-breaking within the community. Such a categorisation reveals little about the levels of violence used; rather, it indicates the community processes through which such expressions materialise. Indeed, the latter groups may find themselves in opposition to different elements of the organised community, resulting in a contest over informal social control within geographically defined areas.

A common feature of both is that they are a reaction to 'the vacuum of government strategies to control crime' (Hughes and Edwards 2002: 1) and antisocial behaviour at a community level, which has resulted in a situation where paramilitary and vigilante action occurs. Both the disorganised and the organised community can be viewed as sources of violence that form part of an embedded culture of violence (Steenkamp 2005). The main reason for making this distinction is that the different rationales for, formations and structures of the 'organised' and 'disorganised' community require different types of intervention, in that what 'works' when aiming to affect the practices of paramilitary organisations may not be as effective in relation to various vigilante groups. This is important when trying to estimate the effectiveness of community restorative justice in Northern Ireland, which has been explicitly aimed at the former. Importantly, these two groups of informal social control within the community are in competition with each other, arguably over the ownership of justice at the local level. Such competition is not necessarily a benevolent affair, and I will return to this point later in the chapter, after providing a more detailed narrative of informal justice practices on the island.

Informal justice in a historical Irish context

Informal justice institutions are ... non-bureaucratic and relatively undifferentiated from larger society, [they] minimise the use of professionals, and eschew official law in favour of substantive and procedural norms that are vague, unwritten, commonsensical, flexible, ad hoc, and particularistic. Every instance of informal justice will exhibit some of these characteristics to some degree, though in none will all of them be fully developed. (Abel 1982a: 2)

Alternative systems of justice have developed in many jurisdictions which have undergone political, social or ethnic conflict (Burman and Scharf 1990; McEvoy and Mika 2001), partly because the legitimacy of the state, and in extension the law, is frequently questioned and renegotiated in such contexts. Indeed, one of the defining characteristics of law and justice is a perpetual state of tension – between competing claims, and between civil society and the state – particularly when the very legitimacy of that state is in question (Bell 1996; Feenan 2002). When informal alternatives develop, challenging the sovereignty of the state, such tensions are bound to increase. In Ireland, tensions between formal and informal structures of justice have a long history, from the times of English colonisation to recent struggles in Northern Ireland. This section provides a brief historical overview of informal justice practices on the island of Ireland since the seventeenth century that have provided important precedents for more recent expressions of informal justice in Northern Ireland, at least for restorative justice projects in Republican areas. Such precedent was not relied upon in relation to projects in Loyalist communities, since they do not see themselves as sharing the same Irish legacy of informal justice. Instead, they depended more explicitly on recent models of restorative justice as a framework and basis for practice.

Practices of informal justice in Ireland can be traced back to Brehon law, which comprised the justice system on the island prior to the concerted impression of Anglo-Saxon legal powers in the seventeenth century. Due to the pressures of colonisation, it changed radically until being completely suppressed after centuries of British presence in Ireland. Traditionally, Brehon law encompassed customs, customary laws and legal institutions (Monaghan 2002). The outcome of the legal process, and the punishment prescribed, depended less on the actual crime, and more on the social status of victims and offenders. It also contained a strong emphasis on reparation, restitution and reintegration of both victims and offenders, and its aim was to preserve social cohesion and the status quo of the rural, hierarchical communities of that time. This was essential since 'the legitimacy and authority of the system was dependent on the cohesiveness of the community' (Monaghan 2002: 42). The centrality of both victims and offenders to the process was important, features which have led commentators to see the Brehon law as a type of restorative system of justice (Bell 1996; Auld et al. 1997; Monaghan 2002). Following the collapse of the Brehon legal system, several informal justice alternatives, including a number of secret societies, emerged during British rule in Ireland. The emergence of such alternatives often had a direct relationship with disputes over land and possessed the dual functionality of challenging the dominant British system of justice during the eighteenth and nineteenth centuries, and focusing on resolving land disputes and serving the local community (Monaghan 2002).

During the concerted guerrilla campaign against British occupation by the IRA from 1919, the informal tradition continued with arbitration courts, called Dáil Courts,[1] established by Sinn Féin in 1919. Like their predecessors, they focused mainly on cases arising from disputes over land, but extended their jurisdiction to cover criminal cases as well. This meant that they were similar to the dominant British system, effectively creating a direct challenge to British authority (Bell 1996). The Dáil courts operated at parish, district and national levels, and involved lay arbitrators and jurors. Judgements were largely administered and enforced by the IRA of the time. These courts were seen as operating outside the British system and, with the onset of the War of Independence in 1922, ceased to exist after an Act to this effect was introduced in the following year (Kotsonouris 1994; Bell 1996; Auld *et al.* 1997; Conway 1997; Monaghan 2002).

Nationalist communities in Northern Ireland generally see themselves as sharing this legacy of informal justice. This was important during the armed struggle and is also one reason why current restorative justice programmes have resonated so strongly with the community activists who were involved in their establishment. The following section investigates contemporary expressions of informal justice in Northern Ireland, from the beginning of the Troubles to the present time and, more particularly, the role of paramilitaries in Republican and Loyalist communities respectively.

Paramilitary justice in Northern Ireland: the organised community

Contemporary discussion regarding informal justice in Northern Ireland generally refers to acts which fall under the term 'punishment violence'. These are 'policing' activities undertaken by Republican and Loyalist paramilitary groups in the working-class communities in which they live and operate. Such practices have their origins in the Troubles, beginning in the early 1970s when the police were engaged in fighting insurgents and consequently paid less attention to 'ordinary'[2] crime. In addition, the police were seen as an illegitimate force in Republican communities and were denied access to such areas. Paramilitaries consequently took on the role of dealing with crime and conflict at a community level at the same time as they were involved in the 'war' effort against the British state and Loyalist paramilitaries (Munck 1988; Bell 1996; Feenan 2002).

Punishment violence exists for a number of interrelated reasons, but the most commonly cited are the absence of legitimate or adequate policing, rising levels of crime and antisocial behaviour, the perceived failure of the formal criminal justice system to prevent and effectively deal with crime, and a consequent community pressure to 'do something' about crime and antisocial behaviour in both Republican and Loyalist areas (Feenan 2002; McEvoy and Mika 2001, 2002; Monaghan 2002, 2004; Jarman 2004). In addition, Loyalist punishment violence in particular is associated with internal discipline among their own members and feuds between different Loyalist factions to a larger extent than for their Republican counterparts (Winston 1997; McEvoy and Mika 2001; Mika and McEvoy 2001; Monaghan 2002, 2004).

The methods of punishment violence traditionally[3] involve either shootings (of arms, legs, joints or a combination), or beatings (using baseball bats, iron bars, cudgels or hurley sticks). In addition, measures such as warnings, curfews, and exclusion from the community were common at the lower end of the tariff system (Bell 1996; Feenan 2002; Hamill 2002; Monaghan 2002; Jarman 2004). The main organisation responsible for punishment violence in Republican communities has historically been the Provisional IRA, although smaller dissident groups have also been sporadically involved in such attacks.[4] In Loyalist areas, there are several groupings which engage in this type of activity, a feature of the more factional and territory-oriented nature of Loyalist paramilitaries (Bruce 1992). The largest group, the UDA, and the somewhat smaller but equally violent UVF, have been responsible for most punishment attacks over the years. The LVF, a splinter group formed in 1996, has been one of the later additions to the arbitrators of 'justice' in Loyalist areas.

As part of the research for this book, an analysis of newspaper clippings reporting punishment attacks between January 2004 and August 2005 was undertaken. Generally, the news reporting of punishment attacks is short, to the point, and based on limited information. During this time period, a total of 143 cases were reported, and below are some typical examples of such attacks, carried out by both Loyalist and Republican paramilitary organisations:

The victim, a 30-year-old man, was attacked in his house in East Belfast at 10.45 pm by three men who shot him in his hands, knees and ankles (*Belfast Telegraph*, 30 May 2005).

37

The victim was a 30-year-old man, and the attack took place in the victim's home. Four masked men broke into the victim's house at 5.50 am and shot him in one leg. Baseball bats were also used (*Irish News*, 3 February 2005).

A 37-year-old man was abducted from a local bar, beaten by seven men with pickaxes, baseball bats studded with nails, and iron bars. He was also shot nine times in both legs. The victim has since been subject to continuing threats from the Provisional IRA and has contacted a solicitor, who is keeping recorded statements about death threats (*Irish News*, 14 January 2004).

The victim was a 47-year-old man in North Belfast, dragged at 10 pm from his home into his driveway by six masked men, and shot in both legs (*Irish News*, 14 January 2004).

The attack took place at 10 pm, when four masked men approached the two victims, aged 20 and 21, on a road in Newtownards. The victims were led to a nearby car park where they were shot in the lower leg (*North Down and Ards Telegraph*, 27 October 2005).

Four masked men forced their way at 1 am into the home of the victim, a 28-year-old man, where they beat him with iron bars (*Irish News*, 19 March 2005).

The victims, two young men aged 16 and 17, were shot in the legs in an alleyway in Newtownards at 9.40 pm (*Belfast Telegraph*, 15 April 2005).

The victim was walking near the canal in Newtownards at 1 am when he was approached by an unknown man, armed with a handgun. The victim was ordered to roll up his trouser leg and was shot once in the calf (*Newtownards Chronicle*, 26 May 2005).

A 20-year-old man has been shot in Poleglass on the outskirts of West Belfast. He was attacked by two men while walking on Ardcaoin Drive about 1 am on Monday. The man was taken to hospital with an injury to his left leg after what appears to have been a paramilitary-style incident. Police in Lisburn have appealed for anyone with information to contact them (*BBC News*, 18 August 2008).

The reasons for and the practice of punishment violence differ between Loyalist and Republican areas and will therefore be discussed separately. This is important since interventions to challenge such practices will necessarily differ, both in their form and ultimate impact – a fact often overlooked by uncritical commentators. Much of the discussion will be in the past tense, since Northern Ireland is moving rapidly away from this type of organised 'policing' of working-class communities. However, punishment attacks still take place, albeit on a much lesser scale, but the involvement of the main paramilitary groups in such practices has largely ended. Current attacks are mainly carried out by dissident groups who want to continue the armed struggle, or as 'policing' of feuding between different groups involved in criminal activity.

Practices of punishment violence in Republican communities

As mentioned earlier, the Dáil courts of the early twentieth century served as a model and source of inspiration for Republican communities in Northern Ireland during the Troubles, when different varieties of informal justice were utilised. The earliest forms of contemporary expressions of informal justice were the Citizen Defence Committees, established in many Catholic areas in the early days of the Troubles (late 1960s – early 1970s). Their aim was to protect Catholic enclaves from Loyalist attacks by building and supervising barricades and patrolling interface areas by foot or car (Munck 1988). In Derry in the early 1970s, local defence associations in Catholic areas such as the Bogside, Brandywell and Creggan[5] responded to increased pressure from the community for informal social control by setting up their own 'police force' where punishment usually consisted of a stern talking-to regarding the need for solidarity (Thompson and Mulholland 1995).

During a short-lived IRA ceasefire in 1974, the Republican movement[6] created so-called People's Courts, filling a vacuum of social control in Nationalist communities (Munck 1984; Conway 1997). Mainly due to community pressure, the IRA found itself occupying the role of community 'police' in Nationalist areas (Burton 1978; Munck 1988), with the task of engaging with community disputes, local crime and antisocial behaviour. These informal justice initiatives were run by local people who carried moral authority in the community and who during this time took the responsibility for dispute resolution in Republican areas (Morrissey and Pease 1982; Auld et al. 1997). These courts, however, were short-lived. Their demise has been attributed to a number of factors, including disruption by the Royal Ulster Constabulary (RUC)[7] because the IRA (a clandestine organisation) was required to operate more openly (Munck 1988).

The ceasefire broke down in 1975, but some of the characteristics of community control continued. The IRA continued with 'policing' activities, especially in administering punishment,[8] and Sinn Féin established incident centres which soon became locally known as 'Provo police stations',[9] as they were easily accessible to the local community (Monaghan 2002). Such centres were hearing cases and trying to resolve disputes with 'local notables such as teachers, doctors or shopkeepers who would be called in to ensure the "impartiality" of Republican judicial procedures' (Munck 1988: 45). These developments indicated a shift in the administration of informal justice in Republican working-class areas. The IRA was, however, still a central feature of the administration of informal justice but conducted its affairs less publicly to avoid exposing itself to the police or security forces (Morrissey and Pease 1982; Feenan 2002).

In 1982, the Republican movement reconsidered its policy of punishment after acknowledging that shootings did not solve the problem of rising crime. A wide-ranging debate occurred within Republican circles and in Nationalist areas on how to combat crime. At the time, physical punishment was still used against the more hardened and persistent criminals, but young people involved in offending were 'to be involved in a process of discussion with the Republican movement as to the consequences of their behaviour for their victim and larger community' (Monaghan 2002: 48; 2004). However, rising crime rates during the mid-1980s led to increased community pressure on the IRA to deal more harshly with young offenders, as they eventually did, abandoning this attempt to create a more humane way of dealing with crime and antisocial behaviour for the time being (Thompson and Mulholland 1995; Feenan 2002).

The situation changed after the signing of the 1998 Good Friday Agreement when the use of firearms became politically unacceptable. As a result, beatings increased, and the results of such attacks were often much more serious than those of shootings. Hence, attacks did not become less punitive. The serious injuries which resulted from beatings were due to the types of weapons used. As mentioned above, baseball bats and iron bars were the most common, but when axes, hammers, cudgels, and baseball bats studded with nails are used, the consequences can be horrific. Indeed, those 'punished' sometimes claimed to prefer being shot to being beaten, since the latter may cause injuries that take much longer to heal (Bell 1996: 156; Nolan and McCoy 1996; Feenan 2002). Moreover, attacks were often carried out by a group of people, increasing the risk of serious injury. Typical injuries after a punishment beating included fractured and broken limbs, fractured skulls, and puncture wounds if the weapon used was studded with nails (Monaghan 2002).[10]

A tariff system was in place in Republican communities (Thompson and Mulholland 1995), which included warnings and curfews for the less serious, first-time and young (under 17 years) offenders; beatings and shootings for more serious or repeat offenders; and exclusions from the community or from Northern Ireland altogether[11] for crimes that were deemed the most serious, such as informing, drug dealing and sex offending (Thompson and Mulholland 1995; Feenan 2002; Silke 2000b; Jarman 2004). These last three offences also carried the threat of offenders being subject to a death sentence if they returned to the community (Thompson and Mulholland 1995). In some cases, those due to be punished were told to turn up at a certain time and location to receive their punishment. Failure to do so often resulted in harsher punishment. Even though the overall severity of punishment is greater than would be the case in the formal criminal justice system, the informal system was similar enough in its construction – with mitigating factors, number of previous offences, age, and family connections taken into account – for two authors to refer to it as 'the black criminal justice system' (Morrissey and Pease 1982).

Republican paramilitaries were generally perceived as more organised (Bruce 1992; Conway 1997) and their tariff system more sophisticated and stringently adhered to when compared to their Loyalist counterparts. Keeping in mind Abel's definition of informal justice as non-coercive, decentralised and unprofessional (1982a: 2), the informal system operated by the IRA was the opposite as it was 'coercive … relatively bureaucratic and centralised' (Munck 1988: 50), lending credibility to the argument that the IRA and other paramilitary organisations belong in the category of the 'organised' community.

Traditionally, punishment of women was rare and limited to occasions where a woman from a Republican community was found fraternising with members of the army or police during the Troubles. The punishments were tarring and feathering, placarding (the guilty woman having to stand in a public place with a placard around her neck spelling out her crime), or shaving the woman's head (Munck 1988; Conway 1997). This was often perceived as an expulsion ritual in that punished individuals knew that they had to leave the area (Burton 1978), and the same reasoning occurs in relation to shootings. As mentioned by one interviewee, 'normally the process was very much you get shot, you heal, you get out. And that was very much a warning to everyone else, that not only do you get shot, you also get excluded from the community'.[12]

Punishment violence against women and young people under the age of 17 increased during the 1990s and early 2000. According to police statistics, 23 females received punishment beatings between

41

1989 and 2000 (total number for both Loyalist and Republican areas), but no one was shot. Based on the interview data, such a development is usually seen as mirroring the trends in offending elsewhere, in that the participation of young females in serious offending has increased, and if more women are being punished by the formal criminal justice system, similar developments are likely to take place at the community level.

In more recent times, when the IRA has abdicated its 'policing' role, a change has occurred in the way the organisation is perceived by the community. For example, many young people subjected to paramilitary punishment have less of a perception of the IRA as a local law and order organisation or as protectors of the community, and more as 'the people who shoot you'. As was mentioned by one interviewee in relation to how young people perceive the role of the armed groups today:

> Many young people in these communities today do not have a grasp of the history and rationale behind the Struggle, and judge them [paramilitaries] for their present actions only. Among the hoods,[13] some are very aware of the history of the place even though they have not grown up during the conflict, and they would be active Republicans. Others, on the other hand, would not have heard of the hunger strikers, Bloody Sunday, and know very little about the conflict and the role that the IRA played in it. To them, the IRA is a group that deals with punishment violence and will tell you when you stepped out of line.[14]

Such a change in community perceptions has also put pressure on the IRA to find alternative ways of dealing with crime and antisocial behaviour in the community. Perhaps it should come as no surprise that a community that for several decades has experienced the futility of such stigmatising shaming[15] as a feature of punishment would have a genuine interest in more reintegrative measures of community shaming. As a result of such changes in community support for punishment violence, along with broader political developments, internal discussions within the Republican movement have taken place over a long period of time, during both the Troubles and the subsequent transition, about alternative ways of addressing crime and antisocial behaviour at the local level (McEvoy and Mika 2001). Community restorative justice projects were the direct result of such discussions (Auld *et al.* 1997).

Practices of punishment violence in loyalist communities

Whereas local people are well aware of the several different paramilitary organisations in Northern Ireland, this is generally not the case for many international observers, particularly in relation to Loyalist paramilitaries. The Provisional IRA tends to be perceived as the only major paramilitary organisation in Northern Ireland, but this is far from the case.[16] It may be the largest, and certainly the one making the international headlines, but Loyalist paramilitaries have arguably made their presence felt in equal measures.

While Republican communities draw on a history of informal justice in Ireland going back centuries, such a precedent is not relied upon in Loyalist communities. Instead, informal justice expressions stem from the much more recent practices of community defence, arising since Partition, which increased greatly during the Troubles (Bruce 1992). Hillyard (1985) has noted that 'while there have been examples of popular justice in the Protestant and Loyalist community these raise very different issues because of the relationship of Protestants to the state in Northern Ireland' (p. 250). One feature which added to the complexities of Loyalist punishment violence is that Loyalists claimed to defend the union with Britain, while at the same time attacking the very security forces they claimed to support (Conway 1997).

It has also been problematic to comment accurately on the position and practices of Loyalist paramilitary groups due to a scarcity of research in these communities. A lack of nuanced analysis regarding the nature of Loyalist paramilitarism is also likely to stem from methodological approaches to research within Loyalist communities. In general, there is a lack of representative samples, in that much research has been carried out by interviewing people in prison (a convenience sample) or by talking to a few high-profile leaders, but rarely with the rank-and-file members who carried out most of the attacks (see Bruce 1993; Cusack and McDonald 1997; Silke 1998a, b, 1999, 2000a, b; Taylor 1999; Crawford 2003). There is also a tendency to sensationalise and pathologise the actions of Loyalist paramilitaries, instead of treating them as a 'natural' part of their communities and a consequence of the Troubles (Winston 1997). Members of paramilitary organisations are also someone's father, brother and husband, and not necessarily, as Silke (1999) has argued, mentally disturbed individuals with a strong intrinsic propensity for violence.

Traditionally, and by default, Loyalist groups were supportive of the police and would sometimes hand over suspected offenders to them. However, with the signing of the Anglo-Irish Agreement in November 1985, it has been argued that a mistrust of the Northern Irish state began to develop, and feelings of being 'sold out' to the Irish due to pressure from the IRA increased (Bruce 1993; Graham 1998; McKay 2005). Such sentiments have, according to Shirlow and Murtagh (2006), continued to grow with every perceived move by the Unionist government away from Britain and closer to Ireland. This resulted in an increase of informal justice measures in Loyalist communities, with a sharp increase in the number of punishment shootings and beatings since 1985 (Monaghan 2002). Similar developments were seen after the signing of the Good Friday Agreement in 1998, where Loyalists argued that the agreement was a bad deal for the Protestant community and represented a shortcut to a united Ireland. A consequent erosion of the legitimacy of the police and a lack of trust in their political representatives ensued, occurrences which are arguably the opposite to developments in Nationalist communities since 1998.

As mentioned previously, Loyalist paramilitary recruits were generally seen as being of a lower calibre than their Republican counterparts (Bruce 1993; Conway 1997). This was reflected both in terms of their 'policing' activities and their efforts to 'take on' the IRA during the Troubles (Bowyer-Bell 1993). There are several reasons for this difference; for example, that the police and the security forces drew recruits from the same population as Loyalist paramilitaries – the Protestant population in Northern Ireland – resulting in potential high-calibre recruits choosing employment with the police and military. Working for the state had the advantages of being better paid, being legal, and offering higher levels of job security (Bruce 1993), while still offering the opportunity for people to 'do their bit' for the defence of their community and the union with Britain. For Republican paramilitaries, there was no such drain on resources since joining the police or military would be viewed as a betrayal of Republican ideology; therefore, those who joined paramilitaries in Republican communities included those with considerable military and political acumen.

The motivation for practices of punishment violence in Loyalist communities may differ from that of their Republican counterparts, yet the methods have been very similar (Conway 1997; Knox and Monaghan 2002). Punishment attacks for the purposes of addressing internal discipline or inter-factional feuds were much more common in Loyalist areas than in Republican communities (Cusack and McDonald 1997; McEvoy and Mika 2001), and have continued up until the present day. Involvement in crime and antisocial behaviour were the most common reasons for a punishment attack. No agreed tariff system was in place, and warnings were hardly ever issued – instead people were often shot or beaten as a first measure (Monaghan 2002).

Punishment violence in both communities was meant to act as a general and specific deterrent, but there is little evidence of the effectiveness of such measures. For example, one study suggested that young people who had been punished by the IRA were likely to return to antisocial and offending behaviour with greater intensity and severity (Thompson and Mulholland 1995). Munck (1988) has noted that some of the 'hoods' attach a certain pride to having been 'kneecapped' by the IRA, since it confirms their status in the community as someone to be reckoned with, hence making punishment violence not only ineffective but also counterproductive. According to interviewees in both Loyalist and Republican areas, these issues are acknowledged by paramilitary organisations. One interviewee who had been active in a Republican punishment squad commented on the case of a young man who had been shot in both legs for involvement in joyriding and spent three weeks in hospital as a result. When the young man came back to the community in a wheelchair, he ripped out the driver seat in a car so that he could fit his wheelchair inside and managed to crash the car after an evening of joyriding around West Belfast.[17] Moreover, interviews conducted in Hydebank, the juvenile detention centre in Northern Ireland, clearly demonstrated that the absolute majority of young offenders had been either shot or beaten by paramilitaries at some point, but this had not deterred them from further offending. This ineffectiveness of punishment violence is another underlying reason for the establishment of community restorative justice projects, with the hope that inclusive and non-violent responses to conflict with a concurrent focus on reintegration would prove more effective in deterring future offending and the re-emergence of conflict.

The extent of punishment violence in Northern Ireland

Levels of punishment attacks in Northern Ireland are officially measured by the Police Service of Northern Ireland (PSNI),[18] which has collected and published a statistical summary of shootings since 1973 and beatings since 1982. These figures suggest that since 1973, 3,285 people have been the victims of punishment shootings and

2,265 people have been assaulted since 1982. Figure 3.1 summarises the more recent data from 1998 to 2005.

Levels of punishment violence fluctuate, however, in response to political developments and events on the ground (Silke and Taylor 2000). For example, around the 1994 IRA ceasefire, the number of shootings decreased dramatically. There was also a drop in rates of punishment violence in 2006, mainly because of the decommissioning of the IRA in July 2005. However, this did not mean that the IRA abandoned its policing role, a fact which can be gauged from the increase in the number of assaults during the same period in Table 3.1.

Such statistics provide an indicatory measure of the fluctuating levels of punishment violence. However, as with official police statistics elsewhere, the validity of such measures can be questioned.[19] Apart from the problems with official crime statistics noted by Maguire (2002), Northern Ireland adds its own peculiarities. There may be a reluctance to report these incidents for the reasons mentioned earlier in relation to the perceived illegitimacy of the police, and because the formal system has proven that it can do very little in terms of prevention and prosecution of such incidents. Moreover, many disputes at a community level are seen as a private matter to be dealt with internally.

Additionally, some young people punished are involved in serious offending behaviour and thus have no desire to tell the police about such punishment activities,[20] and many attacks are unreported for fear of paramilitary reprisal (Knox and Monaghan 2002; Monaghan

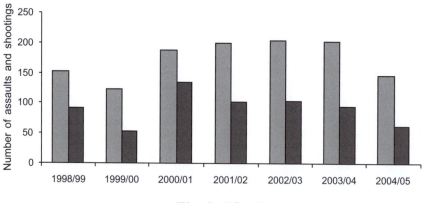

Figure 3.1 Paramilitary-style shootings and assaults in Northern Ireland

Table 3.1 Paramilitary attacks 1989–2006

Year	Shootings (by group)		Assaults (by group)		Total casualties
	Loyalist	Republican	Loyalist	Republican	
1989	65	89	51	23	212
1990	60	46	21	47	174
1991	40	36	22	40	138
1992	72	61	36	38	207
1993	60	25	35	6	126
1994	68	54	38	32	193
1995	3	0	76	141	220
1996	21	3	130	172	326
1997	46	26	78	78	228
1998	34	38	89	55	216
1999	47	26	90	44	207
2000	86	50	78	54	268
2001	121	65	93	53	332
2002	117	56	89	50	312
2003	101	55	103	46	305
2004	89	23	74	41	227
2005	74	11	60	29	174
2006	25	5	28	14	72

2004). Official statistics, however, are not only comprised of incidents reported *directly* to the police. Most attacks come to the knowledge of the police because victims of attacks are often admitted to hospital due to the seriousness of their injuries, and information is passed on to the police via that route.

Paramilitary punishment violence was, and to an extent continues to be, an extensive and deep-rooted problem in many communities in Northern Ireland. It is also a problem which occurs due to several interrelated reasons as discussed above, reasons which may be difficult to understand from an 'outside' perspective. This is arguably why previous attempts to end such practices through top-down means have largely failed, and why bottom-up initiatives are needed.

Top-down pressure to end punishment violence has been a long-standing feature in Northern Ireland, and increased with the beginning of the peace process and the release of political prisoners after the signing of the Good Friday Agreement (McEvoy 2001; McEvoy and Mika 2001). Condemnation by local politicians in media outlets was also common, particularly during politically sensitive times. As noted by Knox and Monaghan (2002), what was needed to address the social problem of communal violence perpetrated by paramilitaries against those suspected of crimes within their own communities was a multi-agency approach due to the complex nature of the problem. Such an approach, however, was being hindered by a deep mistrust and suspicion of statutory agencies in many working-class communities in Northern Ireland, and also by the perceptions of the 'undeserving' nature of victims of paramilitary attacks. As noted by Knox and Monaghan: 'Statutory bodies either minimise the problem of community violence or remain indifferent to it. The net result is a disjointed response at both the inter-sectoral and inter-agency levels' (2002: 89).

Practices of punishment violence have their basis within local communities, and hence any effective strategy to challenge such practices arguably needed to adopt a bottom-up approach (McEvoy and Mika 2001), since that is where the most important dynamics take place. Such a strategy also had to be sensitive to the differences between Republican and Loyalist communities and the relationship between paramilitary organisations and their communities. The community restorative justice projects in Loyalist and Republican areas are examples of such bottom-up approaches that are inherently sensitive to the community context in which they work due to all practitioners being from the local community, several of whom have been actively involved in the armed conflict or have close relatives who were.

Before moving on to a detailed exploration of these restorative justice projects, it is important to mention another aspect of informal social control in Northern Ireland – vigilantism – which has existed alongside the more organised paramilitary groups. Indeed, some groups such as the UDA arguably began as a vigilante reaction to the threat posed by the IRA in the early 1970s. This is an important aspect of an embedded culture of violence, created through conflict and which has continued in the transitional phase.

Vigilantism: the disorganised community

This section discusses vigilantism, which for the purposes of this book I have termed 'disorganised' expressions of communal violence. The term 'disorganised community' stems from the fact that these groupings *lack* the organised military structures, permanent membership and leadership that signify paramilitary groups such as the IRA and the UVF. Vigilantism is usually employed by 'ordinary' community members, concerned about high levels of antisocial behaviour in general, or as an ad hoc response to particular incidents. Vigilante actions, as expressions of a disorganised community, are relatively frequent in Northern Ireland and are similar to paramilitary punishment violence in that they represent a reaction to increasing levels of crime and antisocial behaviour in the community. They are also a result of a concurrent perception of the criminal justice system as illegitimate or ineffective in dealing with these issues. These types of activities generate many case referrals to community restorative justice projects in both communities. However, due to the characteristics of the disorganised community, their practices are more difficult to challenge and change, as the community restorative justice projects were designed to challenge practices undertaken through organised paramilitary structures.

Defining vigilantism

'Vigilantism' is a term commonly used in the Northern Irish context but often without adequate conceptualisation. Such a lack of theoretical distinction between different expressions of informal justice has led to pessimism and misconceptions about different forms of informal justice in general (Cain 1985). This has occasionally resulted in the practices of paramilitaries, vigilante groups and community restorative justice being 'lumped' together by critical voices, with the assumption that they are all different disguises of community oppression and control by paramilitary organisations.

The term 'vigilantism' is rarely defined beyond the cursory, with some notable examples (see Rosenbaum and Sederberg 1976; Johnston 1996; Abrahams 1998, 2002). Rosenbaum and Sederberg (1976) have provided a typology of vigilante violence that focuses on the *intention* of the actor, which they see as fitting into three categories: crime control, social-group control, or regime control. The first, crime control vigilantism, tends to occur when a group of people are dissatisfied with the formal legal system, due to its perceived slowness, its inability to address issues of importance to a certain group of people, and its leniency, often coupled with rising crime rates. Social-group control vigilantism, on the other hand, is not so much concerned with the ineffectiveness of the formal system, but instead deems it irrelevant as an avenue of redress. This type of vigilantism can be engaged in both by private citizens and agents of the state, and is generally aimed at a social group – identified by its communal (ethnic, religious), economic, or political characteristics – who are perceived as threatening the status quo and, as such, the dominant classes in society.[21] The authors also mention that this type of vigilante activity can be engaged in by official groups such as the 'B Specials'[22] in Northern Ireland, a Protestant police force which abused the Catholic minority. Such observations have led commentators to argue that 'although the formal system is supposedly even-handed in enforcing the law, the occupants of official positions may identify with the dominant communal groups and essentially support their efforts to maintain the status quo' (Rosenbaum and Sederberg 1976: 14). Lebow (1976) included the original UVF and other paramilitary groups of both Republican and Loyalist persuasions as belonging to the same type of vigilante group as the B Specials. The final category – regime-control vigilantism – describes violence which threatens the existing regime, such as revolutions or *coups d'état* (p. 17).

Johnston (1996) has provided a useful criminological conceptualisation, in opposition to the somewhat dated socio-legal definitions, which have tended to focus on political violence and to group all such expressions under headings of 'establishment violence' (Rosenbaum and Sederberg 1976). Johnston (1996) argues that by equating vigilantism with establishment violence – acts which the police and military can participate in just as well as 'ordinary' citizens – the concept becomes all-inclusive and consequently loses much of its explanatory power. He asserts that vigilantism, properly defined, has six necessary features: (1) it involves planning and premeditation by those engaged in it; (2) its participants are private citizens whose engagement is voluntary; (3) it is a form of 'autonomous citizenship' and, as such, constitutes a social movement; (4) it uses or threatens the use of force; (5) it arises when an established order is under threat from the transgression or the potential transgression of institutionalised norms; and (6) it aims to control crime or other social infractions by offering assurances of security for both the participants and others (Johnston 1996: 220). A similar conceptualisation of vigilantism has been noted by Abrahams (1998, 2002), who distinguished between vigilantism as a means of crime control that seeks to compensate for state failures in law and order, and vigilantism that is defending 'sectional interests' for political or other advantages, both of which have clearly been part of the informal justice picture in Northern Ireland. It is important to note that the vigilante groups, as an expression of community, are heterogeneous and reflect the tensions and hierarchies of power within the community from which they draw their members. Further, they may very well exploit community institutions for their own ends (Abrahams 1998).

Vigilantism in Northern Ireland

Foster's (1995) research on informal social control in high-crime areas indicates that residents often prefer to deal with low- and medium-level crime informally, through existing social networks, rather than reporting them to the police.[23] Her conclusions resonate closely with the Northern Ireland context. The vigilante groups under consideration here exist in both Republican and Loyalist communities, but, according to the primary research for this book, they seem to be more frequent in the former.[24] They tend to operate under semi-legitimate names such as Community Watch and Safer Neighbourhoods Schemes. The problem is not the presence of such groups – after all, they are a common feature across the UK (Bolton 2006; Crawford 2006; Farrow and Prior 2006), where their activities are supported by the police – but the *quality and nature* of such a presence. While some people participate in ad hoc vigilante groups following a particular incident which angers the community, such as a murder or sexual assault when the perpetrator is known, others have joined Community Watch on a more permanent basis. As noted by one interviewee in West Belfast:

> I think people just have decided that they want to live in a better place, and that they want to make their own community safer. A lot of people who are out on the streets would themselves have been victims at some point of crime and antisocial behaviour. For instance, people would have tried to steal their cars or whatever, so people feel that they need to be out there and protect theirs and their neighbour's property.[25]

Some of the actions taken by these groups have on occasion been questionable, resembling those of punishment squads rather than concerned citizens. When these groups were first established, they sometimes employed 'older' types of community enforcement such as the wearing of face scarves and the use of baseball bats. Interview data indicated that some people who have joined Community Watch are former members of paramilitary organisations, usually of a lower rank, dissatisfied with the increasingly non-violent route taken by the IRA and the UVF. Arguably, the number of Community Watch-type groups increased after the Good Friday Agreement when political violence became less acceptable and the IRA and UVF endorsed non-violent practices such as CRJI and Alternatives.

As these groups are defined by a *lack* of leadership and organised paramilitary presence, it has been difficult for community restorative justice groups to challenge and change their behaviour. Considering that CRJI and Alternatives were established to work with the organised structures of paramilitary organisations, they lack the tools necessary to challenge effectively all of the violent practices of disorganised vigilante groups. Although these are organic relations at the grass-roots level between CRJI staff and volunteers and Community Watch activists, it would be wrong to overstate the influence of the former over the behaviour of these groups. Certainly, it is easier to make restorative justice-style interventions designed to encourage non-violent responses to crime with a relatively centralised and hierarchical paramilitary organisation such as the IRA than with a much looser and less disciplined organisation such as the Community Watch collective.

There are, however, positive aspects of Community Watch and Safer Neighbourhood groups, particularly evident in more recent years. In some instances, these organisations mirror their English counterparts (Bolton 2006; Crawford 2006; Farrow and Prior 2006), in that they consist of ordinary residents within an area who report suspicious and antisocial behaviour. In England, however, such behaviour would be reported to the police (Bolton 2006), whereas in Republican communities the situation is somewhat different. In the recent past, they would have reported it to a paramilitary organisation, while today they report mainly to CRJI. The aim for the future, as this research indicates, is for them to have a more effective working relationship with the police so that both organisations, the PSNI and Safer Neighbourhood/Community Watch, can support each other. At the time the majority of interviews were conducted on the Republican side (late 2004/early 2005), it was said by a CRJI practitioner[26] that Community Watch volunteers

> are our eyes on the street. I am not out there 3 o'clock in the morning. They would bring us cases about kids who are on the street at 3 am sniffing glue, and the parents say that the kids were in bed all night, and they weren't. So that gave us information, and I supported that. ... They now use our referral sheets, and I passed those on to social services.[27]

Later interviews (2007/2008) indicate that the Safer Neighbourhood Projects in particular have consolidated their own identity, working separately from community restorative justice projects, and are also less engaged in questionable activities.

Violence by members of the disorganised community also takes place outside of Community Watch-type organisations. For example, a 39-year-old man was stabbed to death in West Belfast on 3 February 2006 as part of a long-running neighbour dispute. Several other families in the area became involved, and a number of people were put out of their homes by threats and acts of violence by vigilante-type groups. There were 600 related incidents reported, ranging from threats and arson attacks to murder.[28] By October that year, the PSNI had spent over £1 million on dealing with retaliation between the two feuding families.[29] It is not unusual for disagreements between neighbours or rival groups of young people to rapidly escalate, resulting in petrol bombs being thrown at houses;[30] assaults with baseball bats, clubs and axes; and families being forced out of their houses by intimidation and fear for their safety. Such incidents can be viewed as expressions of violence by the disorganised community.

Vigilante action in Loyalist communities received much media attention during large-scale riots in September 2005. These riots followed the rerouting of an Orange parade, and escalated into several nights of serious rioting within several Loyalist areas in Belfast.[31] There seems to be less violence, however, emanating from Safer Neighbourhood groups in these communities, possibly because of the more prominent role played by the various armed organisations in relation to social control in these areas, and the consequent lack of space for other competitors.

The fact that paramilitary groups such as the IRA have been labelled vigilante groups in the past does not mean that such classifications hold true today. Before 1998, communal expressions of violence and defence arguably were usurped by the organised structures of paramilitary groups. In the transitional period, however, a split can be discerned, whereby organised paramilitary groups moved in one direction and the more loosely organised vigilante groups in another. This has resulted in a competition between different modes of informal social control at the community level. The largest Republican armed group, the Provisional IRA, has taken the road towards peace and support of the Northern Irish state for the first time since its formation. However, there are elements within the community who disagree with such an approach altogether. One consequence of such views is the formation of vigilante groups and, indeed, dissident Republican armed groups that often lack the discipline and hierarchical structures of the IRA.

In Loyalist areas, there is also a change, albeit of a somewhat different nature. Fewer of the paramilitary groups have committed explicitly to a peaceful road, with the exception perhaps of the UVF. The structure of Loyalist groups, as noted above, differs from their Republican counterparts, and there is no hegemonic group such as the IRA, resulting in a more fierce competition over informal social control in Loyalist areas. There are several different, and strong, voices of community opinion, and some of these groups also have access to weapons and the label/name of well-known paramilitary organisations. Instead of the clear shift that has taken place in Republican communities, Loyalist areas have witnessed several of their armed groups metamorphosing into more or less organised criminal gangs, but without the ideological component that was so crucial during the conflict.

By way of summary at this point, this chapter has outlined the sources of violence in Republican and Loyalist areas in Northern Ireland, which arguably form part of what can be called a punitive community. It was demonstrated that paramilitary punishment violence occurs as a result of several interrelated factors intrinsic to the organisations' *raison d'être* and to community pressure to 'do something' about crime and antisocial behaviour in the area. It was also discussed that such reasons differ somewhat between communities. What is clear is that efforts to challenge and change such practices need to contain an in-depth understanding of such factors – and of the construction of 'community' – and ideally be indigenous to that community, as opposed to outside and top-down. Importantly, the existence of several paramilitary organisations within both communities makes social control – both within each community and between community and state – a highly contested and controversial site. Debates about ownership of justice are central to these tensions and contribute to the construction of a complex set of community relations.

Community in Northern Ireland is clearly a fundamentally political concept, and the construction of community is saturated with hierarchies of power, making communities not only political but highly contested places (Hoggett 1997). Power struggles take place within the community and between the community and the state, particularly in a transitional society. Awareness of such constructions and contestations of power and control are essential when exploring the utilisation and expression of informal social control within any community, and when tracing the competition over ownership of justice between community and state. The function and expression of such hierarchies of power within the community should also form a central part in any analysis of restorative justice. After this overview of the theoretical and factual dynamics which preceded the development of community restorative justice projects in Loyalist and Republican communities, we now turn to a closer exploration of the process through which the projects were established.

Notes

1 The Dáil was the revolutionary assembly established in 1919 by Sinn Féin following the 1916 Easter Rising. Today, it is the term for the lower house of the parliament in the Republic of Ireland. The term Senate (former upper house) is called Seanad Éireann.

2 For the purposes of this book, this distinction applies to Northern Ireland and similar transitional contexts. Most writers make the distinction between 'ordinary' and 'political' based on differences in form, context and motivation. Political crime has been defined by Hagan (1997) as criminal activity that is committed for ideological purposes rather than private greed or passion. It has also been argued that the definition should include crimes committed by the state (Turk 1982). In Northern Ireland, this debate took on additional urgency when the British Government abolished the special category status, which resulted in the hunger strikes of IRA prisoners in 1980/1. Mrs Thatcher, the then prime minister, expressed the now famous aphorism: 'A crime, is a crime, is a crime' (Hillyard 2001: 211). Also see McEvoy et al. (2007) for a detailed exploration and international comparison of political prisoners and the discourses around their status and management.

3 The levels of punishment violence have decreased substantially during the course of researching and writing this book, partially because of the efforts of community restorative justice projects in both communities.

4 During the latter part of 2008, dissident activity increased in Northern Ireland, including some incidents of punishment violence, but also attacks on police stations and other targets that, in the eyes of the perpetrators, represent the British state. This will be discussed in more detail in Chapter 8.

5 Three areas in which community restorative justice projects are today thriving.

6 The 'Republican movement' is a collective term which generally includes the Provisional IRA and Provisional Sinn Féin, and Ogra Sinn Féin, which is their youth wing.

7 The Royal Ulster Constabulary, the name of the Northern Irish police force before its name was changed to the Police Service of Northern Ireland in the aftermath of the 1998 peace agreement.

8 Silke (1999) has also noted that the people within the IRA who were responsible for the so-called punishment attacks tend to be in the lower ranks and in the periphery of the Republican movement – what he refers to as 'cannon-fodder'. Some authors have referred to the people who carry out punishment attacks as 'psychopaths' (Silke 1999), or as 'the more sadistic elements' among Loyalist and IRA members (Kennedy 1995).

9 'Provo', or 'Provie', is local slang for the Provisional IRA.

10 An article written by five medical practitioners at the fracture clinic in the Royal Victoria Hospital in Belfast (Nolan *et al.* 2000) detailed the physical and financial cost of punishment violence. They compared the nature and extent of injuries before and after the ceasefires in 1994, which, as mentioned above, resulted in a sharp decrease in shooting injuries and a corresponding increase in injuries caused by beatings with clubs and sticks. They reported that in the 10-month period before the ceasefires, 31 patients were treated for gunshot wounds. All patients were male with a mean age of 25.2 years. Mean time spent in the operating theatre was 2.6 hours, mean hospital stay was 7.6 days, and mean cost per patient equalled £3,102. In the following 10-month period, there was only one shooting injury; the other 27 were due to beatings. Again, all were male, with a mean age of 27.4. Time spent in the operating theatre was 2.6 hours, mean hospital stay was 12.4 days, and the mean cost per patient was £3,849. Overall, the injuries sustained from beatings were more serious and required longer time spent in rehabilitation. According to the authors, there were, on average, three punishment attacks per week requiring hospital treatment and with a mean cost of treatment of £3,849 per patient. The annual costs exceeded £600,000.

11 Exclusion from the community could be time-limited, such as 6 or 12 months, or be permanent. Usually, the person to be excluded received a warning that he or she had to leave the area within 24 or 48 hours. Sometimes whole families were excluded, and when one parent was told to leave, he or she would often take their children with them. People from Republican areas usually went to the Republic of Ireland when excluded, whereas people from Loyalist areas tended to go to Scotland or England. Many people returned to the community without 'permission' from the paramilitary group that was responsible for the exclusion, often with serious consequences. However, as many people had never been outside their community before this incident, they preferred to take the chance of going back to the place they knew, instead of being forced to live in a different country without friends or family (Thompson and Mulholland 1995; Feenan 2002).

12 Interview with CRJI caseworker, 11 November 2004.

13 A local derogatory term for juvenile delinquent.

14 Interview with CRJI coordinator, 14 February 2005.

15 The deterrent effect of punishment violence was minimal, as will be discussed in more detail below.

16 See Appendix A for a more detailed overview of the different paramilitary organisations.

17 Interview, 7 February 2005.

18 Or the RUC, as the police service was called up until midnight of 3 November 2001, when the name was changed as part of the recommendations of the Patten Report, following the Good Friday Agreement 1998.

19 For a detailed description of the problems of validity and reliability associated with official crime statistics, see Maguire (2002) and Muncie (2001).

20 These are also important reasons why quantitative victim surveys cannot be carried out with any accuracy, a technique which is used elsewhere to bolster the reliability and validity of official crime statistics. Smaller qualitative studies exist, however, which provide important information about the lifestyles and experiences of the young people subjected to punishment violence: e.g. Hamill 2002.

21 Examples include the Ku Klux Klan and other 'anti-black' violence aimed at 'keeping black people in their proper position'; racial riots in places like India and China, and more recently in France; and similar situations where private citizens 'take the law into their own hands' (Rosenbaum and Sederberg 1976: 12–14).

22 The B Specials were a part-time, unpaid and armed force of the Ulster Special Constabulary which was created in 1922 to deal with the 'rapidly deteriorating situation' in Northern Ireland. In 1922, it was said that the B Specials was 'Northern Ireland's main counter-insurgency force' and when the IRA stood down for a period in that year, it was commented by supporters of Unionist rule that this was a consequence of the service and selfless duties of the men of the Ulster Special Constabulary. More critical voices, however, tend to point to the abuses committed by the force, and view it as a Protestant paramilitary group, inherently sectarian and an instrument of oppression. The B Specials were disbanded in 1969 after the reports of the Cameron inquiry, which told of the assaults, battery and malicious property damage the force had committed against Catholics in Derry's Bogside (Hezlet 1972; English 2003).

23 The use of such informal networks was evident in several interviews with both victims and volunteers in Loyalist and Republican communities. Respondents told of how they could use the informal network to find out more information about a specific perpetrator, information which then could be taken straight to the paramilitaries, or in some instances, to the police. Others, however, used the neighbourhood's network of

informal contacts to confront the parents of the perpetrator, which was seen as preferable to involving other organisations.

24 On the other hand, there is a common opinion in Northern Ireland that Loyalist paramilitary groups, who in the post-peace agreements era have largely metamorphosed into criminal gangs, are nothing more than vigilantes now that the political reason for their existence has largely dissipated.

25 Interview with CRJI caseworker, 2 December 2004.

26 Throughout the remainder of the book, I use the term 'practitioner' to refer to those people employed by CRJI and Alternatives as managers, administrators and mediators. The term 'volunteer' refers to all people volunteering for the organisations who receive no monetary compensation for their work.

27 Interview with CRJI coordinator, 16 November 2004.

28 *Ibid.*

29 *BBC News*, 6 October 2006, 'Policing of Estate Feud Defended'.

30 *BBC News*, 23 November 2006, 'Teenager Critical After Fire Bomb'.

31 *BBC News*, 13 September 2005, 'Third Night of Loyalist Violence'.

Chapter 4

The beginning of CRJI and Alternatives: legitimising restorative justice in a punitive community

This chapter outlines the establishment of community restorative justice projects in Republican and Loyalist communities in Northern Ireland, beginning with the initial discussions held in 1997–8, in which former combatants and ex-political prisoners were a central driving force. The development of community restorative justice reflected the divided nature of Northern Ireland, and, importantly, the process of establishing the projects occurred independently of each other; there was no cooperation or exchange of ideas across the community divide at this stage.[1] However, common themes emerged from the establishment processes in both communities, notably the organic development of practice which characterised the first years of operation for these grass-roots organisations, competing modes of social control between paramilitaries and restorative justice projects, and changing community perceptions of this new and radical initiative.

Establishing community restorative justice in Northern Ireland

The legitimacy and moral authority to operate is derived firmly from the geographical communities in which they operate. (McEvoy and Mika 2002: 547)

Community restorative justice initiatives in Loyalist and Republican communities in Northern Ireland emerged in 1998 with the explicit intention of providing a non-violent alternative to practices of punishment violence. Both CRJI and Alternatives were preceded by extensive community consultations which aimed to achieve credibility, moral authority, and community ownership. This process has been referred to as one of legitimisation (McEvoy and Mika 2001), and was essential in building community support for restorative justice (Pranis 2004). Interestingly, however, restorative justice per se was not a guiding or organising principle of practice at this early stage. Instead, the design of the projects reflected community needs in relation to punishment violence specifically, and to crime, antisocial behaviour and victimisation more generally.

Each community – Loyalist and Republican – will be discussed separately, as the projects grew out of very different community contexts, and because several interviewees made it clear that they did not wish to be compared and contrasted to the 'other' community. Thus, the comparisons which inevitably are made in this chapter are limited to discussions of restorative justice as a framework of practice, and care has been taken to highlight the distinctiveness of the two projects.

Community restorative Justice Ireland (CRJI)

In Republican communities, a group consisting of criminal justice practitioners, one academic from Queen's University Belfast and community activists led the discussions that preceded the first working model of community restorative justice. These initial discussions resulted in the publication of the *Blue Book* (Auld *et al.* 1997), which outlined the background to and design of an alternative to punishment violence based on restorative justice principles in Republican communities. It defined the parameters of practice as 'operation within the law, non-violence, respect for the human rights of the offenders, accountable community involvement, restoration of both victim and offender, and proper training of those involved' (Auld *et al.* 1997: 2). In interviews and discussions, the original authors of the *Blue Book* were quite clear that the origins of these projects did not lie in a commitment to restorative justice theory and practice. As one of them summed up:

> Our dialogue with the Republican movement began explicitly on the subject of trying to find an alternative to punishment violence pure and simple, it did not grow out of a commitment to restorative justice per se. In fact, none of us knew very

much about restorative justice in those days in 1995–6. The early discussions were more based on the informalism tradition summed up in Richard Abel's work. It was just serendipity that Harry Mika was on sabbatical in Northern Ireland at the time. He was working out of the Institute of Criminology at Queen's as we were writing it and in discussions with him and others, it just seemed to fit perfectly. It also resonated almost immediately with the Republicans' value base, especially their notion of their responsibilities in local communities, and then it just took off.[2]

Once the *Blue Book* had been published and circulated, a grass-roots community consultation process began which aimed to receive feedback from as many local interest groups and individuals as possible.[3] Such a bottom-up approach to the establishment of the project was seen as vital (McEvoy and Mika 2001). As Pranis (2004) has argued, restorative justice should not be mandated in a top-down authoritarian process, but the work of implementing its principles must be done at the local level and must involve all stakeholders, that is, all interest groups in the community. A bottom-up approach to the establishment of community restorative justice projects is even more important in a transitional context due to state–community relations being severely damaged during conflicts (Criminal Justice Review 2000), and in the Northern Ireland context a lack of legitimacy of the state in Republican communities (McEvoy and Mika 2001).

This grass-roots approach was exemplified in Republican areas by the use of a Community Charter as part of the widespread consultation process which preceded the actual establishment of restorative justice in west Belfast, and later in Derry.[4] The Community Charter was distributed to all the homes in the relevant geographical area where the establishment of a restorative justice project was proposed. The initial Community Charter is outlined below:

A Draft Community Charter

Accepting that recognition and acceptance of the collective, and individual, rights and associated responsibilities of all the members of our community is the foundation of freedom, justice and peace for all of us and acknowledging the need to consistently promote and advance a supportive social and physical environment as essential to the development of the potential of all in our neighbourhood we, the residents of

---

'........................', commit ourselves to the promotion of a new spirit and infrastructure to build a better community.

In keeping with this commitment we agree to work collectively, jointly and separately as appropriate to ensure and reaffirm the dignity and worth of all who live here regardless of gender, race, religion, language, disability, sexuality or age and to strive to the best of our abilities to promote social justice, supportive relationships and an associated physical environment for all who live in our community. This dignity and human worth is enshrined in a combination of rights and responsibilities:

We affirm that everyone in our community has the right to:

Be free from torture, inhuman or degrading treatment;

Fair trial;

Shelter, warmth and basic living necessities;

Freedom from externalised fear and anxiety;

Privacy;

Own property alone or in association with others;

Free association;

Information and freedom of opinion and expression;

Choice of sexuality;

Education and learning opportunities and resources;

Appropriate care and support;

Open expression or celebration of their religious, cultural or political affiliation;

Political participation;

Equal protection under the law;

Equality of access to public service;

Work to free choice of employment, to just and favourable conditions of work and to protection against unemployment;

Rest and leisure and to share in the cultural and artistic life of the community.[5]

We also hold that we each have a responsibility to ensure that we do not create, or enhance, any condition, relationship or situation which may prevent our neighbours from exercising or enjoying their rights as outlined.

Given that a major factor in the negation of the rights of our residents is crime and the fear of crime, we believe our community must address this issue, its causes and its consequences, with humanity, consistency and as a matter of urgency. Ensuring that our model of justice includes both restorative elements and proportionate treatment, recognising that we must distinguish between the various criminal, deviant and anti-social behaviours and differentiating between crime against the person, against property and that which can generally be classified as nuisance. We commit ourselves to confronting crime and its effects on our community.

Each signatory to this Charter pledges to respect the rights of his/her neighbours in the community and appropriately exercise his/her own responsibilities.

In keeping with this pledge we reject violence as a tool for resolving disagreement between individuals or families and as an alternative we will initiate and/or will co-operate in any agreed community systems or processes involving informal or formal mediation to resolve disputes or respond to crime, and to criminal and anti-social behaviour within our community.

Should such extensive processes of mediation prove not to be effective in resolving a dispute due to unwillingness or refusal of any of the parties to the dispute to co-operate or meet their responsibilities we will further commit ourselves to participating in any non-violent activity collectively agreed in open discussion within the community. Such activity should be designed to ensure that those who refuse to comply with their responsibilities are subjected to the collective disapproval of the community expressed if necessary through boycott or any other non-violent process as may be necessary to protect the rights of individuals or groups in the area.[6]

Used with permission by Community Restorative Justice Ireland, 2006.

The Community Charter was also published in the local press with the clear endorsement of the Republican movement. As one spokesperson noted in a statement in the Republican newspaper *An Phoblacht*:

The community at large, the business sector, Church, schoolteachers, shopkeepers, solicitors, doctors, political parties, residents and tenants associations, but also youth groups, elderly people's groups, women's groups, and statutory agencies all need to be involved, because all are involved. The first step to setting up a CRJ scheme is for such groups to meet and discuss the notions of CRJ, its standards and values. This stage is followed by the promotion of a Community Charter door to door. Endorsement of the Charter, the support and participation of the whole community, is what lends CRJ its legitimacy but it also provides the step of empowering the community to take responsibility for itself. (*An Phoblacht*, 12 July 2001)

In Derry, the Community Charter was distributed to all 260 homes in a small Nationalist community called Brandywell as part of the establishment process of the first project there in 1999. A questionnaire was also given out in conjunction with the Charter, in which people could leave feedback if they wanted to add or take away something, a process which took three months to complete. Through this method people received information about restorative justice, and what type of services the project offered – a process which can be described as one of community education.

A strong sense of community ownership developed, exemplified by the swiftness and number of case referrals to the project which began immediately after the first office opened (McEvoy and Mika 2001). In Derry, community restorative justice projects now operate in seven other estates, and similar community consultation processes took place in all locations.[7] Similar developments took place in the four areas in West Belfast where subsequent projects were set up.

As mentioned earlier, practices of mediation and dispute resolution at a community level were not new to these practitioners. As noted by Mika and McEvoy (2001), there were important antecedents for the individuals instrumental in the establishments of the projects:

There is anecdotal evidence that several individuals, most of them ex-prisoners with close ties to paramilitary organisations, have been informally involved in negotiating alternatives to punishment beatings, shootings, exclusions, and other threats on a case-by-case basis since the early 1990s. It is thought that several hundred such cases may have been negotiated, resulting from the direct appeals of those under threat and pressure, from their families or advocates. (p. 295)

Such statements were confirmed during the research where several interviewees discussed these practices, reflecting the internal discussions which had been ongoing within the Republican movement for several years (Morrissey and Pease 1982; Auld *et al.* 1997; McEvoy and Mika 2001; Monaghan 2002). The community consultation was a crucial first step towards building support among the interest groups which make up the community, and achieving credibility, moral authority and community ownership of these new restorative justice initiatives (McEvoy and Mika 2001).

Northern Ireland Alternatives (Alternatives)

Alternatives did not have a written Community Charter like the one used in Republican areas. Instead, a former life-sentenced UVF prisoner, Tom Winston, who is now the manager of Alternatives, undertook extensive initial community consultations. He was commissioned by the Northern Ireland Association for the Care and Resettlement of Offenders (NIACRO) to investigate the possibilities of non-violent alternatives to punishment violence in the staunchly Loyalist area of upper Shankill in West Belfast (McEvoy and Mika 2001; Mika and McEvoy 2001). As in Republican areas, this process formed an important part of gaining acceptability and community ownership. As Tom Winston commented,[8]

> In March 1996, I started the research. What we were going to do, we did not know, how we were going to do it, we did not know. So what I decided to do was to talk to everyone that had something to offer. And that ranged from all the statutory agencies, including police, probation, social services, educational library board (youth division, which had a lot of youth work going on in the Shankill area at the time), victims of crime that came to the attention, victims of paramilitary violence, paramilitaries, young people, local churches – which numbered around 90 at the time – basically everyone within that wide remit.[9]

This consultation process included one-to-one talks and public meetings, which eventually involved hundreds of people in the area.[10] The first two groups to be interviewed were the police and local paramilitary representatives. According to Tom Winston, the police were very supportive and their view was that everyone was condemning the practice of punishment violence, but no one was doing anything about it, and hence they welcomed the efforts. The response from one of the Loyalist paramilitary groups, the UVF, was that:

> If you can come up with a different model that can have wide-spread support, then we will back off it [the practice of punishment violence]. Basically we are being tortured[11] to carry out policing in this community in the absence of the police not doing it.

This quotation also reflects the debates held within some of the Loyalist paramilitary organisations that were looking for a way to reduce their involvement in punishment attacks.

The same widespread consultation process took place as each new project was established. For example, an Alternatives office in East Belfast opened in 2002, and, as on the Shankill, it was the ex-prisoners' groups in the area that initially discussed the concept of restorative justice, looking for an alternative to punishment violence. The manager of the East Belfast project was asked by these groups to sit on the committee that investigated the possibilities for such a development. The committee ran into some difficulties during this period, however, mainly due to local community politics:

> People were holding it up, people wanted different models, because of the situation within Loyalism, and with us trying to make it inclusive we tried to bring all the organisations along with us and have one programme. Unfortunately one of the constituencies wanted their own programme, with their own management board, but with funding and all that it would not have worked. ... So that held it all up.[12]

The constituency which held the process up was the UDA. According to an interview with a senior officer in the PSNI, they wanted their own mediation structure, with their own mediators, who at that time were members of the UDA. The UDA also wanted full control over what, and with whom, they would mediate. This situation illustrates the importance that was placed by these groups on being 'in charge' of social control within the community. The PSNI declined to sign up to this initiative, which in the end never got off the ground.

As in Republican areas, restorative justice did not form part of the initial community consultation. However, as the community consultation progressed, the type of model which could work became clear, in relation to what types of things people wanted to happen in a project which addressed antisocial behaviour. Many of these things resonate strongly with values articulated in restorative justice theory and practice, such as the views that offenders should take responsibility for their actions and should 'put something back' into the community, that offenders should meet with victims if possible, and that offenders' needs should be met in a wider social setting by addressing the underlying causes of their offending. Restorative justice as a concept, however, did not enter the picture until a later stage of the consultation following the involvement of Debbie Watters. Watters had worked with restorative justice in Elkhart, Indiana, USA, and had recently returned to her native Northern Ireland, and brought with her the skills and knowledge needed to proceed with a restorative justice framework.

Their first office opened on the Upper Shankill Road in November 1998. The Shankill is often seen to represent the heartland of Loyalism in Northern Ireland, and many of the paramilitary groups have their headquarters here. Hence, if you want to challenge paramilitary practices, this was the place to start (Winston 1997). The focus was on a geographically small area initially, so as not to dilute their limited resources, instead putting their energies into proving that the project could actually work. However, the first case was that of a young person from Rathcoole, a Loyalist estate in North Belfast about six to eight miles away, who was involved in antisocial behaviour and was under threat of being beaten or shot. This case was an indicator that the widespread consultation process had been successful in 'spreading the word' about this new project, and also of the very urgent need in many Loyalist areas of Belfast for such a project.

The initial model of restorative practice was uniquely tailored to function within the particular context of the Loyalist community, and for working with young people under threat of punishment by a paramilitary organisation. The project manager of the Shankill office said in relation to this:

> The original model was basically around one-to-one contact between a young person and a support worker, with the aim to develop a contract. In terms of adapting it [the RJ model], the work was obviously in a unique setting and we also used it not only to address the prevention of offending behaviour, but also as an alternative to paramilitary punishment beatings. So it was more tailored for the different context in which we were working. We tried a number of different things, and some of the terminology that was used in America obviously wasn't suitable for our setting, so we had to do some basic tinkering.[13]

The practice of this project will be explored in detail in the next chapter. Alternatives now operates at four different locations: three in Belfast (West, North and East) and one project called IMPACT located in Bangor, 30 minutes north-east of Belfast.

Paramilitaries and restorative justice: competing modes of informal social control

The relationship between community restorative justice and para-military groups within the areas in which they operate differs somewhat between the two communities. The broad endorsement of CRJI by the Republican movement meant that the projects enjoyed a wide remit of practice, and only a handful of cases were not referred to a restorative justice office (McEvoy and Mika 2001). As the dissident Republican paramilitary organisations are relatively small in comparison to the Provisional IRA, there was less competition over social control in these areas than in Loyalist communities. Alternatives had to, and still does, operate under a more stringent remit of practice. As mentioned earlier, the Loyalist paramilitary groups are more equal in size than their Republican counterparts and therefore the struggle over social control is more tangible in those areas. Moreover, only the UVF endorsed the philosophy and practice of Alternatives, and even their endorsement was limited.

The main deciding factor regarding the remit of practice of Alternatives was the factional and territorial nature of Loyalist paramilitarism (Bruce 1992; Conway 1997; Cusack and McDonald 1997). For example, disputes relating to the internal discipline of Loyalist paramilitary members and disputes between different paramilitary organisations fell outside the remit of a community restorative justice project (Winston 1997). Moreover, there were (and to a certain extent, still are) offences which the paramilitaries took more seriously and preferred to deal with themselves as instead of referring them to restorative justice projects or the criminal justice system, such as sex offenders, the selling of drugs to minors, and crimes against the elderly. These were areas in which Alternatives was initially not allowed to intervene (Mika and McEvoy 2001; Winston 1997).

These parameters of practice still existed at the end of the fieldwork in 2006, and the main focus of Alternatives remained on young people who were involved in serious and persistent antisocial behaviour. As mentioned by one interviewee:

They [the paramilitaries] are still very rigid on, for example, internal discipline within the organisation. Sex offenders – unfortunately there was one just around here who was shot the other night.[14] His name is up on the gable wall, saying 'sex offender', 'child molester'.[15] But we could not deal with that sort of stuff, we do not have the means for that. In relation to internal disputes, we have offered to mediate, but they are reluctant to take up that offer.[16]

Alternatives will negotiate directly with the paramilitaries, mainly the UVF, in relation to young people who are under threat of being shot, beaten or excluded. Since the inception of the project, the referral base of cases has increased, and now includes parents, youth workers, or young people themselves:

Last week for example we had one young lad whose mother and his school referred him, because his behaviour pattern, he had started to display all the antisocial tendencies and behaviour which was ... I suppose the way we put it, his name is way down here and suddenly it is starting to go up the ladder, if you know what I mean, and people within the community is starting to notice this lad, and before it gets up there we want to, you know, intervene. So yes, we are finding now more and more that families are starting to refer their children.[17]

Awareness of such features of community life is vital, as is an understanding of the activities to which paramilitaries tend to respond. Tom Winston argued that for an alternative to punishment violence to be successful, such an informed awareness of the differences between the types of activities which attract the attention of the paramilitaries is needed. This is necessary so that interventions (at least initially) may be focused on those areas where they may realistically have an effect (McEvoy and Mika 2001).

CRJI, on the other hand, enjoyed a much wider remit, because of the broad endorsement of the Republican movement (Mika and McEvoy 2001). As mentioned by the manager of CRJI, most people in the mainstream IRA support the work of CRJI.[18] Such widespread support has not only resulted in an effective non-violent alternative to punishment violence, but has also enabled CRJI to increase greatly the scope of practice since its inception. Apart from addressing punishment violence, CRJI also deals with neighbourhood disputes, often of a serious nature; children and families whose behaviour has placed them at risk of coming to the attention of the armed groups; drug- and alcohol-related incidents; assaults; and joyriding, to mention but a few.

However, the same endorsement is not forthcoming from dissident Republican groups that want to continue the armed struggle and feel that CRJI is becoming too closely linked to statutory agencies, including the police. Some of the less organised groups, such as Community Watch and Safer Neighbourhood Projects, are also ambivalent in their attitude to CRJI. This is an area about which interviewees were reluctant to talk, but it is obvious that there is a contest over the ownership of informal social control and, importantly, over who holds the legitimate role of 'community representative'. This contest was ongoing during interviews in early 2008, made more explicit by the CRJI's budding partnership with the police.

The legitimisation process preceding the establishment of the community restorative justice projects was characterised by a grass-roots ethos and the prominent role of former combatants and ex-political prisoners. It arguably resulted in the legitimacy and credibility of the projects and moral authority for those who worked within them. The nature of the paramilitary presence in these areas placed constraints on practice, which differed between the two communities. It is important to note, however, that the reactions from the community were sometimes mixed. How such community perceptions and expectations were approached by community restorative justice practitioners and volunteers will be discussed below.

Community reactions to restorative justice

> We are not always the most popular, because we challenge people, and we confront their behaviour ... we don't judge it, we challenge it. And people don't like challenges, so if you are in this sort of work, sometimes word of mouth of our work is a good thing, but sometimes it is a bad thing.[19]

Within both Loyalist and Republican communities, there were suspicions of the motives of Alternatives and CRJI, and some perceived them mainly as an extension of paramilitary control.[20] One of the traditional arguments put forward by those who are cautious of grass-roots involvement in the ownership of justice is the risk that the notion of community becomes idealised, which may in turn obscure the possibility of exclusionary or authoritarian practices (e.g. Dignan 2000; Pavlich 2001). Such arguments have been prominent in discussions about community restorative justice in Northern Ireland. For example, on the Loyalist side, it has been said that Alternatives is just a front for paramilitaries, that paramilitaries control what Alternatives does, and that the project is used by such organisations to maintain control over their communities, albeit in a less malevolent manner. During an interview with a Loyalist ex-prisoner who was engaged in community work in mid-Antrim and had no formal connections with Alternatives, he made it clear that he had reservations about their work and doubts as to their claimed independence of paramilitary organisations:

> The staff of Alternatives sit around the same table as the leadership of the UVF on their monthly meetings, what does that tell you? And maybe they have had a positive impact in their communities, but they have had ten years, surely they should have a bigger impact by now if they really wanted to.[21]

Vocal criticisms of CRJI based on similar reasons were also forthcoming from several camps, in particular from the Social Democratic Labour Party (SDLP).[22] One spokesperson from the party said in an interview:

> Our main points are: we are not opposed to restorative justice, we think restorative justice is a very good idea. We are not opposed to community restorative justice, but we do think that before you have CRJI funded by the state, you need to put in place a hell of a lot of safeguards. We are concerned that some CRJ groups involve paramilitaries and are ultimately aligned to Sinn Féin and that leaves open the possibility of abuse; that the possibility of abuse is particularly high when we know that Sinn Féin and the Provisional movement protects its own members from the rule of law.[23]

In a similar vein, despite the widespread consultation process preceding the establishment of community restorative justice projects, the initial reaction from parts of the community was one of suspicion, and people were unsure about what types of services were offered. Some people were dismissive, and others outright hostile.

A very important factor in dispelling such fears was the feed-back the staff and volunteers at Alternatives received from the young people who were in contact with the project. Many of the participants initially presumed that the project had strong links with the paramilitaries, not only because there were ex-prisoners working on the support staff, but also the reasoning was that 'if Alternatives was going to stop people being beaten up by paramilitaries, then there had to be some connection with paramilitaries in order to do that'.[24] On the Republican side, as was described by several CRJI project coordinators, many presumed that they were the same as the IRA and, as such, offered the same types of 'services' in terms of punishment violence. Time after time the staff had to explain that:

> No, if you want someone shot then you have come to the wrong place, and no, we do not know of anyone who can provide that service for you in this community.[25]

It has taken them a long time to demonstrate otherwise. It was mainly the central involvement of ex-political prisoners and former combatants which contributed to this confusion in both Republican and Loyalist areas (McEvoy *et al.* 2002). When asked how she countered allegations of being an extension of the Provisional IRA in her daily work, one CRJI project coordinator said:

> I don't work for the Provies ... I negotiate with them. I can go in and speak to any of them, and we are supported by the Sinn Féin party – but that is it. We are very much an identity on our own ... [I] had an IRA man saying to me one day something about 'The Provies set you up, don't you know? ...' And he was really arrogant with me, and I just laughed at him and I said that 'if I had wanted to join the IRA I would have done that a long time ago. But don't order me about and don't tell me who I am.' I mean, no-one is denying that the Provisional IRA had a huge part in the organizing of an alternative to punishment beatings and shootings, but that does not mean I work for them. They don't *own* me, they don't give me *orders* as to how I should do my job.[26]

Some people who came to CRJI with a case found it difficult to adjust to the fact that CRJI offered a very different type of service. Occasionally, people would go to the IRA instead after realising that they would not receive the desired result. However, the IRA generally referred people back to CRJI, saying that they were no longer offering to shoot or beat people as a result of their involvement in antisocial behaviour.[27] According to several interviewees, this new way of dealing with community conflict was difficult for many people to get used to, and they found it especially difficult to take ownership of their own issues, after decades of relying on paramilitaries to 'sort things out'. This lack of accountability and responsibility for the consequences of one's actions is not unique to Northern Ireland, and it is one of the key issues which community restorative justice projects aim to address.

How, then, did the perceptions change over time, and through what mechanisms? One of the senior workers with CRJI mentioned four avenues in which such a process took place. First, this occurred on a personal level, through one-to-one meetings with the people who came to CRJI asking for assistance, and through people who participated in actual mediation processes. Second, community groups were influenced through meetings and information, and, in turn, influenced their members and networks through referrals and personal contacts. Third, this change occurred as a result of the presence of high-profile cases. For example, a murder was committed in one area of West Belfast, in which an old man was killed in his own home and the perpetrators (a couple of youths) then burned down the house to 'hide the evidence'. The people responsible were arrested, but the anger and disgust that remained in the community made people turn on the offenders' parents, threatening them and attacking their house. Several CRJI mediators were involved in the case, trying to calm things down. They spoke to numerous people and had several community meetings in relation to this conflict, and through this situation they were able to convey to people what CRJI was about, who worked there, what values they were advocating, and what type of processes they used. Finally, this shift in attitudes was also a result of the use of referral agencies, such as the Housing Executive and Social Services, who saw first-hand the value of CRJI practices. Such changing perceptions, in turn, led to informal partnerships between community restorative justice projects and statutory agencies on the ground.[28]

A similar process took place in Loyalist areas. Interviewees mentioned that there were two sets of variables which influenced public perceptions of community restorative justice on the Shankill. The first challenge was that the concept of restorative justice was something completely new and did not exist in public consciousness prior to the establishment of Alternatives. Hence, as mentioned above, the process of public education through meetings and written information was vital. The second challenge, which echoes the experience in Republican areas, was the presence of ex-prisoners in the project and the initial links to EPIC,[29] which in many people's minds meant that Alternatives was 'a paramilitary thing'. To try to overcome these perceptions, the strategy adopted by the Alternatives staff was to

> sell restorative justice in a practical sense, saying that 'What you are looking at here is restorative justice as a model and a concept and a philosophy, but it is also a practical way of being an alternative to punishment violence and to address offending behaviour which are the reasons why a lot of these beatings are taking place.'[30]

This practical way of 'selling' Alternatives and CRJI is significant, and takes place on a case-by-case basis. Perceptions could only really be changed through personal contact with and experience of the project, community education, word of mouth from people who had participated, and news of high-profile cases. As part of these processes, the perceptions of Alternatives and CRJI also changed in the wider community through a process of information 'filtering down', from direct participants to their family and friends, which was referred to as 'the ripple effect' by practitioners and volunteers of all projects. As such, the consultation process did not stop with the opening up of the first office, but rather it moved into a new phase.

This new phase of practice can be defined as 'organic development' (Mika and McEvoy 2001) because of three distinct features. It was characterised by a strong grass-roots ethos, the practice was a response to community needs, and it represented a learning curve of effective practice experienced by practitioners and volunteers in relation to what cases to take on, and how to handle them most effectively. For example, one danger of community projects like these is that they can spread themselves too thin by taking on all types of cases (Thigpen *et al.* 1996). This is particularly a risk at the start of a project when staff and volunteers are keen to establish themselves and gain credibility in the community, and can also be due to uncertainties in the community as to what services are offered. As mentioned by one of the CRJI practitioners:

> Some people think that we are everything to all people. For example, we had someone phoning in yesterday asking if we could contact the local council to have his rubbish picked up.

We gave him the phone number to the council and told him to make that phone call himself.[31]

Practitioners and volunteers alike agreed that, after a period of time, they generally learned which types of cases they should avoid (even if that meant they could refer people to another organisation over the phone), and what types of practice might be less effective:

One thing we learned not to do was to make house calls. At the beginning we would have been working day and night. We also learned that we cannot respond like a fire service – people would have phoned and said that there is a fight in the street and we would probably have put our boots on and gone up there, to try and sort it out. We have learned to not do that anymore, you can sort it out afterwards ... because you can actually make the conflict worse by being there while the conflict is going on, because people would think you have taken sides ... Another thing I don't encourage is people visiting my house when they need help, so I have learned to regulate that. People are a bit disappointed if I don't help them there and then, but that is how it has to be if I am going to do my job properly. And they ask, 'What do I do if I am attacked in the middle of the night?' and I say, 'Call 999 [emergency services], that's what I would do'.[32]

The research indicated that it was initially difficult to make people understand that they had to come to the office with their cases, rather than arriving at the doorstep of a practitioner's house. It was important for the staff at the projects to convey to people that such refusal did not mean that the client was not taken seriously, but rather that it was about good practice:

Yeah, that was very difficult. Because people in our community used to do their business on street corners, in shops, in bars, wherever you met people. And that was happening when we first started on the ground. I had people coming up to me in the supermarket ... I mean, I could not even go for a loaf ... like 'Oh, thank God that I met you, blah, blah.' And I was taking it all on, I was thinking, 'This is what I am, this is what I have to do, these people own me.' That is how naive I was. But certainly we had to change that, big time. And I think that is about showing assertiveness and leadership. And that has now filtered through, that 'You do not go near her home. She works during the week, you can come to the office or you can call and make an appointment, but you do not go near her door'.[33]

This quotation also reflects the need which exists in these communities for people to find assistance with their problems, and in the transitional period they are still relying on older and familiar ways of achieving this. Hence, the organic development of practice reflects the values and expectations in the community, and all projects in both the Republican and Loyalist areas have changed and amended their working practices over time to reflect such needs (McEvoy and Eriksson 2006).

In conclusion at this point, it can be argued that a number of features of the community consultation process emerged which were seen as equally important for projects in both areas. An important factor was the resonance with restorative justice values, which was demonstrated by the wider community, as it wanted offenders to take responsibility for their actions, contribute to the community, and meet their victims if possible, and that the needs of offenders and victims should be met in the wider social setting.[34] Such views, as evidenced in interviews with practitioners in both areas, made it easier for the projects to 'sell' restorative justice to the community.

A central shared feature is clearly the grass-roots, bottom-up character of these projects. This was highlighted as the most important feature for effective practice within the transitional context:

I think what has happened is that Alternatives have successfully done what they have done because they work from the bottom-up, so they are [at the] grass-roots level. They have met people on the ground, both paramilitaries and the residents of the Greater Shankill, and saying, 'This is what we hope to do, are you supportive of this?' In contrast, what the government seems to want to do is to force things *upon* the Loyalist working-class communities, and in reality they don't have a clue what the Loyalist community needs, and to be honest with you, I don't think they care very much.[35]

The initial legitimisation process for both Alternatives and CRJI arguably resulted in the widespread legitimacy and credibility of the projects within their own communities. Restorative justice initiatives in local communities in Northern Ireland were built on local capacity, knowledge and experience for devising appropriate solutions to conflict within the areas in which they function. The affirmation and development of new social norms through participatory practices such as restorative justice (Braithwaite 2002b) constitute an especially important feature in a transitional society, where different modes of informal social control and the relationship between them are in a continual process of renegotiation. The ripple effect of community restorative justice practice is also a vital feature of their work in this regard. However, moving away from violent conflict, where severe punitiveness characterised people's responses to norm transgression, towards a strong, peaceful, inclusive and democratic community requires a significant mind shift[36] for many people, and there are no short cuts. The next chapter continues the exploration of restorative justice practice in both communities, with a more explicit focus on the day-to-day work of the projects, and in particular discusses how the praxis of Alternatives and CRJI can contribute to challenging a culture of violence within the transitional context.

Notes

1 Interviews with CRJI and NIA managers, 9 November 2004 and 27 May 2005 respectively.
2 Interview with Kieran McEvoy, 15 January 2006.
3 This initially took place in the Andersonstown area of West Belfast, where the first project was established.
4 Derry/Londonderry. The first form is usually the name of the city preferred by Nationalists, and the latter by Unionists (Whyte 1991). I have elected to adopt the form used when undertaking the fieldwork in respective communities. Hence, the city will be referred to as Derry when discussing CRJI projects, and Londonderry in relation to Alternatives.
5 The influence of international human rights instruments in the formulation of this Charter is evident in many of the points expressed, and the interview data clearly demonstrate the importance placed on human rights as an organising concept, particularly in Republican communities where such rhetoric has a long history (McEvoy 2003).
6 The last point here regarding community boycott has never been implemented in practice.
7 Interview, 31 March 2005.
8 Tom Winston's current role is as a manager for NIA. As such, he is responsible for supervising all the different sites, helping them with training and guidance and to maintain an ethos based on restorative justice. It is also his job to try to attract funding, to negotiate and try to develop cooperation with the police, and to develop the overall practice of NIA for the future.

9   Interview with Tom Winston, 27 May 2005.
10 The Greater Shankill area had a population of around 22,000 in 2001. The Alternatives project, however, initially focused on only the upper Shankill (the population of which is substantially less, but no exact figures for this area were found). This was because this area was UVF territory, the only Loyalist paramilitary group at the time that had a working agreement with Alternatives. The lower Shankill was UDA territory and consequently Alternatives had no remit there.
11 Local slang for 'being put under pressure'.
12 Interview with East Belfast Alternatives manager, 2 June 2005.
13 Interview, 19 May 2005.
14 The man in question was shot in both hands, feet, and knees: a punishment reserved for the most serious offenders on the scale used by Loyalist paramilitaries.
15 A common means of official community 'naming and shaming', which often has very serious consequences for the person in question. In restorative justice language, this is a method that can be firmly placed in the 'stigmatising' category.
16 Interview with East Belfast Alternatives manager, 2 June 2005.
17 *Ibid.*
18 Interview, 9 November 2004.
19 Interview with CRJI coordinator, 16 November 2004.
20 Such suspicions have by no means disappeared, but in later years they have been vocalised mainly by political parties such as the SDLP and the DUP. Most of the critiques have been aimed at CRJI as opposed to Alternatives. This issue of extending paramilitary control under the guise of community restorative justice has been a hotly discussed topic at both community and state levels in Northern Ireland. Several of the Independent Monitoring Commission (IMC) reports pay close attention to the relationship between paramilitaries and the communities in which they are based, in particular in relation to the violence, threats and intimidation used in such communities with the aim of exercising power and exploiting the very communities that they claim to protect and from which they draw support. These dynamics will be discussed in more detail in Chapter 7.
21 Interview, 29 June 2005.
22 The Social Democratic Labour Party, the main contender with Sinn Féin over the Nationalist constituency.
23 Interview, 17 February 2006.
24 Interview with project manager, Shankill Alternatives, 19 May 2005.
25 Interview with CRJI coordinator, 16 November 2004.
26 Interview with CRJI coordinator, 16 November 2004.
27 Interview CRJI caseworker, 2 December 2004.
28 Such partnerships will be detailed in Chapters 7 and 8.
29 The Ex-Prisoner Interpretative Centre on the Shankill, a large Loyalist ex-prisoners' organisation.

30 Interview with project manager, Shankill Alternatives, 19 May 2005.

31 Interview with CRJI practitioner, 2 December 2004.

32 Interview with CRJI practitioner, 2 December 2004.

33 Interview with CRJI coordinator, 16 November 2004.

34 Views of a much more punitive character were also expressed. These will be explored in more detail in the next chapter in relation to cultures of violence.

35 Interview with Alternatives project manager, 19 May 2005.

36 The term 'mind shift' was frequently used by practitioners and volunteers in community restorative justice projects in both Republican and Loyalist areas when talking about the transition and the changes that were occurring. This was in relation to both the 'ordinary' community and paramilitary organisations. Even though the term may seem informal within an academic context, it is used here, as it reflects the understanding of the challenges of restorative justice practice as perceived by practitioners and volunteers themselves. Facilitating this mind shift is seen as one of the most important tasks of their continuing practice.

Chapter 5

The practice of community restorative justice in Northern Ireland

The restorative justice projects analysed here are unique in relation to the complexity and levels of violence which characterise much of their casework. As indicated in the previous chapter, they were established and have operated independently of the state and as such represent a truly grass-roots response to crime and antisocial behaviour. The models of restorative justice utilised by Alternatives and CRJI differ in terms of the remit within which they have been able to work, due to paramilitary influences, and the organic development of practice that reflected the needs of their particular communities. There are also differences among the projects within each community. For example, the practices of Alternatives on the Shankill and in North Belfast are mainly concerned with young people and victims, whereas the Alternatives IMPACT project on the Kilcooley estate in Bangor has had a much wider remit for reasons related to the physical make-up of the community, the nature of the paramilitary presence, the needs of the community, and the leadership displayed by practitioners. Even though several models of practice belong within a restorative justice framework, the community projects in Northern Ireland mostly employ a combination of victim–offender mediation and family group conferencing. Many of the values evident in restorative circles (Stuart and Pranis 2006), however, such as involving the wider community and paying greater attention to both preparation and follow-up support for victims and offenders, also form a prominent part of the practices in both communities.

The first section of this chapter provides a descriptive overview of the practices of both CRJI and Alternatives, while the second part explores whether they can be viewed as examples of transformative justice. This is arguably achieved by affecting broader community structures through utilising existing social networks and empowering individuals and groups to engage with statutory agencies within and outside the community.

Community Restorative Justice Ireland

Previous publications on community restorative justice in Northern Ireland (see McEvoy and Mika 2001, 2002; Mika and McEvoy 2001; McEvoy *et al.* 2002; Knox and Monaghan 2002; Mika 2007; Monaghan 2008) have focused almost exclusively on restorative justice work in relation to punishment violence. This book extends the analysis, focusing on the remaining 95 per cent of the case load. Since its inception, the remit of CRJI has become much wider in scope than was initially intended, and the following section provides descriptive data illustrating the current work undertaken by the four projects in Belfast.

As mentioned earlier, the working models of practice within CRJI were not imported as ready-made solutions but have instead developed organically from the needs of the particular community. Since their initial purpose was to be a non-violent alternative to punishment violence, and to address effectively the complex issues surrounding such practices, a multifaceted approach was needed (Auld *et al.* 1997). Consequently, interventions could not focus solely on dealing with people under threat (of shooting or beating), but also on the very people who carried out the attacks. Such an approach necessitated direct dialogue with local paramilitary groups, mainly the Provisional IRA – an approach which would have been impossible without the active involvement of former combatants and ex-prisoners (McEvoy and Mika 2002; McEvoy and Eriksson 2006).

Referrals, process and outcomes

Referrals to the different CRJI offices currently emanate mainly from individuals directly involved in a dispute or conflict, whether a victim or a relative of an offender. This is in contrast to the first years of practice, during which a substantial number of referrals were received directly from a paramilitary organisation or from the now largely defunct Community Watch. Figure 5.1 provides a summary of all referrals from 2007.

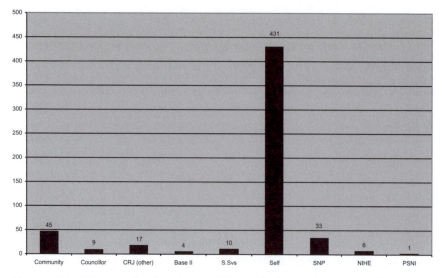

Figure 5.1 Source of referrals to CRJI Belfast in 2007. CRJ: community restorative justice; S.Svs: social services; SNP: Safer Neighbourhood Projects

The grass-roots character of these projects is confirmed by the very small percentage of referrals emanating from non-community organisations such as the Housing Executive, Social Services, or the police. Self-referrals make up the majority, indicating a widespread endorsement of CRJI within the community. Referrals to the project generally occur either by telephone or personal visit. A caseworker then contacts the parties to the dispute as far as they can be identified, usually by a letter inviting them to attend an initial meeting. Sometimes people ignore letters and telephone calls, or contact CRJI to let them know that they do not want to participate, and the process ends here. For cases that do continue, many are subsequently resolved through shuttle mediation, without the parties meeting directly. Shuttle mediation is frequently used as a primary strategy, as it is a useful tool to employ when a face-to-face meeting might be too confrontational or challenging (Roche 2003). People are only brought face-to-face when they all consent to do so.

When a face-to-face meeting takes place – and as a consequence of the often large number of participants in cases – conferencing is the restorative justice process that has been deemed most appropriate. Conferences follow a preset script which provides facilitators with an agreed upon process to which to adhere – a working strategy commonly used in many Australian and New Zealand jurisdictions (Moore and O'Connell 1994; Van Ness *et al.* 2001; Maxwell and Hayes

2007). Consequently, the conference process used by CRJI adheres strictly to certain ground rules, agreed upon by all participants at the beginning of the meeting, such as respectful listening, and refraining from derogatory language, interrupting and violence. Victim–offender mediation practices are rare in CRJI, mainly because there are always attempts to include suitable support people and others who may have been affected by the particular conflict – an approach which fits better within a conference format.

As mentioned previously, CRJI deals with a wide range of cases, and Figure 5.2 illustrates the categories and number of cases handled by the four offices in West Belfast – Falls, Upper Springfield, Andersonstown and Colin – between January and December 2007. In total, they dealt with 819 new cases, a decrease of 186 cases from the previous year. The three most common types of cases were 'youth-related', 'neighbourhood dispute', and 'threats', all of which made up a total of 53 per cent of all cases.

A high number of cases involved youth, which is arguably reflective of the situation in many working-class areas in the UK, often signified by social, economic and structural disadvantage. This situation is arguably amplified in Belfast, a city that is trying to cope with the rapid social change resulting from transition. Some areas of Belfast, however, such as Colin, were characterised by even greater problems around youth-related incidents, this area having a higher caseload for this particular category than any other office. One reason for this

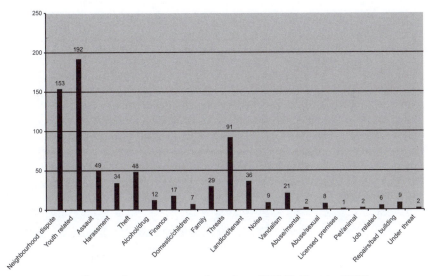

Figure 5.2 All cases by category referred to CRJI Belfast in 2007

difference could be that the Colin area has a higher proportion of young people than any other part of Belfast: according to the 2001 census, 52 per cent of the population in this area was aged 16 or below. Youth Initiative, a project which works in this area, notes that Colin is marked by generational unemployment, a destructive peer environment, large-scale teenage pregnancy, and a strong paramilitary presence and recruitment. Such variables are likely to affect levels of crime and antisocial behaviour, as reflected in the caseload of the CRJI project. Moreover, in all of West Belfast, only 38 per cent of those aged between 16 and 60 were employed in 2001. When CRJI staff indicate that they are trying to address the underlying causes of offending and antisocial behaviour, it is these kinds of variables they have to take into account.

As part of the research for this book, data were collected on several key variables in relation to the practice of CRJI. Figure 5.3 provides an overview of the relevant statistics for 2007, including the number of new cases, unresolved cases, and type of restorative process used.

A noteworthy feature that differentiates CRJI practice from many restorative justice initiatives elsewhere is the high number of participants in cases, and also the number of hours spent by volunteers working on their resolution. In the 819 cases in 2007, 3,174 people were directly involved as participants, with an average number of 3.8 participants in each case. In particular, cases involving

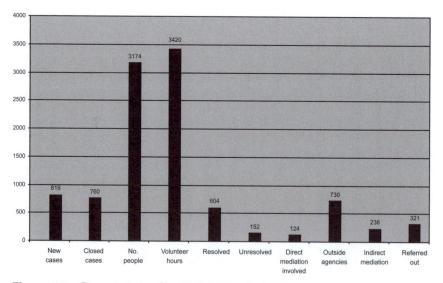

Figure 5.3 Case statistics for CRJI Belfast in 2007

neighbour disputes and youth-related issues tend to involve large numbers of people. A total of 3,420 hours was spent dealing with these cases. Considering that these four offices are staffed by a total of four full-time coordinators and approximately 30 volunteers, the numbers are impressive. Such high numbers are also, I would argue, an indicator of not only the local legitimacy of the project, but also of the community need for such a service.

Irrespective of the model used, number of participants, or type of case, the values and principles of restorative justice are central. As mentioned earlier, it is in particular the *process* of *doing* restorative justice that was referred to by practitioners and volunteers alike as the cornerstone of their practice. Interviewees saw the process as their safety net, providing principles of practice upon which they could rely when facilitating discussions on highly emotive issues and serious incidents of communal or interpersonal conflict. These opinions reflect long-standing debates within the restorative justice literature on whether the process or the outcome should be the focus of practice, with both views being staunchly defended (e.g. Zehr and Mika 1998; McCold 2000; Walgrave 2000; Daly 2003). Outcomes are obviously important and the goals of community restorative justice in Northern Ireland include reintegration of offenders, reducing fear of crime, repairing harm, and transforming attitudes to violence. However, to achieve all of these goals, the restorative process is seen as a crucial means by which such aims could be achieved. According to one senior CRJI caseworker, by participating in the process, or by going through the CRJI training, people are empowered to resolve issues in their own families, among friends and in their own communities. Participation in restorative justice teaches people about alternative ways of conflict resolution, a component of practice referred to by practitioners of CRJI and Alternatives as an 'education process'.

Outcome agreements resulting from the consensual decision-making processes incorporate a range of different actions: apologising to the victims; agreeing to desist from certain behaviours, such as associating with particular individuals – this is often used for young people involved in substance abuse; repairing the harm – which can include monetary compensation for objects stolen or broken through vandalism; reparation through some type of community work – for example, gardening for elderly people or helping to clean up a local area; returning stolen goods; and neighbours agreeing not to talk to each other and/or refrain from shouting abuse at each other. Some cases result in mutual agreement with no further incidents. In other cases, particularly neighbour disputes, participants return for further help, or CRJI involves other organisations such as the Housing Executive or the PSNI.

Practitioners argue that they not only aim to resolve a particular dispute at a surface level, but also strive to address the underlying causes of antisocial behaviour and crime (Auld *et al.* 1997). This includes attending to the needs of the wider family and victims of crime and antisocial behaviour. Outlined below are a number of cases which illustrate the process used, the outcome, and the multifaceted needs-based practice of CRJI. The first case is an example from the early days of practice in 2000, from a CRJI office in West Belfast. It relates to a person under threat of punishment/exclusion from the community by the Provisional IRA:

> The client was a young woman who had alcohol and drug abuse problems. She was in conflict with the community and had been physically abusive against members of her local area. She had married and divorced young, and came from a single-parent family where she had been abused as a child. These issues had never been dealt with and drugs and alcohol were used as coping mechanisms. The woman had a younger brother who had died of solvent misuse three years earlier. She also had a young daughter and there had been allegations that the daughter had been a victim of sexual abuse by her extended family. The young woman had attempted suicide on two occasions, one of them very serious from which she ended up in intensive care.
>
> A caseworker from the CRJI office met with the woman, who admitted the allegations in regards to being violent towards the community, and agreed to engage with the CRJI process. The caseworker consequently met with a representative from the IRA to discuss the case and explained the importance of this young woman remaining in the community for support. The IRA representative agreed and the threat was lifted. This was explained to the young woman in the next meeting, where referral needs were identified and a contract was drawn up. CRJI also contacted Social Services and the mother of the young woman, who both agreed to work with CRJI and to provide the support needed. As part of the contract (outcome agreement), the young woman started attending local AA meetings, a rehabilitation centre and local counselling.
>
> A six-month follow-up meeting revealed that the young woman was still attending her courses, her relationship with

> her family had improved greatly, and she had been allocated a new home in the local area. Social Services were still involved and kept monitoring the case. The young woman had stayed sober and settled during this time. At the 12-month follow-up meeting, the woman had a new baby and she was doing fine. She kept in contact with her caseworker at CRJI during this time for ongoing support.

This case reflects the reality behind many of the cases dealt with by CRJI. Often the issues are not of a criminal nature per se, but rather an intersection of serious personal and social problems. Hence, even 'simple' cases of individuals under threat reveal a multitude of correlative factors that have resulted in someone coming to the attention of the armed groups. The needs-based focus of CRJI allows them to take this into account and address needs accordingly, something which restorative justice that operates as part of the formal criminal justice system often cannot do. In the formal system, this is often due to 'new' crimes being uncovered in the process, for which there is an obligation for criminal justice actors to follow up, sometimes resulting in prosecution. To avoid such a conflict of interest, the offender's story is effectively repressed and only allowed to be told in part. This is not usually a concern for a process that operates outside the criminal justice system, and such independence allows a more holistic approach to practice. Two more cases further illustrate these points:

> The case took place in the Colin area of West Belfast in 2004, and was classified as 'under threat'. A young man aged 17 had been involved in house break-ins, vandalism, and other abusive behaviour towards the community, and was caught by the police while driving a stolen car. Representatives of the IRA had visited his house on several occasions due to behaviour problems with the community. He had also been curfewed by the IRA, a warning which he had ignored. At the time of referral to CRJI, he was under threat by the IRA of being shot or beaten. The first intervention by CRJI was to contact the IRA to confirm the threat. They then met with the boy's mother to establish the facts surrounding the boy's behaviour.
>
> The boy was the youngest of four children, and he had suffered serious grief after the recent death of his father who had passed away after a long-term illness. His mother was nervous and anxious and had several problems since the death

of her partner that she had not been able to address. The family had only recently moved to the area as a consequence of the father's illness.

A caseworker from CRJI met with the family, explained the process of working with them, and both the boy and his mother agreed. The threat by the IRA was lifted and the CRJI caseworker attempted to help the family address their problems. The outcome agreement included a promise by the boy to 'stay out of trouble', and also involved both mother and son in further support services. At the six-month follow-up meeting, the boy was no longer involved in antisocial behaviour; he had been assessed by a child psychologist and was now attending a new school. The mother was attending a local counselling service, and overall the family was doing well.

A young man aged 18 was involved in burglaries, vandalism and 'death riding'[1] in 2005. He was generally perceived as abusive to the community, and drug and alcohol misuse featured strongly. The IRA had called at his parents' house and made them aware of their son's behaviour, and the young man had been curfewed by the IRA on this occasion. The case was referred to CRJI by the IRA. A caseworker from CRJI met with the IRA and the threat of exclusion was lifted, allowing the young man to stay in the community. The IRA, however, did not agree to remove the curfew. The CRJI caseworker assessed the needs of the young man and his family, and the key focus was his need to work or train for a job, which was included as part of the outcome agreement.

At the six-month follow-up meeting, the young man was still involved in work training and there had been no further incidents of criminal or antisocial behaviour. He had broken away from his former friends and associates and CRJI continued to support him throughout this time.

These two cases are typical examples of many of the cases involving 'youth' which are handled by CRJI. Today, few of them are characterised by paramilitary involvement, but the behaviour of many young people is still seen as a substantial problem by the community. In some instances, however, the person under threat chose not to engage with CRJI, or began the process but refused to sign a contract. In such cases, there was little CRJI could do, and up until the decommission of the IRA in 2007, people involved remained under threat of being excluded and/or punished as a result of continuing antisocial or criminal behaviour. This is obviously not an outcome CRJI desired, and in such cases they continued negotiations with the armed groups for as long as possible to avoid further violence.

These cases also illustrate the complexities behind the use of punishment violence as a form of social control, and the work of CRJI is but one factor affecting such practices. As mentioned in Chapter 3, community politics, competition for turf, and the ownership of 'justice' at the community level, as well as the larger political picture in Northern Ireland, all had a substantial impact on the levels of punishment violence. However, every instance of a punishment attack or exclusion being prevented must be seen as a satisfactory result. Importantly, the approach taken by CRJI (and Alternatives) allows for simultaneous identities of victim and offender, taking into account that serious victimisation is often the root cause of criminal behaviour. This is a strength of informal restorative justice processes, in that they do not require unambiguous and imposed labels of 'victim' or 'offender'. Instead, the approach is holistic and labelling is avoided, arguably facilitating empowerment and reintegration.

Not all cases, however, are successfully resolved. The main reason for such an outcome, as illustrated in Figure 5.4, is non-participation, such as parties choosing not to engage with the process in the first place.

This figure reflects the voluntary nature of participation. Apart from people deciding not to use CRJI in the first instance, there are also participants who begin working with CRJI but at a later stage decide not to continue for a range of reasons. For example, some did not want to expend the time and effort required, or they wanted to be responsible for their own solutions. Participants may also be concerned that standing up to their neighbours or to large groups of youths in the area might make things worse.

Reintegration and restorative justice

The consequences of offending in one's community can be exclusion by paramilitary organisations (McEvoy and Mika 2001, 2002; Feenan 2002; Monaghan 2002, 2004; Jarman 2004), eviction by the Housing Executive (due to serious antisocial behaviour), or being forced to leave due to intimidation by one's neighbours or the wider community. As an example of this, I have included below a notice that was placed

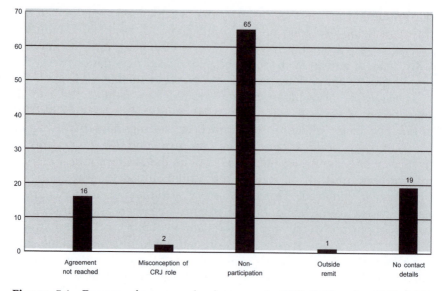

Figure 5.4 Reasons for unresolved cases at CRJI Belfast in 2007. CRJ: community restorative justice

on a local website and also placed in residents' mailboxes in this particular community. The notice was passed on to CRJI since some residents were concerned about the safety of these four young men. It is not clear whether the authorship of the notice lay with an armed group, but it was more likely to be the product of a local vigilante-type organisation described in Chapter 3.

In these instances, CRJI makes contact with the named individuals, making them aware of the allegations and offers to involve them in the restorative process. Some of these particular young men agreed; others declined. The fact that these individuals were named and hence were well known within the community exemplifies strong measures of informal social control supported through tight-knit community networks, arguably the darker side of high levels of social capital and collective efficacy.

As mentioned earlier, a consequence of continued criminal activity and antisocial behaviour within these communities may be exclusion from the area by different means. According to Housing Executive figures, in 2003–4 17,150 households claimed to be homeless in Northern Ireland. Of these, 1,245 claimed to be homeless due to intimidation by neighbours, paramilitary organisations or vigilante-type groups. Base 2, a project run by NIACRO which works with offenders and ex-offenders and assists in the relocation of individuals

---

Gallery of Rouges
Do you know these Thugs?

Name Name has been selling drugs to our children and when he isn't racing around our streets in stolen cars he is paint bombing houses in the area.

Name Name has established a reputation as burglar and ram raider and when he isn't in stolen cars he is selling drugs.

Name Name was part of a gang that murdred a pensioner in the area four years ago. He is heavily involved in the drug trade, theft of stolen cars as well as the looting of these vehicles.

Name Name has a reputation for robbing local houses, selling drugs, car crime and mugging unsuspecting people.

Don't let your children near these thugs!
Don't harbour these thugs in your home!
Protect your children, the elderly and the community!
Ostracise and boycott them NOW!

---

who are intimidated out of their communities, reports that often relocation is made to another city in Northern Ireland, but if the safety of the individual cannot be guaranteed, relocation is made to the Republic of Ireland, Scotland or England. In 2004–5, 956 people were referred to Base 2, and in 2005–6, 880. Many of these referrals are undertaken by the Housing Executive, but both CRJI and Alternatives have referred people also. In all of these instances, people may need to be reintegrated back into the area at a later stage. Such reintegration may also be appropriate after a prison term has been served, or while on parole.

Reintegration work has been a key aspect of restorative justice in both communities since the projects began, as the young people who are under threat from paramilitaries have generally been involved in some type of behaviour deemed to be unacceptable by members of the community (Auld *et al.* 1997). As discussed previously, the process of punishment beatings can be highly stigmatising and excluding (Bell 1996; McEvoy and Mika 2001, 2002; Feenan 2002; Monaghan 2002, 2004; Jarman 2004), and for people who have been excluded from the community altogether, reintegration processes are vital (Braithwaite 1989; Braithwaite and Mugford 1994) if further punishment is to be avoided.

Reintegration processes are often time-consuming, as they involve addressing the underlying reasons for the young person's offending and require negotiations with paramilitary groups, neighbours and the wider community:

> What happens in this area, and I know it happens in other certain areas too in Northern Ireland, when there is a young person shot or beaten, their name is sprayed up on a wall together with the accusation of what they have done. But that also affects their relationship with the community – it is going to be very difficult for the young person to come back into that community, having their name up on the wall. Because not only have they been punished by the paramilitaries, they also have the eyes of the community on them, you know. And you are now dealing with young people who are stuck in a rut anyway, they cannot really afford to go and live in another community, because of the insecurities they have, because of the poverty they live in, they can't move on, so they have to go back into the area where they were beaten or shot, which psychologically is not appropriate for them.[2]

Below are three examples of reintegration agreements signed as an outcome of participation in the CRJI process in 2003 and 2004. They concern three different young men who had been referred to a CRJI office after being placed under threat by an armed group in the area.

CRJI has also worked with so-called Christmas reintegration, a policy whereby a person serving a sentence in an adult or juvenile prison is granted temporary parole for the Christmas holidays. As many young people who are in prison are also under threat from a paramilitary organisation, their re-entry into the community is often a complicated affair. Furthermore, there is also the risk that they will reoffend while at home. According to the interview data, CRJI practitioners are somewhat reluctant to work with these types of cases, as they are often very complex, and CRJI is unable to guarantee that the person will not reoffend while at home. As explained by one CRJI coordinator:

> I have done loads of Christmas reintegrations. But you need to sit on them. Because we as a community also give out to Probation and Young Offender Centres. Because they seem to open their gates and they flood out at Christmas time. And nobody knows where they are or where they are residing. I mean, their mates can sign them out. ... My neighbour's child was killed. She refused to take him home. She said, 'No way can

---

Community Restorative Justice
Reintegration Agreement

I, Name Name, of Address A, am committed to changing my ways within the community. I have been made aware of and understand the conditions of this contract.

- I will not associate with any individuals who are involved in criminal or anti-social behaviour.
- I will not consume alcohol on the streets.
- I will pay for the damage I caused to one of my neighbour's cars.
- I am committed to developing a more positive attitude to all those individuals in the community who are working to make our area a safer place for all to live, work and play.

I, Parent of Name Name, am committed in supporting my son to help him fulfil his commitment to the local community.

Signed:

We in Community Restorative Justice will support Name and his mother with his contract with the community, and make him aware of any accusations made against him.

Signed:

I watch him over the Christmas holiday, he is not coming here.' So his sister signed for him, and he was killed two days before Christmas. He wrapped himself around a mountain [e.g. driving and crashing stolen car]. So ... there are negotiations going on between these young offender centres and the community who say; 'OK, they behave, they behave because they want out for Christmas.' And as soon as they get out of the gates ... Jesus, this community suffers mega. It just comes down on them as a dark cloud. People dread the bloody doors of those prisons opening. ... So for us to be seen doing the same, we have to be very careful. ... And they are running havoc, because they know that they are leaving in five days to go back in anyway.[3]

Hence, the issue of reintegration as a part of restorative practice is complicated by the additional factors of paramilitary involvement,

---

Community Restorative Justice
Reintegration Agreement

I, Name Name, of Address A, understand that it has become necessary for me to sign up to this contract due to my involvement in anti-social behaviour, for which I was excluded from the community in the Summer of 2002.

- I will not be keeping company with previous associates who are known to be still participating in anti-social behaviour.
- I will put an end to all criminal or other anti-social activities that I have been involved in.
- I will not be intimidating or harassing any of my previous partners, either in their own homes or anywhere else.
- To enable me to gain access to my children, I am committed to doing this through Social Services and other legal processes.
- I am committed to working with any of the community support groups within my local community in order to help with my reintegration.
- I am in agreement that this pledge will be visited on a regular basis and can be altered in accordance with ongoing changes which may occur in the future.

Signed:

We in Community Restorative Justice will support Name with his contract with the community, and make him aware of any accusations made against him.

Signed:

---

a punitive community, and a perceived lack of support from relevant statutory agencies such as the Probation Board. Moreover, strengthening a person's ties to the community is by no means a straightforward process, particularly considering the make-up of the community in which exclusion and hierarchical power structures are central features. Empowerment of participants and the wider community is crucial if such negative community features are to be challenged. Such aims form part of CRJI's work both on a case-by-case basis and for their long-term commitment to the community. Mika (2006) provided a detailed evaluation of the impact the projects have had on levels of punishment violence in their respective communities,

Community Restorative Justice
Reintegration Agreement

I, Name Name, am committed to changing my ways within the community. I have been made aware of and understand the conditions of this commitment.

- I will not be keeping company with previous associates who are known to be still participating in anti-social behaviour.
- I am willing to participate in the victim, offender process offered to me through Community Restorative Justice.
- I will not be in a car unless it is legally owned, insured and taxed.
- I will not be involved in either domestic or business break-ins.

I am committed to working with any of the community and support groups within the community in order to help with my reintegration.

Signed:

We in Community Restorative Justice will support Name with his reintegation within the community, we will as necessary make Name aware of any further accusations made against him.

Signed:

noticing that both projects have 'contributed to increasing tolerance in local areas for marginalised members of the community, including delinquent youth and former combatants' (p. 9).

To sum up, CRJI processes a high number of cases every year and includes thousands of people in restorative processes. They use models of restorative justice such as shuttle mediation and conferencing, depending on the needs of the participants in each individual case, and engage in a wide range of types of mediation, from minor nuisance behaviour to complex and sometimes violent neighbourhood disputes. The sources of referral clearly indicate a strong community base, and the projects also aim at community empowerment and community building as macro-outcomes of individual cases. Furthermore, a large proportion of the casework relies on volunteers, and this is very similar to Alternatives.

Northern Ireland Alternatives[4]

On the Loyalist side, the projects are considerably smaller, targeting more exclusively young people under paramilitary threat. These projects involve intensive work with clients including a one-to-one mentoring system (McEvoy and Mika 2001). Between 1999 and 2004, a total of 132 cases were processed, and between 2003 and 2005, formal contact was registered with 2,139 young people and 1,719 engagements with victims. Hence, like CRJI, each individual case often involves a large number of people, including victims, young people and their families. This work is supported through a network of 268 community volunteers (Mika 2004: 23).

Initially, the vast majority of referrals came directly from the armed groups, particularly the UVF. Today, the five main sources of referrals are armed groups (but less so than previously), offenders or family, community organisations, statutory organisations, and self-referrals (Mika 2007). These sources of referral reflect the organic development of practice:

> Particularly in the early stages a lot of the referrals came from the paramilitaries ... I think now as the programme has evolved, I think there is a different shift even within paramilitaries, there are less instances where we have to get involved, whereas in the past they would have been shooting or beating them. You can see a shift in certain aspects of moving away from punitive measures even within the paramilitary organisations.[5]

It is interesting to note this shift in paramilitary practices regarding punishment violence,[6] as reducing such violence was the primary motivation for Alternatives to be established. Yet, reduced levels of punishment violence have not led to a reduced caseload for the project. The opposite has happened, as the types of cases and sources of referrals have diversified. Like CRJI, Alternatives adopted a multifaceted approach to address the complex issues surrounding punishment violence. Its practice relies on effective communication with the UVF (Winston 1997) and, according to several interviewees, with other local paramilitary organisations that choose to engage.

The main focus of Alternatives's work is the behaviour of young people that led them to come to the attention of paramilitaries; that is, the work is to address the underlying causes of offending in the community (Winston 1997). Alternatives also has had to work within a more limited remit, due to the presence of paramilitary groups in these communities, as mentioned earlier. The decision to avoid working in certain types of cases was also based on the expertise available within the projects:

> What we decided at a very early stage, and I think we have been proven right up till now, was that we would not touch anything of a violent or sexual nature – that should be left to the proper authorities; we don't have the expertise to deal with anything like that. And it is not our role, we are not here as an alternative police force, we are here as … our main aim was to bring the police and the community closer together, to look at the issues, and put pressure on the police to deal where they can, and where they can't, then let the community take over and try to deal with it themselves.[7]

This quotation also reflects the willingness to work in cooperation with the police which Alternatives has displayed since its inception. The relationship between Loyalist communities and the police is less complicated than is the case for their Republican counterparts, as was particularly made evident in 2007 when Alternatives became the first project to be formally accredited by the state; for CRJI, this process took longer.[8]

The work of Alternatives can be categorised into three main areas: intensive youth work, focusing specifically on young people under threat by paramilitaries; a preventative project, aimed at young people who are at risk of coming to the attention of the paramilitaries due to their antisocial behaviour; and victims work, an important component of Alternatives' present work, involving different processes being employed to meet victims' needs. Alternatives has also extended the impact of its practice to include the wider aims of community building and empowerment. Each of these different models will be discussed below.

Intensive youth work

The main model of restorative justice used by Alternatives is generally referred to as 'intensive youth work'. The same type of model is used at all of their sites with some slight variations depending on the particular needs of each area. In this type of intervention, the focus is on young people who are under threat from paramilitaries of being shot or beaten, or who are at risk of moving into more serious criminality. Alternatives, will negotiate with the paramilitary group in question, primarily the UVF, so that once the young person has signed up to participate in Alternatives the threat is lifted. Alternatives describes this model of restorative justice as very successful, and it is sufficiently flexible to work in different community contexts:

> You can't lift the model from the Shankill and put it in the East or North (of Belfast), because they are slightly different. And I think the success on the Shankill is down to the model being simple but effective, and the dedicated people who worked 24/7 to set it up. The committed team was absolutely key to making it very successful.[9]

Most of the young people who come into contact with Alternatives do not have a single problem, such as a specific incident of offending or being under threat from a paramilitary organisation, but several interrelated issues which have contributed to their current situation. For example, they might need to address a dependence on drugs and/or alcohol; failure at school and consequent dropout or expulsion; aggression; a lack of insight into the consequences of their actions; and involvement in widespread antisocial behaviour in the local community such as joyriding, theft, or verbal or physical abuse of other members of the community. The contract, which is drawn up between the young person and Alternatives, tends to reflect this complex picture, and the intervention is tailored accordingly:

> Most young people I have found that come on the programme, even if they recognise the hurt and harm they have caused, they also throw the accusation at the community for harming them. And in some cases it has, if a young person has already been punished by paramilitaries in the past. So there is a lot of work to be done with the self-aspect of the contract, where the young person is encouraged to look at themselves and the causes of what has led them into that sort of behaviour.[10]

Such work requires a strong commitment to individuals' needs and expectations of the restorative process. Practitioners in general take great pride in this aspect of their work and argued that such a commitment would never be seen within the formal criminal justice system:

> One example of that is, we have one young lad who has been through the Youth Justice Agency etc., and the YJA said to the

lad that 'You have to make an apology to the victim within four weeks.' The young lad who is working with us has to have his letter of apology in for next week. And he sat here, and said to me, 'I am not sorry.' No problem, he is going to write that letter, but he is sitting here saying he is not sorry for what he has done. ... On the Alternatives model of restorative justice, that is where our work *starts*, that is where we begin if you know what I mean. And in relation to VOM [victim–offender mediation], it could be a year, it could be two, before people are ready to meet, because you have to work through all the issues. And anyone who is from Northern Ireland *knows*, there are people here who were offended against 20 or 30 years ago, and they are *still* trying to work through their issues. These things can't be rushed.[11]

The first few weeks of contact are focused on building a relationship of trust between the young person and his or her support worker. The initial meetings are concentrated on discussing such questions as 'What is antisocial behaviour?', 'How does antisocial behaviour affect other people around you?', 'What is your sense of community?', 'What do you think your obligations are and are you living up to them?', 'Who are your victims and what is your responsibility towards them?', and 'What do your peers do for you?' Subsequently, the meetings focus on developing a kind of contract and action plan. As the project manager of Shankill Alternatives explained:

Then our job would be primarily to support them and keep them focused on the action plan. We work as much as we can with their families, trying to build relationships with them, and to have a network with different services like education or counselling. We would also take them out to different activities to try and involve them in more positive activities, and try to build their confidence and self-esteem, trying to help them feel good about themselves, that they are not being judged, not as a person but by their actions.[12]

Some support workers meet with the young person three to four times a week. They also work with other staff at Alternatives who are responsible for the victims work, to set up a possible victim–offender mediation, although that is something not everyone is willing to do. A key point emanating from the interviews was the amount of time spent working on cases. For some young people, it may take several months before they feel ready to sit down in a meeting with the victim, and victims may also need similar time and preparation to feel comfortable with participation. One youth worker at Alternatives made a comparison in terms of preparation for face-to-face meetings between victims and offenders, between his project and the practice of the Youth Justice Agency.[13] His experience of working with young people and victims who had been through the formal restorative justice conference scheme was that too little time was spent preparing the participants for a face-to-face encounter. He gave the example of one young man with whom he had worked for 120 hours before he was ready to meet his victim, in addition to 30 telephone calls and 15 meetings with all parties who had a vested interest in the young person. It was also mentioned that 'now, the example I gave you was an exception. Another case took 12 hours before a face-to-face mediation. And that is about identifying needs – anyone's particular circumstances determine how we work with them'.[14]

Other common goals set for a young person could be to re-engage with education or secure employment, or attend drug and alcohol awareness counselling or anger management training. The staff will assist in liaison with relevant statutory agencies, such as the Housing Executive, Probation, Social Services, and the Youth Justice Agency. Some kind of community service is almost always part of the contract, not only for the purpose of paying back the community for the harm caused, but also, importantly, to *be seen* by the local community to be doing so. It was argued by several practitioners that it is vital that the community sees that these young people act in a pro-social, responsible manner – a component of restorative justice which is also viewed as an important part of successful reintegration (Braithwaite 1989; Braithwaite and Mugford 1994). In common with CRJI, Alternatives also works with negotiating access back into the community for people who have previously been excluded by paramilitaries and who are now returning, as well as some reintegration work with young people who have finished serving a prison term.

As part of this research, I spoke to two boys,[15] aged 17 and 19, about their experiences after they had completed their contract.[16] Both youths had been involved with Alternatives for about a year, and kept visiting the office on a regular basis. The 19-year-old had been told by the UVF to go to Alternatives, as he was under threat of exclusion from Northern Ireland for involvement in drugs and antisocial behaviour. When asked whether he had felt under pressure to attend Alternatives, he indicated that:

We were told that if we left the programme, nothing would happen, it was up to us if we wanted to stay or not. If we continue with antisocial behaviour then we might get beaten by the paramilitaries, but that is not the fault of Alternatives. If Alternatives weren't here, kids would just get beaten or shot, so Alternatives are really important here. ... I would definitely recommend this programme to someone else in my situation, but it is important to keep in mind that *you* have to want to change, no-one can do that for you, and some people simply are not ready for that yet.

The 17-year-old, on the other hand, was told by his social worker that he should engage with Alternatives.[17] Throughout their time at Alternatives, they both felt that they were treated fairly and with respect, and that they could talk with the staff about their concerns. The fact that everything was confidential facilitated conversation and engagement with the project. Both agreed that they would not have been so open about their problems if they had known that their issues were being reported to another agency. One of them compared his experience to one he had while participating in another programme called Opportunity Youth,[18] where he felt that the staff had based their interventions on a manual without relating to him or his background. In contrast, at Alternatives he felt that

People here can relate to you better, perhaps because they had also been in a bit of bother when they were younger. They deal with the real issues, they do not work from a manual ... they are from the community and can understand the issues that I had to deal with.

The most difficult thing about completing their contract was giving up drugs. As part of the contract, they were no longer spending time with their old friends, but had to find a new social network. However, both of them thought it was worth it. At the time of the interview, both had a permanent job and a new place to live, and the positive reaction from their families had also meant a great deal to them.

Preventative project

Alternatives also engages in preventative work, focusing again mainly on young people between the ages of 10 and 16. One of the reasons for this development, according to the interviewees, was that

Alternatives did not want to be perceived as only taking an interest in young people once they had offended or when their antisocial behaviour had escalated to the point of coming to the attention of the police or the paramilitaries. Hence, at least two nights a week (this varies slightly among the different offices), they run workshops with groups of young people, focusing on similar issues to those that they initially explore with the older youths. The practitioners in Alternatives see these themes as crucial to the process of taking responsibility for one's actions and preventing future offending. The discussion can also revolve around other issues such as racial awareness, teenage pregnancy, identity and culture, photography, computer skills, and art.

The groups of young people initially become involved in Alternatives by being approached by a member of staff or volunteer from Alternatives, usually at a time when they are congregating on street corners, 'hanging out'. Often such 'hanging out' involves the consumption of alcohol and drugs, and the occasional shouting of abuse at passers-by. Some of these groups were quite receptive to the suggested involvement in Alternatives, and many tried it for a while. Even if they do not change their behaviour within a certain time frame, Alternatives will not give up on them. However, some young people are, of course, less willing to engage, and because of the voluntary nature of Alternatives, nothing more can be done at this time.[19]

As part of the research, I spoke to a group of six young people, aged 16–17, who were participating in the preventative programme on the Shankill.[20] They had become involved with Alternatives after being approached by one of the staff members. Alternatives can also be alerted by family members to a young person that has come to the attention of paramilitaries as a result of antisocial behaviour. If the youth is seen to be 'at risk' of further involvement in antisocial behaviour, this could lead to more serious attention from paramilitaries. Hence, this is the preventative aspect of the work. When I spoke to the group, they had been meeting every Tuesday for the previous four months, and the programme was set to continue for as long as they wished to engage.

As part of the programme, they had been talking about what antisocial behaviour is (most of them did not realise that hanging out on street corners, drinking and shouting abuse at passers-by, was seen as antisocial, or the impact this can have on other people), the history of Ulster, their community, information about drugs and alcohol, and education. They also went on field trips, and Alternatives has tried to involve them in positive activities within the community, such as helping to paint a new antiracism mural that was under way at the time. Overall, they were very satisfied with their experience of Alternatives, especially that they were treated with respect and listened to – new experiences for many of them. They were also very aware that if they continued with their antisocial behaviour, there was a real possibility that they would come to the attention of the paramilitaries or the police – something which they did not want to occur.

Victims and community development work

Alternatives uses victim–offender mediation processes and, importantly, also works with victims whose offender has not been caught. The main part of victim intervention is often to provide victims with someone to whom they can talk and from whom they can receive support. Staff and volunteers from Alternatives call and visit when needed, and victims can also telephone the office at any time. Alternatives, in cooperation with the PSNI, has also helped to provide physical security measures such as personal and property alarms. According to the interviewees, this work rates very highly in terms of satisfaction for the victims involved. For example, one woman who was interviewed had been supported by Alternatives for about nine months. She came into contact with Alternatives through one of her brothers, who himself was involved in the intensive youth programme. She said that she had gained self-confidence and felt more secure in the community thanks to her contact with Alternatives:

> I was very afraid that the paramilitaries would come knocking on my door, that was my biggest fear. And not knowing when they could come and how many there would be. I am the only girl in the family and have been responsible for my three brothers, and it was always worrying not knowing what they were up to and if the paramilitaries would get involved. I was not feeling safe in my own house. So I am very grateful that Alternatives could help me. I can now go to bed without worrying, and I can now go down to my kitchen during the night, which I could not do before because I was worried that someone was going to come to my door. Now I am OK.[21]

One important aspect mentioned by the victims interviewed is that the staff at Alternatives are from the local community and, as such, are seen as better able to understand and respect local needs, and this has not been the experience with victim workers from 'the outside'. As mentioned by one practitioner who coordinates the work with victims,[22] Alternatives aims to provide frequent, regular and ongoing support and is not concerned with closing cases, but recognises that even if people have overcome the initial fear of crime and have moved on as far as possible, they are still much appreciative of ongoing contact:

> You have to think about restoration in the broadest possible sense. Even if the police have done all they can, it may still not be enough. We can address their emotional health and fear of crime ... we have undoubtedly decreased the isolation of certain individuals in the community ... restoring their faith or belief that community is still possible.[23]

Restorative justice interventions with victims are also vital for reducing fear of crime in the area, and as these programmes become more established, people are starting to approach Alternatives directly (Mika 2007). During a focus group with nine victims, many expressed feelings and opinions common to people who have been victimised (Strang 2002), such as anger, frustration, and the need for answers and reassurance. These were reactions and needs for which Alternatives actively seeks to provide support (Mika 2007). Moreover, according to the practitioners of Alternatives, the positive effects of starting the work with victims are probably more wide-reaching than was initially thought:

> Now a rather large section of the community is phoning us. Especially since the victims side was brought in, because they have been really good in getting a large section of volunteers from within the community, and that has had a really positive effect in that more people are aware of what we do.[24]

All four of the Alternatives projects are also involved in a range of community development initiatives in and around their geographical area of practice, a feature of restorative justice work they have in common with CRJI. In regards to such efforts, the manager of Alternatives mentioned how important he felt it was that Alternatives provides a model for alternative ways of dealing with conflict at the individual level, but also of strengthening the community on a wider scale:

I think that Alternatives is now the leading community development organisation in the Shankill area, even though others might view it differently. But I believe that what we have delivered to the Shankill is benefiting victims, offenders and everyone in between. It was about drawing up a package that was holistic in its view, that everyone has something to offer here. We are finding now that other organisations such as schools and some statutory agencies are calling us for help trying to settle a dispute, using the expertise we have developed over the years. Restorative justice is not just about victims and offenders, it is a much wider remit than that, trying to heal relationships no matter where they are.[25]

Such work aimed at the wider community is an example of 'holistic practice'. This type of work with victims can also have important benefits in terms of reducing fear of crime in the community (Skogan 1986; Grabosky 1995). It can also contribute to people feeling that they themselves can do something to address these issues in the community in a non-violent way. Through such processes, the reliance on paramilitary organisations can be reduced, as the latest research data on community restorative justice and levels of punishment violence clearly indicate (see Mika 2007).

As indicated throughout this book so far, the communities in which these projects operate can be very punitive, and they are used to quick, visible and starkly retributive solutions to conflict at all levels, with a simultaneous reluctance of people to take responsibility for their own actions. To place this within a more theoretical framework, such a situation can be characterised as a 'culture of violence', as is often prominent in transitional societies. An important and arguably unique aspect of community restorative justice praxis in Northern Ireland is the aim to challenge and change such a culture. This reflects restorative justice that moves beyond more traditional applications and an individual focus, towards a wide-reaching practice that aims for transformative justice and communal efforts of peace-building in transition. The next section will explore these issues in more detail.

Challenging cultures of violence through restorative justice: transforming communities in transition

It has been argued that a period of protracted violent conflict gives rise to 'a culture of violence', creating a socially permissive environment within which violence continues. Violence is used to resolve interpersonal conflict and to respond to communal problems of crime and disorder, even after peace accords have been signed and the violent political conflict has ended (Steenkamp 2005). This section explores how the day-to-day practice of community restorative justice projects in Northern Ireland can contribute to challenging and perhaps even changing such embedded cultures of violence at the individual and communal levels.

These restorative justice projects are characterised by three key features which make such an endeavour possible: the presence of former combatants and political ex-prisoners who provide leadership during such transformations; a strong grass-roots ethos and an emphasis on local community members as volunteers; and, finally, a firm adherence to certain key restorative justice *values* in combination with a flexible approach to the *process*, which results in the projects being able to respond to a wide range of communal and interpersonal conflicts. It is important to note that I am not arguing that community restorative justice will provide a complete solution to the complex issues experienced at the community level, during a transition or otherwise. Rather, what will be suggested is that a well-run restorative justice project may act as a vehicle and facilitator for some of the transformative practices that are taking place in this particular societal context.

Cultures of violence

In general, the expression 'cultures of violence' is used as shorthand for the assertion that there is a direct link between exposure to violence over a long period of time and an acceptance of violence as a means of resolving interpersonal conflict or of dealing with frustrations in everyday life (Hayes and McAllister 2001; Steenkamp 2005). Hence, the experience of prolonged violent conflict in areas such as Northern Ireland has arguably resulted in the use of violence as a means of conflict resolution becoming embedded in the broader values and norms which guide behaviour in any one community; that is, the local culture (Vogelman and Lewis 1993; du Toit 2001; Ferme 2001; Knox and Monaghan 2002; MacGinty and Darby 2002; Kynoch 2005). When such violence remains after a conflict is over, a culture of violence is said to exist within the transitional society. According to Steenkamp, violence thus 'loses its political meaning and becomes a way of dealing with everyday issues ... a socially accepted mechanism to achieve power and status in society' (2005: 254). Violence continues to be central to informal social control approaches when dealing with interpersonal and community conflict, arguably mirroring the formal social control measures used throughout the conflict.

There are studies that consider the *emergence* of a culture of violence (Rupesinghe and Rubio 1994; Curle 1999; Hamber 1999; Bourgois 2001), but which pay little attention to how such violent cultures are *maintained* in the transitional society and beyond. In general, the communal aspect of a culture of violence has been covered more comprehensively than the individual (for some excellent exceptions, see Staub 1989, 1996, 1999, 2003), such as a culture of violence in the American South (Gastil 1971; Cohen and Nesbitt 1994), and the Sicilian Mafia (Cottino 1999). This literature is, however, mainly exploratory and descriptive, focusing on the original formation of such violent cultures, not their persistence. The lack of a more in-depth analysis is a missed opportunity, an omission that prevents an exploration of the factors and processes that not only maintain such cultures, but also can challenge them as part of broader peace-building and crime prevention efforts in the transitional context. Arguably, such an analysis can also be an important component of crime prevention efforts in high-crime communities in more 'settled' societies.

Steenkamp (2005) has constructed a framework to explain the maintenance of a culture of violence that differs from previous attempts at definition. It aims to provide an analytical mapping of factors that create a context for violence whereby it is allowed and even encouraged. As such, 'the question is not why people are violent, but rather, how are the norms and values that underpin the sustained use of violence created and entrenched in society?' (Steenkamp 2005: 255). Hence, if one is to challenge such a culture of violence, a comprehensive understanding of the values and norms which underpin and sustain it is necessary. Such a conceptualisation also justifies the focus on grass-roots responses, since the behaviour of people in any one community is more likely to be a reflection of communal values than those of the far removed state.

A culture of violence in Northern Ireland

The existence of a culture of violence in Northern Ireland has been noted by several writers (MacGinty and Darby 2002; Knox and Monaghan 2002; Jarman 2004), although the actual expression 'culture of violence' has been used sparingly and with little attempt at analysis as to why such a culture has been maintained in the transitional phase. Importantly, a culture of violence and its maintaining factors can exist, according to Steenkamp (2005), on several levels: international, state, collective and individual. The last two are the focal points of discussion here, and it is argued that it is at these two levels that community restorative justice can have the greatest impact. It is important to note, however, that the different levels are interconnected, as micro-processes take place within and are affected by larger macro-processes – for example, violence committed by an individual takes place within a broader social, political and economic context.

The key to understanding a culture of violence is that culture is learned through socialisation, using the symbols and behavioural codes available to members of any one society. It is also passed down from one generation to the next (Groff and Smoker 1996). In the Northern Irish context, such a transfer of knowledge and values forms part of a 'socialisation which is restricted almost exclusively to a reproduction of the values of one's own respective political community' (McAuley 2004: 545).

As mentioned earlier, this has resulted in sharply defined borders between Republican and Loyalist communities, where local community identity is symbolised through the construction of community borders and so-called peace walls, which work to facilitate an ingrained communal segregation (Shirlow and Murtagh 2006). The glorification of violence at the communal level is a central maintaining factor for the continuing use of violence as a means of informal social control. Steenkamp (2005) mentions that 'communities glorify past acts of violence in order to strengthen group boundaries and emphasize the distinction between them and the other' (p. 263). This is an obvious strategy in both Republican and Loyalist communities, and one which tends to result in an affirmation of segregation:

> Apart from the more obvious influences that living through a sustained militarised conflict has on the people and their society, one can also point to the legitimising impact of a wider culture of commemoration and celebration, the annual cycle of parades that are held to mark the anniversaries of wars, battles, risings and martyrs. There is also a growing popular culture of paramilitarism and resistance which has been elaborated through the media of writing, song, music and the painting of elaborate murals and which is maintained through the numerous informal social clubs in working-class areas ... such activities help to legitimise certain forms of violent or criminal activity – by claiming they are being undertaken in opposition

to the state or to further struggle. It thus helps to maintain an underlying rationality, which accepts that violence and conflict are endemic, necessary and a persistent part of life in the north. (Jarman 2004: 435)

In the transitional period, the socio-economic conditions for many of the poorest sections of society remain unchanged. It has been argued that continuing structural violence in such circumstances (found, for example, in deprivation, poverty, economic inequality and unemployment) 'can provide the conditions that make the micro-level use of violence more common' (Steenkamp 2005: 260). It is important to note, however, that the impact of such experiences may very well differ among communities, with the experiences being mediated by social structures and people's relationship with the state. This highlights the obvious point that communities in Northern Ireland are neither homogeneous entities nor necessarily 'nice' places. Indeed, as noted by Crawford and Clear (2001):

> In order to consider the genuine potential of restorative and community justice, we need to shed the rose-tinted glasses worn by many advocates and confront the empirical realities of most communities. The ideal of unrestricted entry to, and exit from, communities needs to be reconciled with the existence of relations of dominance, exclusion, and differential power. The reality is that many stable communities tend to resist innovations, creativity, and experimentation, as well as informal social control, and the way these processes play out lacks inclusive qualities and offender-sensitive styles. They can be coercive and tolerant of bigotry and discriminatory behaviour. Weaker parties within such communities often experience them not as a home of connectedness and mutuality but as a mainspring of inequalities that sustain and reinforce relations of dependence. They are often hostile to minorities, dissenters, and outsiders. (p. 137)

When we consider utilising restorative justice initiatives to address communal conflict within such areas, such features must be explicitly recognised. It is against this larger backdrop of a divided society and strained relationships between communities, and between communities and the state, that the values and norms that maintain a culture of violence in Northern Ireland exist.

As discussed earlier, paramilitary organisations in both communities were largely responsible for informal social control in the absence of a legitimate and effective criminal justice system during the armed conflict. One result of such reliance on paramilitary organisations to manage conflict at the community level was, according to the interviewees, an abdication of responsibility for their own conflicts, by individuals, families and, by extension, the whole community. Moreover, an ineffective criminal justice system and weak state control over informal alternatives (McEvoy and Newburn 2003; Roberts and McMillan 2003; Cartwright *et al.* 2004; Shearing *et al.* 2006) are two important sustaining factors of a culture of violence in transitional societies (Steenkamp 2005). Hence, where the state is unable to consolidate its monopoly over violence through effective sanctioning, the norms and values that legitimise the personal use of violence are likely to linger (MacGinty and Darby 2002).

The social and economic position of young people within the transitional context is also an important contributing factor to the maintenance of a culture of violence. This group can emerge from protracted periods of conflict as one of the most marginalised groups in society (Higgins and Martin 2003). They are likely to have limited, if any, experience of institutional civil life and participation, and a mistrust of the political system and its actors (Simpson 1993). They are socially isolated because of the break-up of family networks, are economically vulnerable with (at best) an interrupted education, and have direct experiences of violence. Consequently, they are at risk of becoming involved in violent actions as a means of acquiring a sense of belonging and status, resulting in a situation where violence and social rewards become interlinked (du Toit 2001; Steenkamp 2005). As was mentioned by Jarman (2004) in relation to Northern Ireland:

> These types of activities, whether it's rioting, antisocial behaviour, low-level crime, or just hanging around on street corners, also bring many young people into frequent contact with the police and here too a relationship based on mutual suspicion and hostility and a lack of mutual respect serves to increase the marginalisation of many young people. For many young people, there is little expectation of anything outside the boundaries of their local estate; they have low educational attainments, few job prospects outside the black economy, and in such a situation, drugs, crime and violence provide the parameters of their expectations. (p. 434)

These issues were frequently mentioned during the research, as the continuing presence of paramilitary groups, particularly in Loyalist areas, plays a central and detrimental part in the lives of many young people, who continue to join different armed groups, even though the 'war' is over.[26] This arguably occurs because Loyalist paramilitary organisations held considerable degrees of power in their communities during the Troubles, and even though efforts are being made by several organisations and individuals, the process of reversing this power relationship is difficult and slow. As noted by Winston (1997):

> With the considerable social, political and symbolic significance attached to these organisations, it is a quite natural progression for young men to join one of the paramilitary groups in their late teens. Membership is high, and the organisations have tended to represent an important locus of power in the area. (p. 124)

Moreover, paramilitary organisations, particularly Loyalist ones, have been linked to the drug trade in Northern Ireland (Silke 2000a; Monaghan 2002), and the distribution of illegal drugs is part of a wider network of organised crime (Higgins and McElrath 2000). This particularly affects young people who are vulnerable to such influences. The manager of East Belfast Alternatives, in an interview in June 2005, was only too aware of the effects of such communal dynamics. The following quotation is somewhat lengthy, but illustrates the effects of a culture of violence in transitional Belfast and the work faced by community organisations trying to challenge and change it:

> The young ones, they are what we would call 'ceasefire soldiers' who join for various reasons. We would say, in our analysis, from talking to them, that peer pressure is incredible in these areas. It is hard to stand on your own two feet and say, 'No, I am not joining', when all your friends are telling you to. And you have people coming to you, pressurising you, and 'I am going to hit you', they have a whole team behind them. And a lot of kids would join just to get that team behind them, for protection if nothing else. This is one of the main reasons, we are finding. And once they are in they are getting sucked into drugs etc. Drugs are a massive problem in east Belfast, massive. Thankfully we have, in this area, a leadership that are trying to stomp it out.[27] The young people are leaving school without any qualifications, they have no jobs to go to. Their role models

within the community are the ones driving the BMWs wearing gold chains, etc. And where are they getting their money? Drugs ... We had one young lad, 11 years old, sitting in this office telling us that his only goal in life was to become a drug dealer, because he sees them as role models. And it is about breaking that vicious cycle, and it is going to be a long, slow process. It is not going to change overnight.[28]

Significantly, several of these maintaining factors of a culture of violence exist at the grass-roots level, emphasising the importance of intervention approaches that are bottom-up, and indigenous to the local communities in which they work.

The principles and practices of restorative justice can provide a useful framework through which communities can themselves take a lead in the transformations required. At the individual level, this can arguably be achieved by involving individuals and their families in processes defined by restorative justice values such as non-violence, inclusiveness, respect, reparation, integration and empowerment. Importantly, it is an opportunity to *experience* the use of such values in interpersonal interaction – for some people, it may be for the first time – and this is a powerful agent of change at this level. At the communal level, restorative justice can potentially challenge cultures of violence by affecting conflict resolution practices in both paramilitary organisations and wider community networks.

The field research indicated that restorative justice practices can also be a catalyst for change for both the Republican movement and the UVF. The work of CRJI and Alternatives informs and questions the role of the armed groups, now and in the future, in relation to methods of conflict resolution and partnerships with the police and other statutory agencies (McEvoy and Mika 2002; Mika 2004, 2007). This, in turn, can permeate wider community structures in relation to modes of conflict resolution in the community – a combination of education and the ripple effect. Contribution to such events is the 'mind shift' in practice within transition. As the manager of East Belfast Alternatives framed the issue:

[Alternatives is] very, very important. It – and I am sure you have heard this like a million times – you know, we had 30 years of conflict, 30 years worth of mind-sets that needs to change. I believe we are starting to make an impact with the paramilitaries. We are starting slowly to change mind-sets that you do not solve every crisis through shooting someone, through violent actions, and that there is another way where things can be resolved without violence. But it is a slow change, it is very, very slow. But thankfully, we have in place here in east Belfast, especially within the UVF/Red Hand constituency, people who, I would say, are mature enough to listen to what you are saying. ... The fact that last week, one of the leaders was able to walk into my office with a young lad and sit here. Whereas two years ago he would just have shot him.[29]

On the Republican side, several CRJI practitioners mentioned that their work can particularly affect the Republican movement, through talking directly to people involved in it, and educating people about the direct benefits of restorative practices. According to the manager of CRJI, when the Republican movement previously dealt with a case, there was usually a win-lose outcome, which was the clear result of a punishment attack: for example, the paramilitaries 'win' by re-establishing order and meting out 'deserved' punishment, and the people shot or beaten 'loses' due to their physical injuries and lack of redress. However, through the use of a restorative justice process, there can be a win-win situation. Moreover, community restorative justice has also provided the paramilitary groups with a 'new' language in terms of talking and thinking about conflict and its resolution. As opposed to the old methods of informal social control, the rhetoric of restorative justice provides a wider range of options that can be used by people with very different interests and personal investments without losing face.

It was also mentioned during the interviews with CRJI staff, in relation to the impact they can have on changing attitudes within paramilitary groups, that it is generally the people who are the most keen to work with CRJI who are the easiest to convince about the advantages of restorative justice. These people are often senior members who have had their fair share of exposure to the administration of punishment violence and who are acutely aware of its ineffectiveness. One practitioner at CRJI said that he and other senior staff met on a regular basis with members of the Republican movement in a type of workshop where they talked about community restorative justice, educating the IRA in restorative justice practices:

The work we do ... it gives CRJI an opportunity to create awareness among the armed groups in the area about community needs. Like when you talk to the armed groups about a particular person, then there is a better understanding by the armed groups about where the person is coming from. Whereas before, none of that would have been taken into consideration, there was just a person who was causing problems and 'Let's deal with him.' But they, just as our volunteers, would now have a better understanding of what the issues are that need to be taken into consideration.[30]

The multifaceted approach adopted by CRJI and Alternatives allows them to challenge embedded cultures of violence from both individual and collective angles – including a direct impact on the practices of paramilitary organisations – arguably increasing their potential effectiveness in this regard.

Today, when paramilitary groups have largely relinquished their responsibility in relation to informal social control, and the police have still to gain full legitimacy and effective practice within these working-class communities, a void exists that is partially filled by CRJI and Alternatives. This gap in social control, and in effective approaches to the prevention, management and resolution of conflict at the individual and communal levels, is evident in the changing remit and focus of practice for both projects in recent years. It is arguably these changes in practice, changes to shifts in individual and communal needs, which allow them to address several other maintaining factors of a culture of violence, apart from 'just' paramilitary punishment violence.

Affecting wider community practices of conflict resolution

This punitive community is a very good reason for the continuing need for CRJI.[31]

A common theme mentioned in all of the interviews conducted with practitioners of Alternatives and CRJI was a focus on wider practices and expectations in relation to conflict resolution in the community. Such a focus of practice was, and still is, an integral part of their work. Challenging an embedded culture of violence cannot be achieved by a singular focus on paramilitary groups (Mika 2007). As was mentioned by the project manager of Alternatives, there are still some people in the community who put active pressure on the different paramilitary groups to continue their tradition of 'policing':

I think that the biggest problem … if people come to us and say, 'Aye, the paramilitaries have to stop shooting kids this way', then we would have been a hell of a lot further on. It's the appetite within these communities where people go to the paramilitaries and say, 'What do you mean you are not going to shoot them? I want them shot.' And trying to convince people that punishment violence is not the answer, we had it for 30 years and it did not solve anything. We don't say we have a magic wand but we feel that in the long term it is far more valid for our community to address these issues by having residents taking responsibility, to have young people address and own up to the damage they have done within their communities, and to do that in a restorative way, as opposed to beating them.[32]

Several interviewees within both CRJI and Alternatives mentioned that they could see a change in communal attitudes to violence. In particular, there is a change in how young people are viewed, both by paramilitary groups as argued above, and by the community. A practitioner at Shankill Alternatives noted:

I think there is an acceptance by most people that things need to change. I do understand that there is a dilemma and that some people believe, especially with serious repeat offenders, that things need to be handled in a punitive way. However, there are genuine people within paramilitary groups who do not want to have to do these sorts of things. It is a case where people go 'shopping' – they go to one [paramilitary] group and if that group does not do what they want to do, then they will go to another, maybe from a different area. It is so complex, but I do think that there is a shift gradually … and I believe Alternatives has been part of that. And there is also things going on within paramilitary groups themselves … they are moving on like. And people have come here and said that they would normally go to the paramilitaries but that they don't want anyone shot, they just want it to stop. I think that slowly but surely it is a trickle towards that. There is still an appetite among people towards a punitive way, but there is a shift, there is a change.[33]

However, this process of change is slow. Knox and Monaghan (2002) have pointed out the difficulty that communities, which for 30 years demanded and witnessed 'rough justice', must experience in accepting an alternative that is centred on apologies, reparation and community service. Such a mind shift, they argue, would necessarily take time. In relation to community restorative justice practice, one interviewee mentioned:

> We do have to combat the attitudes of some people out there who do go to the paramilitaries, who don't go to the police, who don't want another alternative but who go to the paramilitaries for justice. Because it is seen as a swift and immediate type of justice ... it is very visual if a young person has been shot, you know.[34]

Attitudes supportive of violence within the community clearly emerged in research undertaken by Hamill (2002) in relation to practices of punishment violence in Nationalist West Belfast. Hamill was present at several public meetings where the problem of high levels of antisocial behaviour among young people in the area was discussed. The meetings were attended by local residents and representatives from youth and community projects, but also by people from statutory agencies and political parties. The dominant mood during these meetings was one of anger and frustration, demanding that harsher intervention was needed in relation to 'hoods', who were seen as destroying their community. Hamill (2002) noted that the demands for harsher intervention against hoods all came from local residents: 'They can't stab other people and get away with it; they need to be taught a lesson they'll never forget' (2002: 61).

The people involved in the efforts to persuade local communities regarding the potential of restorative justice during the *Blue Book* consultation (e.g. Auld *et al.* 1997) reported similar harsh community attitudes, which had continued throughout their practice. On several occasions, mothers had come into a CRJI office with their sons, asking to have them beaten up, since they simply could not handle them any more. Such requests were explained by practitioners as due to the long-standing practices of punishment violence in the community, and it was mentioned that some people in the area had become used to solutions that were punitive, quick and very visible. Hence, the argument went, when people asked for someone to be beaten or shot, they were basically doing what they knew.

People's fear of victimisation, combined with inadequate protection from the criminal justice system, can lead them to use violence to restore order and security. One interviewee in a Loyalist area commented on such punitive tendencies in the community:

From the victims' perspective, they say that 'I hold off going to the paramilitaries and you have eight weeks to fix the problem', and then they see the kid out and about every weekend misbehaving. ... 'Where is the evidence then that your approach is working, whereas if I went to the club and say that this kid is bothering me, and then I see him hobbling around, that would be much more satisfying.' And that view is not to be discounted, you know. I find the case persuasive, that [going to the paramilitaries] does not resolve the case on a community level, and it might not resolve the problem on an individual level either in terms of reoffending, but I don't think that you can deny that there is something immensely satisfying with someone who has injured you, getting injured himself, you know. You see that they have been punished for what they have done.[35]

Similar community opinions were displayed in an area in north Belfast in 2004, where a new CRJI project was being established at the time.[36] When conducting a local survey and asking for community feedback via the Community Charter distributed to people's houses, many wrote on the back of the Charter what they would like to do to the 'hoods': for example, 'don't shoot them six times, once should be enough'; 'tarring and feathering and tie them to a lamp post', 'throw them out, they don't deserve any more chances'; and 'bring back public flogging'.[37] Obviously, they did not perceive a restorative justice process to be an appropriate method of dealing with these issues.

There is no grand plan to challenge actively and overcome such punitive attitudes in a transitional society. Instead, as was mentioned by CRJI volunteers in Derry, they view the potential of community restorative justice to challenge cultures of violence as 'case by case, by offering alternatives to the traditional methods of dealing with crime and antisocial behaviour'.[38] As a practitioner at an Alternatives project explained:

People in this area would say that the police are proving ineffective. ... So people go to people like us, or the paramilitaries, or local churches – people within their local community who they can trust. So we have to change that, you know, the community mindset. And hopefully through the paramilitaries we can do that. Because if they say, 'No, we won't do that, we will send him to Alternatives', *that* will make people think. Again, it is going to be a long, slow process and I am making no apologies for that.[39]

Viewed in such a way, practices of restorative justice at the micro-level can have an impact on the macro-community, which includes both paramilitary organisations and the wider community – a dynamic generally referred to by practitioners as the 'ripple effect'. Such a ripple effect of practice can have wide-ranging positive effects within punitive communities. The manager of CRJI in Derry indicated that one of the major contributions the practices of restorative justice have provided in the areas where they work is to raise the threshold of when people ask to have someone shot or beaten. This is a major change for communities that for many years have relied on paramilitaries for conflict resolution.

Importantly, both projects have noted that even though levels of crime and antisocial behaviour in their communities are not decreasing, such events have not resulted in a renewed increase in punishment attacks. Instead, the caseloads of both projects, especially CRJI, have increased in relation to crime and antisocial behaviour in recent years, signalling a reduced community reliance on paramilitaries to deal with such issues, a reduced willingness by paramilitary groups themselves to engage in such practices, high or even increasing levels of offending and antisocial behaviour in the transitional context, and, finally, but importantly, a lingering reluctance to report even serious incidents to the PSNI.

It seems clear that the practice of restorative justice can raise the threshold of punitive attitudes in the community, consequently decreasing calls for punishment violence or vigilante actions. Contributing to ending practices of punishment violence in Loyalist and Republican communities is a considerable achievement by community restorative justice projects in the transitional context of Northern Ireland. Moreover, the effects are seen in relation to participants in the restorative justice process, the views of volunteers, and wider community structures; and by addressing the situation in which many youths find themselves – a situation characterised by disadvantage and marginalisation – another maintaining factor of a culture of violence is affected.

The projects deal with a range of cases, some of which are serious and violent, and others which are likely to escalate into violence if not dealt with in a timely manner. In relation to this, practitioners in CRJI and Alternatives strongly argued that there is little point in restoring people to the situations and the relationships they were in before, since it was precisely those situations which gave rise to the conflicts in the first place. In this instance, the word 'conflict' was used to refer to both the particular dispute which brings people into contact with community restorative justice and the bigger picture, such as the Troubles and the ensuing systems of punishment violence. Hence, most practitioners see themselves as aiming for transformative justice as opposed to 'just' restorative justice. Arguably, restorative justice – with its focus on the (re)integration of young people, addressing underlying reasons for offending, a forward-looking philosophy, and participation, inclusiveness and personal responsibility – can be a well-placed vehicle to address such complex issues within the transitional society.

Importantly, CRJI and Alternatives undertake this work with little or no support from the state, and they have developed independently of any other concurrent changes in the criminal justice system, based on grass-roots needs as opposed to top-down requests or pressures. In all of these ways they differ quite radically from many other restorative justice programmes in stable democracies around the world, and have more in common with organic developments in other transitional societies such as South Africa and Rwanda (e.g. Shearing 2001; Drumbl 2002; Roche 2002; Roberts 2003; Cartwright *et al.* 2004; Waldorf 2006; Froestad and Shearing 2007). The leadership provided by volunteers and staff alike has been crucial for the success of the projects, particularly the leadership of ex-political prisoners and former combatants. The next chapter discusses this in more detail, along with an in-depth exploration of the role of volunteers in community restorative justice in Northern Ireland.

Notes

1 Generally known as 'joyriding', but many people in these communities have started to refer to it as 'death riding' due to the extensive damage caused by such behaviour.
2 Interview with Alternatives coordinator, 2 June 2005.
3 Interview, 16 November 2004.
4 The data collected in relation to the work of Alternatives are largely qualitative due to a lack of access to case files for Alternatives, but a clear picture of their work emerged from the many interviews and field visits conducted during the course of the research, and casework will be illustrated through quotations and narratives. Secondary sources are relied upon in relation to some of the more quantitative information.
5 Interview with project manager, Shankill Alternatives, 19 May 2005.

6 Obviously, the existence of Alternatives is just one variable that has contributed to reducing punishment violence in Loyalist communities in Northern Ireland. Much depends on community politics, the relationships between paramilitary groups, and the overall political situation of the day. However, one important fact which should not be overlooked is the much reduced levels of punishment violence within the specific areas in which there is an Alternatives office in operation (Mika 2007).

7 Interview with Alternatives project coordinator, 27 May 2005.

8 These developments will be discussed in detail in Chapters 7 and 8.

9 Interview with Alternatives project coordinator, 27 May 2005.

10 Interview with youth worker, East Belfast Alternatives, 2 June 2005.

11 Interview with Alternatives caseworker, 21 June 2005.

12 Interview, 19 May 2005.

13 The Youth Justice Agency works according to a restorative justice model, focusing on young people between the ages of 10 and 17. It was set up during the reconstruction of the criminal justice system in the wake of the Good Friday Agreement, but had very little cooperation with the community-based projects at the time of writing.

14 Interview with youth worker, North Belfast Alternatives, 27 May 2005.

15 Interview, 28 June 2005.

16 Obviously, two people do not make up a representative sample, and ideally it should have been larger. Access to the young people who had completed their time at Alternatives had to be organised by the project itself, and hence it became limited to two people. However, they spoke candidly and at length about their experiences, and I felt it was an important insight into not only how Alternatives worked, but also into young people's experiences in these communities. It is quite possible, of course, that the two young people who agreed to speak to me were representative of 'success stories'.

17 After engaging with Alternatives, he was in court for another offence, and he was offered the route of a restorative conference within the formal justice system, facilitated by the Youth Justice Agency, instead of facing disposal in court. At the time, he presumed that the conference would be an easier option so agreed accordingly. At the conference, he had to face several victims whose cars he had wrecked, an experience he felt was far from easy. Moreover, as part of the plan emanating from the conference, he received community service, which he was able to complete through Alternatives. As such, Alternatives supported him throughout his sentence, encouraged him to complete his probation hours, and also arranged victim–offender mediation with some of the people who had not felt comfortable meeting him earlier during the conference set up by the Youth Justice Agency.

18 Opportunity Youth was established in 1993 in response to the diverse needs of young people involved in vocational training in Belfast. Through their work, they encourage the social and personal development

of young people and support them to be the best they can be. The organisation offers guidance, information and support, using peer education methodology for young people aged 8–25. They also work with young offenders in the Hydebank Young Offenders Institution (www.opportunity-youth.org).

19 Information based on the interviews with support workers in Shankill, and North and East Belfast Alternatives.

20 Research note. Since English is not my first language, I expected to have problems at some point in understanding local people's accents, but I suspect that to understand everything these boys said, one would need some type of special training, which I had not undertaken. At the end of the interview, I also asked, as I always do as part of my praxis, if they had anything they wanted to ask me. The 'leader' of the group braced himself, and, in an attempt to show off his knowledge of foreign cultures, asked whether it was true that 'Swedish women didn't shave … under the armpits', it followed after a somewhat tense silence. The answer to that question will stay on the Shankill, but their hysterical laughter was worth the response.

21 Interview, 30 June 2005.

22 Interview, 19 May 2005.

23 Interview with victims support worker, Shankill Alternatives, 19 May 2005.

24 Interview with support worker, Shankill Alternatives, 19 May 2005.

25 Interview with Alternatives manager, 27 May 2005.

26 This was the situation during the field research in Loyalist areas in the summer of 2005. The situation, however, is bound to change somewhat, after the UVF issued a statement on 3 May 2007 announcing that the organisation was transforming into a non-military one and that they were putting their weapons beyond use. In the statement, the UVF also pledged their support for community restorative justice in Loyalist areas (*BBC News Northern Ireland*, 'UVF Calls an End to Terror Campaign', 3 May 2007).

27 This statement reflects the ambivalent relationship within and between different paramilitary groups, where some groups would be involved in importing and distributing drugs in the community, while others work to stop it. Feuds between different factions, especially within Loyalism, are not unusual outcomes of these tensions.

28 Interview, 2 June 2005.

29 Interview, 2 June 2005.

30 Interview with CRJI practitioner, 2 December 2004.

31 Interview with CRJI manager, 9 November 2004.

32 Interview with Alternatives manager, 19 May 2005.

33 Interview with project manager, 19 May 2005.

34 Interview with Alternatives practitioner, 2 June 2005.

35 Interview with victim support worker, Shankill Alternatives, 19 May 2005.

36 This office has since closed due to a lack of funding.
37 Interview with North Belfast CRJI coordinator, 14 February 2005.
38 Interview, 31 March 2005.
39 Interview with manager, East Belfast Alternatives, 2 June 2005.

Chapter 6

Volunteers and practitioners: leadership in a culture of violence

> Community involvement is often seen as an essential element of restorative justice. Therefore, the involvement of volunteers, as members of the community, in the mediation process can make it more restorative. (Pelikan and Tranczek 2006: 81)

One of the defining features of community restorative justice in Northern Ireland is that Alternatives and CRJI have maintained and even extended their community ethos by recruiting volunteers and practitioners from the geographical areas in which the respective projects operate. Between 2003 and 2005, Alternatives had 269 volunteers and the corresponding figure for CRJI was 310 (Mika 2007). Such widespread utilisation of local people, who have been provided with an opportunity for real involvement, is often portrayed as an important measure by which informal justice projects can maintain their independence and at the same time resist professionalisation (Marshall 1988). The projects clearly benefit from their involvement, but the volunteers also benefit from working within the projects, which will be discussed below.

This chapter also explores the different styles of leadership that former combatants and ex-political prisoners have demonstrated through the establishment and subsequent practice of community restorative justice in this transitional context (McEvoy and Eriksson 2006). These different types of leadership – military, political and moral – have been central to the success the projects have had in influencing a shift in social norms, actively challenging the existing modes of violent informal social control at the community level, and also in initiating partnerships between historically estranged communities and the state.

Volunteers in community restorative justice

The number of volunteers in the two projects is high, as noted above. All participate in a training programme before commencing their roles, and CRJI and Alternatives run their own in-house training for this purpose. From a rather rudimentary beginning, the training courses have become more formalised and extensive. At CRJI, the training programme consists of a 10-week course with meetings one evening per week. Over the years, this course has developed to cover more topics – such as child protection, conflict resolution, domestic violence awareness and human rights – and included outside agencies as guest speakers:

> When I joined CRJI in 2003, the training course was quite basic. It was unaccredited. Then it moved on to a course accredited by the Open College Network. So now they get an official certificate. And it gives us a standing within CRJI where we want to go with this. Now we have one evening per week per subject, such as child protection, conflict resolution, and human rights law, but if we had the money maybe we could have one in-depth course per subject and have each recognised as OCN. We also bring in people from Social Services, the Housing Executive and Probation to talk to our volunteers as well, which would not have happened a few years ago. So it has gradually developed.[1]

For many, the reason for becoming a volunteer in community restorative justice was a desire to help improve one's own community, by helping people who have been victims of crime, or by supporting young people who are trying to change their lives for the better. In other contexts, it has been argued that they personally gained a sense of pride and satisfaction from seeing the change in other people, and from being able to help and empower other people, which in turn empowers the volunteers (Roche 2003). Most people in CRJI and Alternatives volunteer for about three hours per week, but some people put in considerably more time, sometimes up to 20–30 hours per week.

It was mentioned that practitioners and volunteers learn, through the practice of restorative justice, to separate people from actions. It humanises conflict, highlighting that there are 'real' people involved, and this counteracts labelling and techniques of neutralisation (Sykes and Matza 1957; Braithwaite 1989). This might be particularly important within a transitional society, and an important aspect of challenging an embedded culture of violence. Coordinators in both communities noted that by working within a restorative justice framework, practitioners and volunteers learn to respect other people, even if they disagree with their opinions or actions. It can also challenge punitive views held by volunteers, helping them to see the overall context of a person's behaviour. In this regard, one CRJI practitioner explained:

> The CRJI training course is not about being able to mediate between two groups of people, it is not about that at all. Some people might have come in here and thought it was OK to shout at your neighbour, or being angry at the 10-year-old standing out on the street corner at night. But it is about making people aware that the 10-year-old may not want to go home because his parents are drinking and shouting at him or whatever. So it is about educating the community about that the problems out there, are problems because of the way in which people have come through society, and they got their own issues to deal with. And they are not getting the support they need because if they did they may not be standing out on the street corner drinking. And I think it is important that the good in the community sees this, and community education is vital in this.[2]

Apart from a focus on addressing the underlying causes of crime and antisocial behaviour, this statement also reflects the importance placed on community education as one of the underlying values of the overall practice, and of the training of volunteers. For a society emerging from conflict, such an ethos of practice makes it possible to challenge long-standing norms of conflict resolution and simultaneously present people with a practical and tangible option. Such a change in perspective can extend well beyond participants in restorative processes and even one's own community. For example, according to a practitioner in a Republican community, to be able to understand the experience of people on the Loyalist side, even though one might disagree with the substance of their opinions, had been a significant personal development.

Such experiences demonstrate the personal impact on individuals who work within this restorative justice framework, and how micro-experiences map onto broader political attitudes. As noted by Merry and Milner (1993) in relation to restorative justice practice, 'the impact on those who handle problems seems to be greater than on those whose problems are being handled' (p. 16). What is of primary importance for the transitional context is the ripple effect of working within a restorative justice framework, which can prompt people to think in new ways about conflict in their everyday lives. Thus, restorative justice becomes a way of dealing with everyday issues, not just a job. This resonates throughout their close community, and as mentioned by one CRJI practitioner:

> Working here definitely affects how our volunteers view conflict and its surrounding issues. There are people here who would have possibly supported the idea of punishment beatings, but since coming in here they are totally opposed to it. They understand the whole story. It also changes your attitude and how you deal with things, how you deal with conflict at home, so it also influences how you do things in your personal life.[3]

Not everyone is open to such change in perspective, however. In a focus group of volunteers at one of CRJI's offices in 2005, it was indicated that (at that time) about 40 people had gone through the training, but few actually continued as a volunteer once their training was over. Some quit after a few months of involvement, realising that they could not handle this type of work, that some clients frightened them or that they could not be sufficiently neutral. Another issue, especially in the beginning, was that people expected CRJI to be more 'Republican', more like the IRA. When aspiring volunteers realised that this was not the case, some of them simply walked out – they wanted nothing to do with 'hood hugging', but wanted more 'hands-on' work.[4] According to the manager of Derry CRJI, the work they do is apolitical: 'Even if you have your own personal politics, you don't let that affect your work. Neither does it matter what political affiliation the victims or offenders have, one has to be neutral.'[5] For some, this is too difficult, and they choose to stop working with community restorative justice.

The majority of volunteers interviewed, however, mentioned that through the training and subsequent work, their understanding of the causes of antisocial behaviour and conflict in the community had increased since becoming involved with community restorative justice, and they felt more able to deal with conflict both at work and at home. They also mentioned that the training had increased their self-esteem and that they had in general acquired a better understanding of other people in their surroundings and were now less quick to judge other people. Moreover, after going through the training and doing some volunteer work, many people move on to further education or to other jobs that are better paid. Through the training, people gain not only skills but also the confidence to use them, and become more aware of their own abilities. In short, this engagement empowers them (Barton 2000).

Apart from the effectiveness of practice, the active involvement of the local community in restorative justice training and practice in a transitional society can have important repercussions for the way conflict is viewed and dealt with on a day-to-day basis. The transformation of the personal attitudes and beliefs of practitioners and volunteers involved in these community-based projects was highlighted in the research as one of the most important consequences of practice, after the impact it could have on practices of punishment violence in the wider community:

> 'Cause remember CRJI is based on the ethos of bringing in and engaging the community, so all our caseworkers will always be volunteers, because we are here to educate the community in that sense. So even if we had the money to pay caseworkers we still would use volunteers, because you are trying to do as big a turnover within the community as possible.[6]

This quotation highlights the importance placed on community education within this transitional period and the positive effect of actively working within a restorative justice framework. The effectiveness of the practice of CRJI and Alternatives is not measured solely on the basis of reduced levels of punishment violence or successful mediation, but also on the changing perceptions of volunteers to violence and conflict resolution more broadly.

Volunteers should ideally come from all sections of the community, including people of different ages and backgrounds. An important consequence of drawing practitioners and volunteers from the local community, and of trying to make such groups as representative as possible, is that the involvement of ex-prisoners is something these projects actively work towards since they make up a substantial percentage of these communities. The staff at Alternatives and CRJI believe that if there is a large proportion of ex-prisoners in the local community, their presence is vital to ensure the credibility and legitimacy of the practice.

In a focus group of eight volunteers at one Alternatives office, I enquired as to their views on including only local people as volunteers for the project. One of them replied, '[v]ery important. It makes people feel safer, that there is someone that they might know, and they understand the issues that affect the local community. It is an issue of trust.' However, it was also mentioned that this could be a hindrance. This was expressed by another volunteer who lived in a different Loyalist area that also has a community restorative justice programme. She felt, conversely, that people might find the close association inhibiting, and therefore she decided to volunteer at another project. This was a personal decision on her part, but such a view has also been highlighted in the restorative justice literature where it has been argued that there may be dangers of too close an association between clients and volunteers/staff (Levrant *et al.* 1999; Wachtel and McCold 2000; Crawford and Newburn 2003). It can raise questions regarding accountability (Roche 2003) and transparency.

However, within these particular communities, the involvement of 'outsiders' can be viewed with suspicion by the community. The coordinators of CRJI and Alternatives were acutely aware of such sentiments during the establishment phases of the projects:

> We hand-picked those who we thought had something to offer, and that was a conscious decision. We did not want people coming in from outside the area, and telling us things that we had already developed ourselves. And if we had done that, we would not have had the support from the community, if outsiders were seen as coming in and trying to fix things.[7]

This quotation reflects not only the grass-roots ethos of restorative justice practice, but also the exclusionary nature of these communities discussed earlier, a legacy of the conflict within which the projects have to operate. However, an important aspect of the strong presence of practitioners and volunteers from the local community means that the project can, quite effortlessly, tap into the general mood of the community. They can consequently tailor their interventions according to the needs or issues prevalent in the community, a feature of practice that state-based restorative justice projects have yet to attain.

Volunteers obviously hold a prominent and valued position within CRJI and Alternatives, and they are guided by the coordinators of each project. The leadership displayed by ex-political prisoners and former combatants in the transition has been central to the practice of community restorative justice in Northern Ireland. A conceptualisation of the different types of leadership displayed during the establishment and subsequent practice of CRJI and Alternatives is discussed below, placed within the context of the wider literature on leadership in transition.

Restorative justice, ex-prisoners and leadership in transition

The fate of ex-prisoners and former combatants in the process of transition from conflict has been widely recognised as central to attempts at peacemaking (McEvoy and Eriksson 2006). In some of the long-lasting and more complex armed conflicts, the failures in planning and delivery in finding new roles for former armed actors have been viewed as highly destabilising for emerging transitional processes (McEvoy and Eriksson 2006). Traditionally, much of the focus has been upon breaking up armed groups as quickly as possible and removing their weapons in order better to facilitate security. However, a more multifaceted approach is needed, and, as Mani (2002) has noted, 'finding employment in a field where they feel their skills and background are being put to relevant use may reduce the grievances of unemployed and disgruntled ex-combatants, which might otherwise find violent expression' (p. 61). In a similar vein, the former UN Secretary-General, Kofi Annan, argued in a speech in Derry, Northern Ireland in 2004, that peace cannot be secured without

> providing the fighters with an alternative, peaceful means of earning their living. Nowadays we no longer contemplate demobilisation and disarmament – the two 'Ds' – without adding an 'R', which stands for reintegration into the civilian economy. Without this, it is a virtual certainty that new weapons will be acquired and violence will resume. (Annan 2004)

The issue of community 'leaders' being representative of the whole community in relation to justice initiatives in general and to Northern Ireland specifically is critical, and one which has been highlighted by several authors (Silke 1998a; Crawford 1999a; Knox and Monaghan 2002; Pavlich 2004, 2005). Such issues relate to internal power structures and have been fiercely debated in relation to these restorative justice projects. In this regard, it has been argued that both CRJI and Alternatives are simply another means for paramilitary organisations to keep control of their own communities

129

by oppression in disguise (Dignan 2000). Yet this research indicates that the moral authority invested in the practitioners of community restorative justice has been vital for the establishment and continued operation of the projects, and the leadership provided by ex-prisoners within this transitional context during a transformation of cultures of violence should not be underestimated. However, the label of 'ex-prisoner' is one with which not everyone is comfortable, and on this point one youth worker at Alternatives commented when asked how his status of ex-prisoner affects his work:

> None whatsoever. What I would say is that no one knows until I tell them unless they know me. And I say this all the time – I am a hell of a lot more than just an ex-prisoner ... I am a son, a father, a grandfather, brother, and husband. I am all those things. You know ... based on my own experiences I am trying to change people's thinking. I want us to cut those ties. ... And even if we should not forget our past, let's move on. Let's move on. I don't want to be known as 'Name Name so and so' for my past, I want people to stay here right now and look to the future.[8]

The social status conferred upon ex-prisoners and consequently held by many community restorative justice practitioners and volunteers has been both beneficial – particularly at the community level – and detrimental, particularly in relation to interaction with statutory agencies. In reply to the question of how his status as an ex-prisoner potentially affected the practice of community restorative justice, both in relation to community and possible partnerships with statutory agencies, Tom Winston replied:

> Within the community it helped me to try and come up with the Alternatives model, because in the eyes of the community I am doing this for the right reasons. I am not doing this for a paramilitary organisation, I am not doing it because I am an ex-prisoner, I am doing it because I am a community member who was willing to go to prison for his beliefs. But in the beginning a lot of statutory agencies looked at me with a great deal of suspicion and some of them still do, thinking that you are closely associated with a paramilitary organisation. But I think that we have proved ourselves that there is no hidden agenda. The organisations out there that really need to know who I am, they do. And our message is starting to get through, that we

are doing this for the right reasons – that we want to make the community a better place.[9]

As I have argued elsewhere (McEvoy and Eriksson 2006), many former combatants and ex-prisoners have been at the forefront in providing leadership in the Northern Ireland transition through seeking to prevent the resumption of organised political and communal violence.[10] Three overlapping styles of leadership adopted by these former combatants and political ex-prisoners can be identified in the Northern Irish transition: political, military, and moral leadership.[11]

Political leadership

In the working-class Republican and Loyalist communities in which these programmes are located, ex-combatants are largely regarded as having 'done their bit' on behalf of their communities (McEvoy and Eriksson 2006). While there are subtle differences between the attitudes of the two communities, the ex-combatants involved in restorative justice bring a considerable degree of credibility, respect and legitimacy to the programmes.

Individually, a number of the most prominent restorative justice activists are highly skilled and charismatic practitioners, and over the years such leadership has become institutionalised in the working practices of the projects. As well as their previous organisational and often 'jail time' experience, many have been involved in community work for many years. As noted above, by working with and subscribing to values of non-violence, human rights, inclusiveness, and respect and tolerance for difference, they are providing small 'p' political leadership in transforming community attitudes to violence (McEvoy and Eriksson 2006).

In addition, and in particular in the Republican communities, which are considerably more politically sensitive, they are also providing leadership towards the building of relations between statutory agencies, the criminal justice system and the communities traditionally estranged from them:

When people see us as community leaders actively using those resources [statutory agencies], then they are more comfortable using them themselves. Historically, working with the state was something you did not do in this community for a long, long time. But I think that now people see someone who they perceive as community leaders doing that, then it filters down.[12]

This 'filtering down' aspect of leadership in transition is a central component of the 'ripple effect' of practice. This is the phrase practitioners from both communities use to describe the impact of restorative justice, not only on the people directly involved in the projects, but also on the wider community. The practice would arguably not have such effects without the moral authority and leadership held by CRJI and Alternatives practitioners. As one of them noted:

> I think that the work we do is invaluable, and sometimes incredible. Like people who were excluded, and we managed to work them back into the community, and who now are fathers and they are working ... they are donating. Without restorative justice four or five years ago, I don't know where they would have been; they could have been dead or become hardened criminals. I think we have a lot of young people who would have been harmed or even self-harmed, or abusing drugs or alcohol, which they did not do because they were put right and helped along. And these kids are not hoods, they are dysfunctional youths, and if you give them a background, give them a life, then people will view them differently. And they are our next adults ... it's about changing a whole generation. The war does not belong to them. Our children are the next generation and what we don't need is anger and aggression, we've had enough of that.[13]

The projects, however, not only have an impact on the wider community, but they can also help affect the inner structures of the paramilitary organisations, by providing alternative ways of thinking about and dealing with crime and conflict in the community, as illustrated earlier. Such efforts can be referred to as military leadership.

Military leadership

As well as working and volunteering in the restorative justice programmes, ex-combatants and former prisoners have been central in efforts to persuade paramilitary organisations to desist from punishment violence, to refer 'complainants' from the community to the programmes, and to consider their own internal organisational attitudes to violence. As mentioned previously, the director of Alternatives, a former UVF life-sentenced prisoner, personally conducted the original research and interviews with the UVF which led to the establishment of the programme (Winston 1997). Similarly, the director of CRJI, a former Republican internee, was one of four individuals involved in direct dialogue with the IRA and other Republicans that led to the establishment of the programmes on the Republican side (Auld *et al.* 1997). Many others working on the programmes have served lengthy prison sentences as a result of their membership of an armed organisation. Consequently, no one within their respective constituency can question the past commitments of these practitioners. Together with other ex-combatants, and precisely because of their collective credibility with the respective paramilitary groupings, the senior practitioners of CRJI and Alternatives have been involved in peacemaking efforts with such organisations (McEvoy and Eriksson 2006).

Importantly, the leadership displayed by community restorative justice practitioners influences not only the armed groups but also the 'ordinary' community including aspects of vigilantism. This influence should not be underestimated in communities that have relied on violence to solve their conflicts for many years, and which still possess a strong punitive element in their responses to crime and antisocial behaviour. As mentioned by one of the CRJI practitioners: 'A very important part of CRJ work is educating community people about alternative ways of dealing with conflict. The ripple effect of our practice should not at any point be underestimated.'[14]

The process of persuasion or leadership in trying to shift attitudes in paramilitary organisations should not be understood as either smooth or easy. As mentioned above, both projects operate under certain limitations in their remit, and the practice of community restorative justice is one of constant negotiation with paramilitary groups so as to allow CRJI and Alternatives to intervene in cases which traditionally were handled by violent means. Such a process of persuasion is part of challenging cultures of violence at the collective level, by demonstrating leadership at the individual level and challenging the military structures of such paramilitary organisations.

On the other hand, it was also mentioned that older former combatants may at times struggle with intergenerational tensions and face accusations that they have 'gone soft' through their involvement in restorative justice. At times, they have to rely on leaders their own age who are still inside the organisational structures to counsel against the tried and failed methods of the past.[15] Despite these difficulties, it is through the leadership and persuasion efforts of former combatants involved in restorative justice that we have seen significant reductions in punishment violence in the areas where the projects are operational. Moreover, changes (for the better) in the ways in which local paramilitary organisations conduct their 'policing' activities, such as referring cases to one of the schemes rather than punishing alleged antisocial offenders (Mika 2004, 2007), have also taken place. Indeed, these restorative justice programmes are examples of the kinds of progressive outlets, aimed at community capacity building, towards which such individuals can ideally direct their political energies.

However, not all are open to such efforts of persuasion – a reflection of the heterogeneous character of these communities, and of existing power struggles over the ownership of 'justice' within the community. During 2008, dissident Republican organisations renewed their commitment to the armed struggle in response to what they perceive as too close cooperation between Sinn Féin and the DUP. Dissident groups, in particular Continuity IRA, the INLA and the Real IRA, voiced their dissatisfaction with CRJI when the organisation developed a closer working relationship with the police. For many, this is one step too far, and practitioners in CRJI have on several occasions received death threats from dissident groups, the latest in October 2008 (*BBC News*, 30 October 2008). Hence, military leadership has proved to be more effective within the more mainstream Republican movement. Similar evidence emanates from Loyalist areas, where groups other than the UVF have been opposed to the practices of Alternatives.

Moral leadership and community building

The third style of leadership provided by former combatants and ex-prisoners is transformative or moral leadership in the process of community building. Bazemore and Schiff (2001) have argued that community building is facilitated by connecting people more closely to existing relationships and to new ones based on trust and reciprocity. Such relationships are then connected to networks of social capital (Putnam 2000) and by skill-building within those networks. The issues surrounding community building and the attention paid to the needs of former combatants are strongly connected in a transitional society (Babo-Soares 2004; Knight and Özerdam 2004; Verwimp and Verpoorten 2004). The reality of the conflict in Northern Ireland, which saw thousands of people imprisoned from geographically small working-class areas, is that, as one seasoned community worker said, 'Everyone has a history here.'[16]

Nonetheless, involvement by ex-combatants in strong and independent community organisations – utilising their existing organisational and political skills as well as demonstrating a willingness to learn new ones – constitutes an appropriately balanced organic relationship between such individuals and the communities from which they come:

> Those people are very much making a contribution to their communities. Especially behind the scenes they are involved in a lot of positive changes. I think that people generally tend to focus on what negative things have happened instead of what positive contributions paramilitaries and especially former paramilitaries have made. If you look at interface trouble and social problems, programmes that are trying to address issues with young people in conflict in schools and so on. People from Loyalist communities are really taking risks and chances to make a difference. Alternatives is one of them but there are a number of others where former prisoners and paramilitaries are involved in. People would not always see that.[17]

However, the status of ex-prisoner is not always a positive attribute. It may confer moral authority, respect and credibility at the community level, but when it comes to cooperation with statutory agencies, things become complicated. When asked about how their status as ex-prisoners affected their working relationship with other organisations and when trying to 'sell' restorative justice to statutory agencies, practitioners responded in line with the comment: 'great message, wrong messenger'. They clarified this by explaining that many statutory organisations were very interested in what community restorative justice could achieve, but wished that someone else was doing it so as to avoid the politically difficult situations that can arise when community and state are dealing with each other directly. This sentiment was also echoed in the interviews with statutory agencies, including the PSNI in 2004 and 2005. It was clear that many wished that the ex-prisoners and ex-combatants would just go away, and that restorative justice should ideally be run by a more 'neutral' organisation. This situation has now changed quite radically, and the PSNI openly acknowledge the benefits of working with CRJI and Alternatives, in particular the leadership provided by practitioners in the attempts to establish closer cooperation between these communities and the police.

By way of conclusion, it can be argued that in the working-class communities which suffered the brunt of violence, these groups of ex-prisoners and former combatants are showing leadership in moving communities away from such long-standing cultures of violence. As individuals who may have been directly involved in committing acts of political violence, and whose organisations have been guilty of punishing alleged offenders, ex-combatants are well placed to communicate the arguments to local communities about the failings of such exclusionary practices directed against the 'hoods'. For those restorative justice practitioners who have both inflicted and been on the receiving end of extreme violence, it holds little allure. Their rejection of the efficacy of punishment violence is itself a powerful exercise in both moral leadership and community capacity building. Consequently, it can be argued that it is often ex-combatants who are taking the lead within Republicanism and Loyalism on how their respective constituencies should deal with the legacy of violence, victim–offender reconciliation work, and cross-community projects designed to lessen tensions at interface areas, as well as the restorative justice programmes under discussion here (McEvoy *et al.* 2004). Indeed, community building around issues such as the ongoing dialogue about the injustices of the past and its legacy is a goal that represents the central potential of restorative principles in the context of political transitions (Leebaw 2001: 286–287). Transitional contexts such as Northern Ireland demonstrate that the potential of restorative justice is not limited to addressing the issues surrounding individual criminal acts, but can contribute to addressing elements of larger social problems that intersect with the criminal act under discussion, by addressing the underlying causes of crime and antisocial behaviour.

This research clearly indicates that the prominent position of former combatants and ex-political prisoners during the establishment phase and the subsequent practice of community restorative justice projects has been crucial to the success of these projects. One of the practitioners at Alternatives noted:

Now, the reason why this programme was able to be sold to the Loyalist paramilitaries, the UDA, UVF, Red Hand Commando, was because of the likes of ... you know ... people that work here. They have proven themselves to be genuinely committed to better their communities, and that has been well proven, and also they are ex-paramilitaries. I think that because they have been involved with Loyalism in the past, they have been able to influence the paramilitaries in saying, 'Well, this is wrong, and there has to be another way.' Obviously, not everyone who works here is an ex-paramilitary, but those who are are able to have that positive influence.[18]

However, the presence of former combatants and ex-political prisoners in community restorative justice has also resulted in major controversy in Northern Ireland, not only during the establishment phase but particularly during developments in 2007 and 2008 when police and communities were moving towards closer cooperation in relation to crime management and prevention. The following chapter explores the gradual emergence of partnership from within the community, and the consequent politicisation of restorative justice in Northern Ireland.

Notes

1 Interview with CRJI caseworker, 22 January 2008.
2 Interview, 22 January 2008.
3 Interview with CRJI practitioner, 2 December 2004.
4 Interview, 2 December 2004 and 9 November 2005.
5 Interview, 31 March 2005.
6 Interview, 22 January 2008.
7 Interview, 27 May 2005.
8 Interview, 27 May 2005.
9 Interview, 27 May 2005.
10 In making this claim, it is important to stress that I am not postulating some form of naive post-conflict eulogising of all of those who once took up arms. Evidence suggests that some paramilitary organisations in both Republican and Loyalist areas have become involved in organised crime in the post-conflict period, at a time when the need to fund their organisations for the 'struggle' holds little credibility (Cusack and McDonald 1997; MacGary and O'Leary 2004).
11 These three styles of leadership were originally based on the conceptual work of Kieran McEvoy, developed for a joint publication (McEvoy and Eriksson 2006). The use of them here is an explicit application to themes emerging from my own fieldwork; that is, leadership and community restorative justice practice.
12 Interview with CRJI coordinator, 16 November 2004.
13 Interview, 16 November 2004.
14 Interview, 9 November 2004.
15 Interview with CRJI practitioner, 2 December 2004.

16 Interview, 16 November 2004.
17 Interview, 19 May 2005.
18 Interview with youth support worker, Shankill Alternatives, 19 May 2005.

Chapter 7

State–community partnerships in transition: a question of trust

> Northern Ireland actually has a more mature debate on standards and principles of restorative justice than any society I know. It is certainly a more sophisticated debate than in my homeland of Australia. I suspect this is because Northern Ireland has a more politicised contest between state and civil society models of restorative justice than can be found in other places. Such fraught contexts are where there is the greatest risk of justice system catastrophes. But they also turn out to be the contexts with the richest prospects for rising to the political challenges with a transformative vision of restorative justice. (Braithwaite 2002b: 572)

The research literature suggests that, even in stable democracies, partnerships between the state and local community structures in the area of criminal justice often struggle to function. Institutional reluctance to cede ownership over justice functions, a distrust of non-professionals becoming involved in justice work, deeply embedded cultural differences, power relationships and conflict agendas between agencies themselves often impede the development of working partnerships that can practically deliver (Crawford 1994, 1999a, 1999b; Hughes 2006). As Crawford (1994) has argued, such challenges in 'settled' societies can arguably lead to a managerial nightmare. In a transitional context, they are likely to be compounded by the previous violent conflict between the different protagonists. Hence, in the aftermath of violent political conflict in which the state was one of the culprits, such as in Northern Ireland, and where the police and military have been accused of gross violations of human rights such as in South Africa, it should come as no surprise that a large part of civil society finds it very difficult to put its faith in the state as a neutral arbiter of justice in the transitional stage. The result can become a keenly fought contest over the ownership of justice.

Control over justice and security was perceived as absolutely central to the state's efforts in tackling political violence in Northern Ireland, and ceding such strongly held control in the transitional phase has not been a straightforward affair (Cunningham 2001). The conflict produced a state system that privileged control over justice and security, eschewed any meaningful community control or accountability over such functions (McEvoy and Eriksson 2008), and was directly challenged by the violent activities of paramilitaries.

There are obvious historical reasons for the state to distrust sections of civil society in so far as it fears they will maintain power over informal justice and sustain armed control over local communities. Considering the experiences during the conflict of paramilitary violence, and the perceived links between community restorative justice and certain paramilitary organisations, there is perhaps little wonder that the emergence of the projects was treated with suspicion by many of the key institutions of the state and influential others whose views were formed during the conflict. Consequently, suspicion and a lack of trust emanate from both state and community in relation to the other, directly affecting attempts at bridge-building between the two. As argued by McEvoy and Eriksson (2008), the initial reaction by the state to community restorative justice projects was one of 'defensive formalism', such that there was considerable pressure exerted to 'impose state control on referrals to the programmes and compel a relationship with the police, regardless of local political and social circumstances' (McEvoy and Eriksson 2008: 170).

The development of a relationship with the police is significant in a transitional society where the relationship between the state and communities (particularly working-class ones) has a long and troubled history (Mani 2002; Cartwright *et al.* 2006). The improvement of such relationships is an important part of the wider normalisation process in a post-conflict society. Indeed, the development of working partnerships between these formerly estranged communities and the police constitutes a groundbreaking transformation in the Northern Irish transition and warrants special attention. In this regard, further fieldwork was carried out in relation to these developments in December 2007 and January 2008.

Hence, the community–police partnerships will be discussed in a separate chapter, while the current one focuses on the developments in relation to partnership with other statutory agencies and the tangible politicisation of community restorative justice, which took place prior to July 2007. Developments in Northern Ireland sometimes happen quickly, and the situation in January 2008 presented a very different scenario compared to June 2007. Consequently, this chapter chronologically traces the developments around the restorative justice projects.[1] So far, the focus has been on the projects themselves, the work they do, and the impact they have within local communities. This chapter explicitly adds a third player to the discussion: the Northern Irish state.

Politics has always formed part of community restorative justice in Northern Ireland and so far the focus has been on such politics in relation to communities and power struggles over social control and ownership of justice at the local level. Here, however, politics with a capital 'P' enters the stage and the picture becomes somewhat more complex. This chapter explores two primary arguments. The first is how the practice of CRJI and Alternatives can, through bottom-up, organic approaches to partnership, contribute to bridge-building and consequent community capacity building within the local areas in which they work. Secondly, top-down approaches to partnerships will be investigated, approaches which in Northern Ireland are characterised by efforts of regulatory capture by the state. Such reactions are arguably due to attempts by the state to bring these unruly justice initiatives under control, and a simultaneous desire on behalf of the projects for long-term financial stability. A tangible politicisation of community restorative justice has been one result of this contest over ownership of justice, as will be discussed in this section.

Bridge-building and partnerships from 'below'

This section focuses on the organic partnerships that constitute the developments in local communities that took place without direct connection to the bigger political discussions in Northern Ireland. They demonstrate bridge-building in practice between state and community, and the potential of grass-roots initiatives to take the lead in such developments.

Partnerships between community restorative justice projects and statutory agencies can be viewed as driven by restorative justice practice and as organic in nature. They have been driven by a need and a conscious effort on behalf of the projects to link participants with the relevant resources in supporting the implementation of outcome agreements. For example, if a young person needed assistance with drug and alcohol counselling, such resources were found and utilised within the local community. A perhaps unique feature of these communities is the strong tradition of self-help which existed, particularly in Nationalist areas, as a consequence of the Troubles, such that a reluctance and sometimes active discouragement to rely on the state for assistance was prominent. As a result, resources needed to be found within the community, and if none existed, they would be created. An illustrative example of such work was provided in an interview with one coordinator of CRJI in West Belfast:

> Well, counselling was our biggest gap. We had no counselling project in the Twinbrook area, an area with 28,000 people. ... So we decided to get one. And we called a meeting with the statutory, voluntary and community groups together and we invited an organisation in from North Belfast who had done exactly the same. They discovered, 'Shit, we have nowhere to refer these people to, let's start one ourselves.' And this priest and nun and another person ... you know with a table and a phone. We did not need big mega funding and we started with two counsellors who were working on a voluntary basis.
>
> There were no resources in Nationalist areas for a very long time. People had to go to Protestant areas to work and they were booed in and booed out, and harassed while they were there. So I think it has been passed down that if you want something you have to kick ass to get it. So we kicked ass and Probation and the Trust came up with the first £20,000. We launched the project officially last year, and we now have a project worker, a coordinator, an admin worker, the Trust has lent us a room in their family centre. We now employ six counsellors, who work with people in the community. It has to be local because if you send these people into town they are not going, Anna, to a great big red building behind City Hall. Half of them don't know where that is. They are wary, closed. So we got the counselling up and running and I am really proud of that, I think it has been a brilliant outcome for us.[2]

In a similar manner, if an individual or family required assistance from the Social Services or the Housing Executive, such contacts were made by the respective projects on behalf of the participants as required. This situation reflects the suspicion of statutory agencies, which is further illustrated in this quotation:

> For years if you spoke to the Social Services you were a tout: 'You didn't speak to those people because they spoke to the cops'. ... Now, that is more and more acceptable. I actually get people to phone the Social Services themselves and they do. And they are OK with it, because they know that the community is OK with it.[3]

Importantly, this mode of operating – with CRJI and Alternatives acting as a facilitator and conduit between the community and the state – has become a key aspect of the emerging partnerships with the police since 2007. Even though some barriers have been broken down in relation to statutory agencies, the relationship with the police is much more complicated, and many people are fearful of contacting the police directly. This is particularly the case in Nationalist areas, and many people approach a CRJI office instead, who can then contact the police on their behalf.

There are also areas of intervention where statutory agencies, including the police, are arguably less effective than community-based justice initiatives. Interviewees mentioned that the transition has resulted in people losing their sense of being part of a larger community, of a common purpose and of being responsible to each other. Community restorative justice has a potentially important role to play here, in terms of bridging gaps, strengthening communities, and increasing tolerance and understanding in a fragmented and fast-changing environment. One CRJI coordinator explained:

> One of the effects of the Troubles was that people became 'gelled' together. ... That feeling is now disappearing and people are losing a sense of independence, of empowerment. This is both sad and dangerous. ... There is a strong sense of isolation and despair in the community, and it is boiling under the surface.[4]

The formal criminal justice system is somewhat helpless in this regard, as it can only deal with the final consequences. This highlights a serious gap in intervention, and in this type of situation, community restorative justice has perhaps one of its most important roles to play. Effective partnerships in relation to such serious issues are something both CRJI and Alternatives strive to attain, since many of these cases, such as domestic violence or child abuse, fall outside their remit of practice. By aiming toward such cooperation, through building bridges between community and state from the ground up, CRJI and Alternatives effectively link people to the resources they need – a practice which arguably helps build community (Bazemore and Schiff 2002; Dzur and Olson 2004).

Staff interviewed in the community projects frequently commented that 'restorative justice is all about building relationships, based on trust and respect'. This refers not only to the actual participants in a restorative process but also to relationships with voluntary and statutory agencies within their communities. CRJI and Alternatives utilise several local organisations in their work. These include community, voluntary and statutory organisations, whose services are used in reaching outcome agreements in the restorative process, and the utilisation of such organisations is an important tool for building bridges within the community and between the community and the state. This aspect of their work – community capacity building and empowerment – was recognised by the Chief Inspector for Criminal Justice in Northern Ireland, Mr Kit Chivers, who in a statement in May 2007 commented that 'most work undertaken by the schemes [Alternatives] relates to community development.'[5]

As illustrated in Figure 7.1, outside agencies such as the Housing Executive, Social Services, the PSNI, voluntary groups and community groups were involved in some capacity in 730 of the 819 of CRJI's cases in 2007, which equals 89 per cent of all cases. Apart from being a part of outcome agreements, such involvement can range from a simple telephone call for advice or an exchange of information, to direct participation in a conference. In 2006, outside agencies were involved in 523 of the 1,005 cases. Hence, the 2007 data demonstrate a 37 per cent increase in the involvement of outside agencies in CRJI casework.

The greatest increase in involvement of an outside agency is that of the PSNI. Prior to 2007, the number of cases in which the police were involved, either as a source of referral to CRJI or as a recipient of referrals from CRJI, was in single digits compared to 85 cases in 2007. This is a significant shift in the relationship between Republican communities and the police in the Northern Irish transition, and will be explored in more detail in Chapter 8. The figure above also highlights the increase in the number of cases in which the Northern Ireland Housing Executive has been involved. Again, this would have been a rare occurrence prior to Sinn Féin's endorsement of the PSNI. It was clear from the interviews conducted in 2005 and 2008 that the

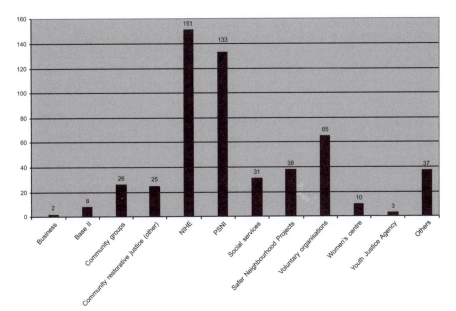

Figure 7.1 Outside agencies involved in CRJI cases in 2007

Housing Executive had some informal contact with CRJI before the endorsement, but is now able to formalise such contact. After the endorsement and since the PSNI has stated that they wish to work with community restorative justice projects in both communities, it is now politically possible for other statutory organisations to follow suit.

Alternatives works with the same types of organisations, although their involvement with statutory agencies is more frequent because of a less complicated relationship between them and the state than is the case for CRJI. Since its establishment, Alternatives has been in what can be termed 'outreach-mode' and has always been very clear about its willingness to form working partnerships with statutory agencies including the PSNI. Due to differences in research access, however, detailed data over statutory involvement in Alternatives practice were not made available. Interview data, however, indicate that Alternatives works with the statutory agencies in a similar manner to CRJI, but has a closer relationship with them.

The number of community and statutory agencies to which Alternatives and CRJI refer is important for a range of reasons, including that this engagement improves service delivery of the projects. Moreover, such relationships can, as mentioned earlier, potentially contribute to local capacity building (Putnam 2000; Dzur and Olson 2004; Crawford 2006). One CRJI coordinator noted:

> CRJI is like the spider in the net in this community. They take referrals from everyone and they also refer out to different community groups. They manage the contacts with the statutory agencies and show people that it is OK to use them. They are at the hub of community building and community empowerment here.[6]

Moreover, community building is not limited to addressing issues surrounding individual criminal acts – that is, micro-community events – but participation at the local community level can also help participants to address the pieces of larger social problems which intersect with the individual act under discussion. Thus, restorative justice practice can address issues at the macro-community level and work towards transformative justice. As has been noted by Dzur and Olson (2004), such links from micro- to macro-levels of social relations can be an exercise in deliberative democracy, highlighted by Braithwaite (1999) as an important feature of restorative justice.

Cooperation with statutory agencies has, however, not been an uncomplicated affair for two major reasons: the strained relationship between Republican communities and the state, which has principally affected CRJI; and the strong presence of former combatants and ex-political prisoners in the projects, which has affected CRJI and Alternatives in equal measures. According to the interviewees, in the first years of practice few statutory agencies were involved in CRJI cases; and when such involvement did take place, it was informal and based on personal contacts. An opinion which was echoed by almost all of the CRJI coordinators was that most statutory agencies work very well with the projects 'on the ground', but it is when CRJI staff start going up the management scale that the difficulties arise:

> We would work with statutory agencies, no problem. But we have found that when you come to work with them, it is all one-way. They want us to refer to them. But they are very, very reluctant to refer to us. It is a major difficulty, a massive difficulty. I don't mind working with them any day, you know my heart is with the young people, and if the statutory agencies can help us with that, great. What we have found is that individuals within, for example, the Social Services, refer to us. But again, it is further up the ladder where it gets difficult.[7]

According to several CRJI staff, this reluctance for equal partnership between statutory agencies and community projects is related to power. Practitioners from both projects noted that the state owns justice and does not want to share it, and the state only seems willing to work with other groups when it suits *its* interest, not when it serves the community. This particular issue is repeated in the restorative justice literature, in which some have argued that professionals in statutory agencies do not share the values of restorative justice and resist moves which could erode their professional ownership in dealing with these issues (Boyes-Watson 1999, 2004; Jantzi 2004; Zehr and Toews 2004). The situation is improving, however, having its basis in several years of informal partnerships. As mentioned by one CRJI coordinator:

> The lovely thing now is that we work in partnership, even if we don't have protocols with them, but you need to work on the ground ... from the ground up here. I would say that we would cover more ground than the politicians would ever do. And it starts on the ground. Now, we work close with the Housing Executive, Social Services, Probation ... all just under the table, within my own community. But there is nothing that goes down that I am not invited to, that my input would not be valued. I would get phone calls from Social Services saying, 'What do you think about this?' ... They are asking for *our* assistance, because we are on the ground. The hardest thing is to convince them that it can work. You know the foundations were already there, and what I had to do was to go to these people and prove that I wasn't the IRA, but there is less and less of that. There is less and less of that perception of us as an organisation, and more and more acceptance of us and more and more acceptance that we are professional and we are serious about this and that we are not going away.[8]

In the interviews with officials from both community and statutory organisations it was acknowledged that there would be immense value in a formal partnership considering that the Housing Executive, Probation, CRJI and Alternatives often work with the same clientele. A senior Housing Executive official had no hesitation in acknowledging that the community restorative justice projects have local knowledge and expertise that is unique, and, as such, they can very useful.[9] A pooling of resources and expertise would, it was argued, benefit all. Community members have a better sense of who is doing what, where, and when in their neighbourhoods, and they can provide a level of informal social control that could never be matched by the police in any free, democratic society (Clear and Karp 1999; Dzur and Olson 2004). Moreover, provision of the necessary and appropriate support for victims and the successful reintegration of offenders require not only community support, but also an understanding of the issues and challenges faced by both victims and offenders in this process.

These features make local restorative justice programmes very important in any democratic and peaceful society, and the cooperation and coordination of resources and information are critical to this process. In a transitional society such as Northern Ireland, these types of programmes become an invaluable tool in meeting the needs of a fast-changing community. At the time of the initial research (2004–6), however, such formal cooperation seemed impossible due to the wider political picture. The next section discusses the developments surrounding attempts to establish formal partnerships between the projects and statutory agencies, including the police. This was a time period signified by strong reactions and vocal opposition from several directions when the state and political parties became intimately engaged in community restorative justice leading up to the endorsement of the PSNI by Sinn Féin in early 2007.

Bridge-building from 'above' and the regulatory state

I think that it will change dramatically when the whole policing issue gets sorted out.[10]

The different expressions of informal justice discussed in Chapter 1 embody and express distinctive ideologies, entailing a vision of the just relationship between the individual, community and the state (Merry and Milner 1993). In a transitional society, however, the role allocated to each of these players and the relationship between them is more fluid and open to interpretation than in stable democracies. The situation in Northern Ireland has resulted in much controversy around community restorative justice, a controversy which has its basis in a redefinition of such relationships. As has been noted by several writers, the existence of an informal community-based justice system raises questions in regards to the legitimacy of the state justice system (Bell 1996; Mika and McEvoy 2001; Feenan 2002), and as long as such an informal system of justice operates outside the state, the question regarding ownership of justice remains unsettled. This was true in relation to the systems of punishment violence discussed earlier, and the same can be said in relation to the community restorative justice projects.

Indeed, Sullivan and Tifft (2006) have argued that restorative justice, at its core, can be perceived as a form of insurgency and as subversive in nature. This is because restorative justice processes, especially those that are community-based and of an independent nature, compete with the state's own way of doing business. As such, restorative justice from a state perspective needs to be 'contained, co-opted, or modified in some way to meet the state's ideological and administrative requirements' (Sullivan and Tifft 2006: 2). As Walgrave has argued, '[i]t is one of the most delicate challenges in the restorative justice undertaking, to conceive the role of the state (or government) in such a way that it does not impede the real restorative process, while playing its norm-enforcing role' (2000: 261). In relation to community restorative justice in Northern Ireland, it has been argued that:

> With the move to new political dispensations there have been attempts at 'regulatory capture' of community-based restorative justice schemes by the state, ostensibly in the interest of human rights protection and securing due process for those accused. (Knox and Monaghan 2002: 139–140)

This is likely to be one possible reason why the state has been so reluctant to acknowledge officially the positive contributions to community crime control and prevention that these projects have made. In Northern Ireland, community restorative justice has come to play a major role in such debates and has subsequently become the object of a process of politicisation.

Since their establishment in 1998, the projects have maintained a permanent presence in the local and indeed national broadcast and print media, and have at times dominated public and professional discourses in the jurisdiction on criminal justice policy and practice.[11] They have been the subject of a specific paper in the Northern Ireland peace negotiations, of a substantial discussion in the review of the Northern Ireland criminal justice system, and of a number of high-profile investigations by bodies such as the International Monitoring Commission and the Northern Ireland Select Committee. Moreover, several attempts were made at draft Protocols in 2005 and 2007, designed to regulate relations between these projects and the formal system, by senior executives of the main criminal justice agencies in Northern Ireland.

Misgivings about community restorative justice were expressed by both statutory agencies and political parties, which tended to fall into two main categories: firstly, concerning the people who are involved in the projects; and second, due to the geographical areas in which they operate. The suspicion of the project due to the presence of several, well-known ex-political prisoners has been covered earlier in this book. The fact that the projects also explicitly set out to work with young people under threat from paramilitaries meant that the staff had direct dealings with active paramilitary groupings, adding to the suspicion regarding the 'real' agenda of community-based restorative justice. In relation to the second concern, all projects operate in sections of communities that are 'hard-to-reach areas' with a strong paramilitary presence. For example, the *Criminal Justice Review* published in 2000 – the first official government document explicitly to mention community restorative justice – clearly indicated the suspicion felt in relation to these new community developments. It stated:

> We heard a wide range of concerns expressed about community restorative justice schemes and their relationship to paramilitary punishment beatings including: The motivations for the development of community restorative justice schemes. Many believed that community restorative justice schemes were being developed by paramilitaries because of the growing unacceptability of punishment attacks within the community, and the need to replace such attacks with other methods of controlling their communities; the risk that those involved in meting out sanctions arising from such schemes would resort to or threaten punishment beatings; the perceived or potential involvement of those with paramilitary links in such schemes; and the risk of schemes being driven by people who did not represent the community as a whole, for reasons that had little or nothing to do with concerns about crime. (*Criminal Justice Review* 2000: 196–197)

As argued by McEvoy and Eriksson (2008), comments such as these 'were reflective of a mindset which *feared* genuine community involvement and ownership in the process of justice, particularly when those communities might be ones traditionally alienated from state structures' (p. 170; emphasis in original). McEvoy and Mika

(2001) have indicated that such suspicions are hardly surprising after three decades of violent conflict, in relation to restorative justice projects that emerged from a direct dialogue with paramilitary constituencies. Such suspicion reflects the fact that many people within the Northern Ireland state were still operating in 'conflict mode', instead of obtaining a real understanding of community dynamics in the transitional phase.

Attempts by the Northern Ireland Office (NIO) to establish a formal partnership with community restorative justice projects in both Loyalist and Republican communities have been evident in the time and effort put into the development, consultation and redrafting of the *Protocol for Community-Based Restorative Justice Schemes*. In December 2005, the government published the first *Draft Guidelines for the Regulation of Community-based Restorative Justice Schemes*. These Protocols can also be seen as an attempt by the government to regulate and control these unruly community developments.

The formulation and publication of the Protocols received much attention from political parties of all persuasions, as government funding would provide CRJI and Alternatives with official legitimacy, which many people felt was undeserved or, as expressed by some political parties, outright dangerous. The perception by many was that community restorative justice in Northern Ireland, especially on the Republican side, was closely associated with parts of the wider Republican movement, in particular the Provisional IRA and their political wing Sinn Féin. Of the political parties, it was mainly the SDLP[12] which voiced the loudest concerns. As one SDLP adviser confessed:

> Our fear is that they [the projects] will try to take the money, without cooperation, working with the police. Meanwhile, Sinn Féin may not get onboard for policing for years yet. ... Meanwhile you have this culture embedding itself. And, also, an alternative method has been given to the Sinn Féin, or what they call an alternative method, for dealing with the problem, which allows them to postpone their decision on policing instead of confronting it. And we want to keep pressure, this is about human rights and protection of individuals, it is also about we want to keep pressure on Sinn Féin to ensure that they do the real solution on policing, as opposed to putting into place something that is very unsatisfactory.[13]

The government was accused of engaging in 'see no evil, hear no evil' (Knox 2002) in relation to punishment violence due to concerns of negatively affecting the wider political process, especially in relation to policing and a will to keep Sinn Féin onboard. As evident from the above quotation, similar accusations emanated from the SDLP in relation to community restorative justice in 2005, and such reactions greatly contributed to an intense politicisation of community restorative justice in Northern Ireland.

After consulting widely[14] on these guidelines, the government announced in July 2006 that a new draft Protocol would be published, in an attempt to address the concerns emerging during the initial consultation – concerns raised mainly by the SDLP in the political arena. The key areas for concern during the consultation process, and the reasons behind the redrafting of the Protocols, were around the issues of the project's relationship with the police, the suitability of those working in the projects (particularly in relation to former combatants and ex-political prisoners), the distinction between criminal and non-criminal matters, the handling of complaints by participants in the projects and the need for an independent mechanism to deal with such complaints, and the nature and extent of an inspections regime in relation to the everyday practice of the projects.

A new draft Protocol was published on 20 September 2006 and was subject to another 12 weeks' consultation.[15] As part of the consultation, the NIO Minister for Criminal Justice visited both projects and undertook an equality-impact assessment (EQIA), and an inquiry was conducted by the Northern Ireland Affairs Committee, at which staff from both projects and a range of statutory and political representatives gave evidence.[16] The extent and range of sources of the evidence given in the House of Commons is an indication of the level of politicisation that has taken place in relation to community restorative justice in Northern Ireland.

Several different solutions were proposed during the consultation to deal with the above controversies. The final Protocol published on 5 February 2007 included several adaptations in response to previous concerns. Summarising the key features for the sake of brevity, the new Protocols included the following provisions.

The provision that schemes could report an offence to the PSNI through a third party (i.e. the Public Prosecution Service (PPS)) was removed. There was a concern among the schemes that the proposed third-party reporting would considerably impede the swiftness with which cases are currently being dealt with at the community level, and that community vigilantism could increase as a result. There was also a concern on behalf of political parties that schemes could effectively avoid direct contact with the police – an unacceptable feature in a stable democracy.

The provision that restorative justice schemes could receive referrals only from a statutory criminal justice agency rather than from within the community was removed. There was considerable concern, expressed by the schemes themselves, in relation to this initial proposal. It would have meant that the schemes would have to abandon completely their current community-based models, and that would effectively undermine their entire *raison d'être*.

The establishment of a panel tasked with determining the suitability of staff will take place. The suitability of staff has been a major issue for political parties and statutory agencies alike who were concerned that not only did ex-political prisoners work within the schemes, but also that there was nothing stopping them from taking on new staff and volunteers with recent criminal records. The NIO Minister for Criminal Justice has consistently stated that individuals with criminal convictions dating back to before the Good Friday Agreement, that is, prior to 1998, should be allowed to work in community restorative justice schemes, but that individuals with convictions after this cut-off date should be excluded from practice. The panel which considers the suitability of individuals will be comprised of representatives of relevant statutory bodies, and it will consider criminal records and other pertinent information provided by statutory agencies, including the police, when determining suitability.

It was agreed that the Probation Board of Northern Ireland will establish an independent complaints mechanism for victims and offenders who may have cause to raise concerns about how a scheme has handled their case. There have been concerns about accountability of practice and what happens when participants in the projects are unhappy with the outcome or the way they have been treated as part of the process. It has been argued by political parties, statutory agencies, journalists and some community organisations that few people would dare to complain about the schemes, considering the perceived close links they have with major paramilitary organisations. The schemes themselves have argued that such statements severely underestimate the capabilities and assertiveness of participants.

It has also been ensured that the final Protocol sets exacting standards that schemes must meet to achieve accreditation, with continued compliance tested by a rigorous, regular, and unannounced inspection regime undertaken by the Criminal Justice Inspectorate, who shall publish their inspection reports. Such an external accountability mechanism has been part of all the different drafts of the Protocols, but the agency responsible for the inspections has been debated. The schemes themselves have continued to argue for the Criminal Justice Inspectorate in this role, as an agency which has some credibility at the community level, but the SDLP commented in 2006 that inspections by the Criminal Justice Inspectorate would be inadequate since it does not have the power to investigate individual cases. Paragraph 22 in the final Protocols says, in relation to regular inspection by the Criminal Justice Inspectorate, that the inspections

> will include, as appropriate, examination of records of offenders and offences dealt with; systems for ensuring that agreed programmes are completed; complaints mechanisms and actual complaints; training initiatives; compliance with the decisions of the PPS on cases appropriate and inappropriate for referral to community schemes; up-to-date awareness of human rights issues; and safeguards for ensuring that for offenders who admit to the offence this is done on the basis of informed consent. Access will also be required to the records of the scheme in relation to non-criminal activity in order to ensure that the distinction between non-criminal matter and criminal offences is being correctly observed. Inspectors will have access to all published material on the scheme or the interventions it provides. (Protocol for Community-Based Restorative Justice Schemes, 5 February 2007)

Following an indication that Alternatives was willing to 'sign up' to the revised protocols in May 2007, the Criminal Justice Inspectorate published a report that recommended that the projects should be accredited by the government.[17] Mr Chivers, Head of the Inspectorate, indicated that he was impressed by the 'high standard of professionalism and dedication' of the staff, and that record-keeping, training and child protection policies were sufficient and in place. He also explored the fears that community restorative justice projects were a front for paramilitary organisations or that people were forced into taking part in restorative justice projects by such organisations, and he 'found no evidence that there was any such problem in relation to Northern Ireland Alternatives or its schemes. There was no evidence of the schemes being driven by paramilitaries and every indication to the contrary' (Criminal Justice Inspectorate 2007: 4).

In February 2007, CRJI wrote to the Minister of State for Northern Ireland, seeking accreditation in respect of community-based restorative justice schemes in Belfast and in Derry/Londonderry. In October of the same year, a pre-inspection by the Criminal Justice Inspectorate was carried out on the project and its different offices.[18] Such action was deemed necessary due to the heightened controversy surrounding CRJI compared to Alternatives, the latter being only subject to one inspection. The conclusion of the report stated:

> The Belfast schemes handle a wide range of business, which includes some serious crime and threats from dissident paramilitaries. They are well run, and great dedication is shown by the small team of staff members as well as by the volunteers. Inspectors were astonished at the commitment shown by many of those they interviewed, and there could be no question about their motivation being to help their communities, not in any sense to control them.
>
> Training was good, and paid due attention to human rights and to child protection. Mediation practice was non-coercive, relying on the forces of social control within the community and the respect in which individual CRJI practitioners are held. Record-keeping was good by the standards of small voluntary organisations and little modification would be required to meet the requirements of Inspectors.
>
> The Belfast schemes are not in the business of patrolling or providing a security presence. They have separated themselves from the Safer Neighbourhood projects, though there is still evidence of some members participating in both. Inspectors agree that CRJI is right to pursue a policy of separation, so that their role does not become confused. (Criminal Justice Inspection 2007: paragraphs 5.8–5.10)

Although the report was largely positive, praising the work undertaken by CRJI, there were some issues which needed to be addressed before a full accreditation could take place. These concerned record-keeping, the importance of being seen not to be aligned to any one political group, and the establishment of proper procedures for recording and investigating complaints internally. In its conclusion, the Inspectorate recommended:

> We **recommend** that the schemes of CRJI Belfast and CRJI North West should be considered for accreditation as soon as they are ready to declare that they are complying with the Protocol, on the

understanding that: They will represent themselves publicly to emphasise that they are a service to all sections of the community equally and would welcome volunteers and committee members from all parts of the community; They continue to move in the direction of distancing themselves from activities not supported by the PSNI that could be interpreted as 'alternative policing'; They strengthen their ability (especially the North West schemes) to keep clear and explicit case records, which can be used as the basis for future inspection; and They introduce proper procedures for recording and investigating complaints and publicise the availability of an independent external complaint mechanism if complainants are still dissatisfied. (Criminal Justice Inspectorate, 2007: 33; bold in original)

At the time of the second part of the fieldwork for this book – December 2007 to January 2008 – CRJI was working hard to comply with the requirements set out by the Criminal Justice Inspectorate with the view of receiving accreditation in the very near future. A closer cooperation with the police was especially difficult, as the police could not enter into official partnerships prior to accreditation, and CRJI could not be accredited without official cooperation with the police. Thus, CRJI faced a catch-22 situation that all involved found frustrating but which they were doing their best to resolve through informal contacts and increased referral and cooperation between the two organisations. New inspections were carried out during the first half of 2008, and in June of that year the final report was published.[19] The overall conclusion of this final report was that:

This report confirms that the necessary progress has been made and that the schemes can now be recommended for accreditation, subject to decisions by the Suitability Panel which is currently considering the suitability of the staff and volunteers who have been nominated to be the authorised practitioners for the schemes. (Criminal Justice Inspection, 2008: v)

In particular, the report noted that cooperation with the police had increased, and that the police overall valued the contribution made by CRJI to the community. Much of the work carried out by the project, as outlined earlier, relates to neighbour disputes, which often require time-consuming and multi-agency intervention. An example of such a case was provided in the report and is included below. It offers a telling illustration of the role CRJI plays in these communities, of its leadership, and of the manner in which informal partnerships are utilised to find the best possible solution:

> In Twinbrook there was an ongoing feud between two Traveller families, which resulted in the murder of one and of the subsequent arrests of members of the other family in Derry/ Londonderry. CRJI in Twinbrook have been working with members of both families to ensure that violence does not spread. They worked closely with PSNI to ensure discreet but effective policing of the funeral and through Colin Neighbourhood Partnership are working with the housing associations and Social Services to ensure that alternative acceptable accommodation can be found.
>
> Another example from Twinbrook also relates to a feud between two well known families from the area. It started after a fight which resulted in one man having his ear bitten off. This was quickly followed by serious threats and attacks on each other's houses. Although the police did respond and recorded as much information as possible, they then left despite the family's concerns that more violence would follow. CRJI were called in by one family, but their attempts to mediate were spurned by the other family. However, they were able to engage with the police and arrange for the two original protagonists to present themselves to the police station. This averted what would have to have been a robust arrest operation. (Criminal Justice Inspectorate, 2008: 7–8)

A full 10 years after the *Blue Book* was published, these developments herald the potential for a real organic partnership developing on the ground between Republican communities, the police, and other elements of the formal justice system. The Protocols designed to regulate relations between the state and community restorative justice projects do not mean that disputes over justice ownership are resolved. Rather, they provide an agreed framework within which such disputes can be addressed. As I have argued elsewhere (McEvoy and Eriksson 2006), the tenacity and durability of the projects to date are due in no small part to the leadership skills of those same ex-combatants whose presence in them has proved so controversial for so long. Their commitment to their respective communities has remained unchanged throughout the long years of conflict and transition. Yet, to judge from the impressions gathered during the course of this research, if any community justice initiatives can receive state funding, be subject to independent oversight, develop strong partnerships arrangements with the criminal justice system, and *still* retain their unique community ethos, it is these ones.

However, while recently there has been significant movement on the macro-political level in Northern Ireland, 30 years of antipathy, violence from and towards the agents of the state, and, indeed, a simple lack of familiarity with the police in particular will not be magically resolved by the formalising of the 'policing deal' (Mulcahy 2006). The next chapter explores these groundbreaking changes, and the attempts to broker partnerships between the police and Nationalist communities in particular, from the perspective of all involved: former enemies who are now becoming 'friends'.

Notes

1 See Appendix B for a detailed timeline of events in relation to community restorative justice in Northern Ireland.
2 Interview, 16 November 2004.
3 *Ibid.*
4 Interview, 9 November 2004.
5 *BBC News*, 3 May 2007, 'Restorative Justice Gets Go Ahead'.
6 Interview, 21 March 2005.
7 Interview, 2 June 2005.
8 Interview, 16 November 2004.
9 Interview, 10 January 2006.
10 Interview with CRJI project worker, 2 December 2004. Indeed it did, as will be further discussed in the next chapter. I included this quotation here, however, since it acts as a stark reminder of the rapid developments in Northern Ireland, after years of stalemate and a focus on preserving the status quo.
11 See Appendix B for a detailed timeline of government publications and key events in relation to these developments.
12 The Social Democratic Labour Party, the main competitor of Sinn Féin for the Nationalist constituency.
13 Interview, 17 February 2006.
14 Comments were received from 56 organisations and individuals across the statutory and voluntary sectors, including many key stakeholders.
15 Thirty-two comments were received this time around.
16 Oral evidence was given by Rt Hon Lord Clyde, former Justice Oversight Commissioner; Mr Kit Chivers, Criminal Justice Inspection Northern Ireland; Mr Ronnie Spence and Mr Brian McCaughey, Probation Board Northern Ireland; Mr Owen Lyner and Mr Pat Conway, Northern Ireland Association for the Care and Resettlement of Offenders (NIACRO); Mr

Duncan Morrow, Community Relations Council; Ms Debbie Watters and Mr Tom Winston, Northern Ireland Alternatives; Mr Jim Auld and Mr Harry Maguire, Community Restorative Justice Ireland; Sir Hugh Orde and Drew Harris, PSNI; Mr David Hanson, Minister of State, NIO; and Mr Stephen Leach, Criminal Justice, NIO. Written evidence was received and considered from: Kilcooley Community Forum; the PSNI; Include Youth; Northern Ireland Policing Board; Police Federation for Northern Ireland; NIACRO; NIA; CRJI; Northern Ireland Human Rights Commission; and Dr Garret FitzGerald. Additional written evidence which was received by the House but not printed out (to save printing costs) was from North Down District Policing Partnership; Criminal Justice Inspection Northern Ireland; Newtownabbey District Policing Partnership; British Irish Rights Watch; NIACRO; the Community Relations Council; Mrs Kathleen Campbell; the Superintendents' Association of Northern Ireland; Ballymena Community Safety Partnership; Craigavon District Policing Partnership; and the Police Ombudsman for Northern Ireland.

17 The full report can be viewed at: www.cjini.org/documents/ProtocolReport2.pdf.

18 The full report can be viewed at: www.cjini.org/documents/CRJIReportWebsiteFeb2008NewVersion.pdf.

19 Full report can be viewed at: http://www.cjini.org/documents/CRJIInspectionJune08FINAL.pdf.

Chapter 8

The road less travelled: policing and partnerships in transition

This chapter continues the narrative according to the timeline of developments around community restorative justice in Northern Ireland. As was mentioned in the previous chapter, the possibilities of a formal partnership with the police seemed a distant prospect at the end of the first period of fieldwork in July 2007. By December of that year, however, both projects had received official accreditation, opening up the prospect of a working partnership with the police for the first time. Hence, the discussions around community–police partnerships have consciously been left to the final chapter of the book, reflecting the order of developments as they took place on the ground.

The development of a functional relationship with the police is a significant undertaking in a transitional society where the relationship between state and communities (particularly working-class ones) has a long and troubled history (Mani 2002; Cartwright *et al.* 2006). The improvement of such relationships is consequently an important part of the wider normalisation process in a post-conflict society. Indeed, an unambiguous working relationship with the police has been one provision that the Northern Ireland Office (NIO) has not been willing to negotiate if the community restorative projects are to receive funding from the state. In the earlier versions of the Protocols discussed in the previous chapter, the provision that the projects must work directly with the police was central and has been an essential tenet of NIO policies since the publication in 1998 of the first document in relation to such practices, titled *Justice and Community Development*. At no point, however, was it acknowledged that a direct working relationship with the police might be at all problematic (McEvoy and Mika 2002).

Communities are sites for a multitude of networks, interests and identities, defined by heterogeneity and complexity. These are dynamics which policymakers and practitioners within statutory agencies often seem to overlook. As argued by Hoggett (1997), 'If public policies are to be targeted effectively at local areas then an appreciation of the differences within and between them must be the starting point' (p. 15). Within the Northern Irish context, this oversight might be understandable, considering that communities have worked long and hard to portray themselves as unified, single-identity places for claims-making throughout the conflict and in its aftermath. That they have been successful in this endeavour is obvious, particularly when viewed from the outside, as most people would refer to 'the two communities' when talking about Northern Ireland. It is only when viewing these communities from the inside that the heterogeneity and power differentials within them become clear.

For many people in working-class areas in Northern Ireland, and particularly Nationalist communities, policing (in the shape of the PSNI and its predecessor, the RUC) is synonymous with violence, alienation and oppression. As argued by Mulcahy (2006), 'policing was perhaps the single most emotive, divisive and controversial aspect of the conflict' (pp. 3–4). 'Community policing', the direction towards which the PSNI is striving, was a term scoffed at by many interviewees, and instead stories of violent house searches, curfews, roadblocks, plastic bullets, torture during interrogations, and shoot-to-kill policies were recounted. Such heavy-handed interventions took place largely in working-class communities, while more 'normal' policing operated in middle-class areas. This reflects the dual mandate of policing in Northern Ireland, where the RUC and later the PSNI were simultaneously involved in broader service provision and counter-terrorism strategies through the control of political dissent (Ellison and Smyth 2000; Wright and Bryett 2000; Mulcahy 2006). As mentioned by McEvoy and Eriksson (2008):

> There were a range of distinct security strategies including brutal army tactics, paramilitary-style policing by the Royal Ulster Constabulary (RUC), internment without trial, torture, emergency legislation, and non-jury Diplock courts. Such measures clearly impacted directly (and largely negatively) on the relationship between the criminal justice system and the community most affected by them. (p. 164)

Consequently, the police have for a long time been actively construed as the enemy, part and parcel of British colonisation and oppression, and as supplementary to the British army.[1] In this regard, from the perspective of the police, Nationalist communities were perceived as the 'sea in which the paramilitary fish swims' (Sluka 1989), and the target of counter-terrorism strategies for many decades of violent conflict. It is between these two former enemies that a working partnership is now being discussed, a partnership in which community restorative justice can be a facilitator of the necessary trust-building exercise between the two parties preceding a more formal relationship.

This chapter explores bridge-building between historically estranged communities and the police in the wake of Sinn Féin's endorsement of the PSNI in early 2007. This is done in an effort to explore the potential of restorative justice as a vehicle for societal transformation after conflict. It will be argued that there is a possibility of developing and affirming new social norms concerning the relationship between state and communities, with the praxis of community restorative justice as an example of transformative justice in transition.

Legitimisation of former adversaries

> Now the police are coming into the community trying to help resolve issues, whereas in the past they would have pulled up in two armoured jeeps and there would have been a riot. So things are changing.[2]

The fraught relationship between Republican communities and the state is well rehearsed (MacGarry and O'Leary 1995; Ruane and Todd 1996; Hayes and McAllister 2001). However, the relationship between the Loyalist communities and the police is not unambiguous either (Ellison and Smyth 2000; Mitchell 2003). While it is often presumed that the police service is seen as legitimate in Loyalist communities, the situation since Patten[3] does not fit this picture:

> I have lived in Loyalist areas and we phone the police and they don't come out for two weeks. I think that one of the problems the police have is a lack of manpower, because that has more or less been destroyed by Patten. The RUC could much better deal with what was happening here, they had much more manpower. Now, with the way the whole situation has changed here, the

police, to me, seem to be perfectly useless. I am pro the police and I totally believe that we have to have a police force, and I want a police force that can speak for everybody but at the moment the police force seems to have been destroyed. ... And this community has completely lost faith in the police. They don't look up to the police, in fact they don't trust the police. They don't think there is any point in phoning the police. And as long as the police are not doing anything, and they don't look like having an interest in doing anything, well then, unfortunately the paramilitaries are going to be used.[4]

In Loyalist areas, Alternatives managed to develop a working partnership with some local police officers soon after its establishment, yet such cooperation was largely unofficial and based on personal contacts. Such unofficial relationships are consequently more vulnerable, especially when that particular police officer is reassigned to a different office. As the manager of Alternatives described:

In the early days we had a great working relationship with the local police, and that is what has helped us to develop to where we are today. Unfortunately, when the Patten measures were implemented, the guy who we were dealing with in our local police station took the retirement package and moved on. So we had to start from scratch with a new person. That has been a hard road, simply because of the Patten situation, there was a high turn-over of staff in our local police station. We then ended up working closely with police headquarters, and building relationships there. And I think we have done that to the extent that all relationships are built on trust and it takes a long time for that to happen. At the beginning, there was a lot of suspicion on us from the police, and I can understand that. But there was also a lot of suspicion from us regarding the police, and I think it took them a wee bit longer to understand that. But now I think that we are at a stage when we have a working relationship.[5]

Alternatives has adopted an explicit outreach mode since its inception, and its partnerships with statutory agencies are much more advanced, reflected in the relatively effortless accreditation of the projects. The development of partnerships between Republican communities and the police, on the other hand, has been much slower and more difficult due to historical reasons as outlined above.

Thus, this chapter will focus more on these latter areas since they represent a truly groundbreaking development in the Northern Irish transition.[6]

Legitimacy is a central concept in discussions regarding state/ community relations in the transitional context. Most writings on legitimacy have been in relation to the state and its agencies, most notably the police, courts and corrections (Tyler 1990; Sparks *et al.* 1996; Sunshine and Tyler 2003), and what measures are taken by such agencies to justify their exercise of power. In a transitional society, the focus is also on the legitimacy of the state – its erosion and eventual reconstruction – but of equal importance for the discussion here is the legitimacy of the community. It is easy to forget that legitimacy is not unidirectional. It also extends from the state to the community, or, in a divided society, it is not extended to a particular community, based on an absence of shared beliefs between community and state (Beetham 1991). Central to such a discrepancy between shared beliefs are complex issues around ownership of justice. The legitimacy of the police has formed a vital part of the official discourse in Northern Ireland since partition in 1921, and, as argued by Mulchay (2006), 'in deeply divided societies where state authority is widely disputed, the question of police legitimacy dominates the social and political landscape' (p. 3).

The argument that the police, and by extension the state, was viewed as illegitimate by the Nationalist community has been made throughout this book. It might, however, be easy to underestimate the passion that debates about policing still generate within the jurisdiction. At the time of Sinn Féin endorsing the PSNI, many people within local communities were struggling to keep up with this rapid development of events. As mentioned by one interviewee:

> If you had said eight years ago that there is a legitimate reason for dealing with the police, you would have been laughed out of existence. Just a *silly* idea, as to be completely nonsensical. But the political argument has moved, so the rationale for having a relationship with the PSNI has *changed*. But people are still using the old arguments and rationales. So, you know, they can't fit the two of them together.[7]

When asked about the community's reaction to these changes from older forms of 'community policing' by the IRA towards this new acceptability of the police, one of the CRJI coordinators said:

I think that when there was conflict going on here – it was a double-edged sword – in that [with] the likes of the IRA and other armed organisations in the area ... it wasn't the done thing to go outside and contact the police or whatever, to deal with criminal acts within your area. I mean, it became the norm to go to those organisations to deal with it. And they would have dealt with the problem in one of two ways: they would either have shot the problem or they would have beaten the problem, and they may even beat the problem out of the country ... they were the police, so to speak. And to go to outside agencies was frowned upon because you were at war with those areas, so why bring them into the area and give them the credibility to deal with the problem? So, in effect, it was a double-edged sword. Now when we had the cessation, the dumping of weapons, and those organisations have come out publicly, politicians have come out publicly and said, 'The police matters when dealing with criminality.' And now they want us to use them. And people are thinking that for over 30 years of people – of *them* type of people – saying, 'You don't go to the police', and now it is reversed and now we *have* to go to the police.

The Nationalist community has for a long time been accustomed to taking care of its own issues, successfully or not, and people find the new role of the police a challenging one. As mentioned by one CRJI worker:

People are passing by the police station to come here and report rape charges. And even when they know that we are going to contact the police, they just won't go there themselves. Because you are going to your own people because they are the ones you know are going to help.[8]

The community relies on local people for local solutions and there is a strong tradition present of not seeking help from the state or any other outside agency; instead, the community looks inwards for help and support. After Sinn Féin signed up to policing in January 2007, there seemed to be an expectation that the community was going to follow suit without further engagement. However, even when the agreement came, other parts of the community felt everything was moving too fast. As noted by the manager of CRJI:

And when they [Sinn Féin] turned around and looked – well, only part of the community was there, because the other part was way ahead of them. But there was another section of the community who said, 'You sold us out'. ... And for Sinn Féin to move from a stance of total disbandment – which was ... it is an easy place to be you know, 'Get rid of them and start afresh' – to 'Well, the same people are actually going to be in place next week, and you are going to have to learn to work with them.' It just ... overwhelmed people. Because, you know, it was a very simplistic way of looking at things. Because, their view was that last week these people were mass murderers and now they are our protectors. People still have problems with that.[9]

This, according to the coordinator of CRJI, is an oversight and an obstacle to progress: 'See, I think that part of the problem is that the debates around policing ... when Sinn Féin got what they wanted, politically, they were content. Now we need to convince the community.'[10] Community change, while certainly rapid, is not accepted equally across the community, and people need time to adjust:

And some people are a bit confused, and it probably came very, very fast for some people in the community because they weren't ... maybe they weren't as politically astute or tuned in as others, and they did not think that this was going to be at their doorstep straightaway and this is what they have to do. And I feel that ... rightly or wrongly, people should have been brought along that route at the same rate – 'This is what we are doing', 'You see, six months down the line, this is what we are going to be doing' – but, in hindsight, it very much depended on how well you were tuned in to the political situation and knowing the way things were going. But I do feel that more and more people are beginning to realise that and to accept that there.[11]

One of the senior PSNI officers interviewed who is currently involved in the practical implementation of the Protocols was acutely aware of this situation, and also of the differences that existed within each community. He said that the community moves at different paces. Some parts of the community are more ready to 'embrace' policing and to report incidents to them. Others still find it unacceptable, or need more time to adjust.

The leadership provided by CRJI and Alternatives in working with the police is positively viewed by many, such as statutory agencies and parts of the community. However, actively working with the police, and being *seen* to do so, are not acceptable practice to other parts of the community. It is important to understand the level of legitimacy that is potentially given to the police by having organisations such as CRJI and Alternatives actively supporting them. This is legitimacy that the police could not have obtained without these projects, at least not at the pace at which it is currently taking place. It is not only about providing adequate redress through accountable justice measures for the community; this is also a leap away from a protracted and violent opposition to the British state and a consequent delegitimisation of the *raison d'être* of the conflict. For some, this is certainly one step too far, too quickly.

These differences in attitudes to policing and the closer cooperation now undertaken by CRJI are reflected in the reactions of some volunteers at CRJI. Not all of them would view a closer working relationship with the police as a positive development; indeed, some would have serious personal misgivings about this. As mentioned by one caseworker:

> And it is difficult for the workers here as well, because not all volunteers would be onboard with this, you know. They have difficulties. I had one person who has left because they don't agree with us working with the police.[12]

The direction taken by community restorative justice in this development is viewed by some groups in the community as wrong, dangerous and something that needs to be stopped. The threat to closer community–police cooperation is emanating in particular from dissident Republican organisations:

> But in my experience working with paramilitary groups would certainly lead me to believe that some of them hate some spokespeople, particularly within CRJI, and some of them would have thought at the back of their heads that we should be killed for the work that we do. *For working with the cops and giving them legitimacy*[13] (emphasis added).

Some people do more than just think about this, and some of the CRJI staff have received death threats from dissident organisations since starting to work with the police. This suggests just how contentious this issue is in Nationalist communities in Northern Ireland today.[14]

Moreover, the threat by dissidents presents a real risk to police in particular, and is not taken lightly by the PSNI. Since the disbandment of the Provisional IRA, dissident paramilitary groups have stepped up their recruitment intake and attacks on both police and civil targets.[15] This also affects the police who work with CRJI, and the assurance of physical safety when visiting the offices in West Belfast and some areas of Derry is of paramount concern. Judith Gillespie, the current PSNI assistant chief constable for rural areas, said in an interview with the *Irish News* that she was 'very concerned' about the threat from dissidents. It was reported that police now are waiting up to two hours to respond to some calls due to the risk of being lured into a trap by dissident Republicans, and that foot patrols have doubled up for safety reasons.[16] In an interview with a senior PSNI officer, this was mentioned as one of the many challenges of working in partnership with CRJI in particular, and that this issue is less of a concern in Loyalist areas. In response to the question of whether he felt safe in West Belfast, he indicated that he felt safe once he was there, but did not feel particularly comfortable entering and exiting West Belfast when on patrol, as there is still a significant dissident threat that cannot be disregarded when policing in Nationalist areas.[17]

This situation is somewhat ironic: police occasionally feel unsafe entering and exiting Nationalist communities, but they feel safe once they are in an office predominantly staffed by former IRA volunteers. That, if anything, is an indicator of how far key individuals within the respective organisations have come in the last 12 months. This emerging relationship between former adversaries in the Northern Irish transition is quite remarkable and is explored in more detail below.

The beginning of partnerships

Since the final Protocol was published in February 2007, Alternatives, CRJI and the police have worked towards a formal partnership arrangement by laying the necessary groundwork for such changes in their practices. Alternatives received accreditation in May 2007, but, according to the police, very few cases have been referred to the police since then. CRJI, on other hand, on which the pressure to engage with the police has always been greater, between January and November 2007 had formal conversations with the police in approximately 200 of their cases.[18] Such formal conversations include direct referrals of cases to the police, but more often take the shape of telephone conversations between a caseworker and a police officer.

Since there is no precedent for these developments, the groundwork for more formal cooperation is laid on a case-by-case basis, an approach taken by all organisations involved. One of the difficulties in negotiating this new relationship is the bureaucratic nature of the NIO Protocols. Two of the senior police officers interviewed were fully aware that CRJI and Alternatives saw them as too narrow and as not taking into account the real working practices of the projects. The police interviewed argued that the NIO designed the Protocols to apply to all community organisations in Northern Ireland that are, or could potentially be, involved in this type of community mediation. As a consequence, it was necessary that the guidelines be narrow, arguably to enable the state to retain as much control as possible over informal alternatives. This was also recognised by the manager of CRJI:

> Well, I think that the relationship will change and they will become more formalised over a period of time. But I don't think the Protocols will be so central. I think they are working guidelines, and I think we have them anyway. Because we all know that the Protocols were written for a specific situation, and they have no real place in the current one. And all of us know that working according to them would just be bureaucratic nonsense.[19]

As mentioned in the previous chapter, a central role in any formal partnership between community restorative justice and the criminal justice system will be held by the Public Prosecution Service (PPS). This was perceived as problematic by both police and CRJI, in effect inhibiting a well-functioning partnership:

> And the difficulty is going to be – and we don't know where the relationship will end up and I think we will have to wait and see how that pans out – but I think it will eventually be us and the cops against the PPS [Public Prosecution Service]. The PPS is going to be the stumbling block, because we are going to say to the cops that 'Here is a case and I think we should be dealing with it', and they say, 'Yeah, you are right, but my boss says we can't do it because we need to go to the PPS.' So

> I think the PPS will hinder a good working relationship because of their bureaucracy.[20]

Apart from such concerns over bureaucracy, one of the main uncertainties is in regards to what constitutes a crime. The Protocols made clear that community restorative justice schemes should deal only with non-criminal matters, and that all cases of a criminal nature should be referred directly to the police. The police will then make the decision as to whether sufficient evidence exists for the case to be referred to the PPS, the problems entailed in which have been mentioned above. One area of contention here appears when there is not sufficient evidence to proceed, and the question arises: should the police refer the case back to CRJI or Alternatives and allow for an informal path of disposal, or are there other options that need to be considered? There are also different views of what constitutes a crime from a community perspective, which often conflict with that of the police:

> Even an assault would sometimes not be seen as criminal by the community, even when someone has to go to hospital, it is still not seen as a police matter a lot of the time.[21]

Notwithstanding the tradition of not reporting to the police in these communities, they have traditionally relied on informal solutions to their grievances. Hence, rarely have people needed to consider whether a situation amounted to a criminal offence, or whether it was 'merely' antisocial behaviour or nuisance. A similar dilemma is now faced by community restorative justice projects:

> In terms of the cases here, and the distinction between criminal and non-criminal – no-one is really sure what that means yet. The police doesn't know and I am not quite sure either. And yet we have to operate under those guidelines – that is a challenge for everyone.[22]

The lack of consensus on definitions of crime and harm arguably obstruct the prospects of closer cooperation based on equal partnership between the criminal justice system and community restorative justice. The former still adheres to a legal definition of crime, whereas the latter has been much more progressive in its definition of harm. As noted by Feenan (2002), '[a] key challenge for the state will be to resist its traditional tendency towards centralised and total control over crime management and instead respect the independence of these schemes within the broader appreciation of local conditions for crime management' (p. 168). The definition of harm adopted by community restorative justice projects in Northern Ireland has allowed a much wider application of restorative justice processes, more responsive to the needs of the post-conflict society.

When someone comes in with a complaint to CRJI, and it is established that it is of a criminal nature and hence needs to be referred to the police, another difficult situation occurs. Most people who come in to CRJI are not comfortable phoning the police because of a long-standing mistrust of them,[23] and out of worry of being perceived as a 'tout' by the community. 'Touting' is something which was punished severely during the decades of paramilitary 'policing' and is still seen as a violation of community protocol by many. Here, CRJI plays a crucial role today, acting as a conduit between the community and the police. As mentioned by one CRJI caseworker:

So us coming in as a first step ... and people are asking if it is OK to go to the police. And I have people asking me permission to go to the police! So it is about insecurities and a lack of knowledge in the community too.[24]

Groups such as residents associations and the Safer Neighbourhood Project would also contact the police on behalf of individuals, even though there are some elements within these groups, particularly the latter, who are still opposed to working with the police. It was also mentioned that these referrals to the police had become more acceptable within the community over the last few months, and one CRJI caseworker was expecting that direction to continue in a positive manner, unless something major happened to reverse the situation:

I feel, over the last few months, that more and more people are becoming amenable and very acceptable toward people going to the police. And I speak from the experience of having people coming into this office, where, if we go back to early last year, when people come in here with an issue of, say, assault or threat, and you say, 'Has this been referred to the police?' and people would say, 'I am not contacting the police!' for one reason or another. It would have been wholly unacceptable at that particular time. ... But since then, people are accepting of you saying, 'Go to the police with this matter', and they would say 'well, that is no problem'. So things are changing.[25]

The position of CRJI as a conduit is equally valued by the police, and CRJI is seen as a gateway into the community, a line of communication previously inaccessible by the police. One senior police officer indicated that the community restorative justice projects had to some degree helped facilitate the debate about closer community–state cooperation, and perhaps even made it happen quicker than would have been the case were there no such community projects.[26] CRJI and Alternatives provide the police, according to the interviewee, with 'a focus point within the communities'. This gateway, when formalised, represents perhaps the first transparent, accountable and legitimate link between community and state in relation to justice ownership and delivery in Northern Ireland for many decades.

Hence, one of the strengths of CRJI and Alternatives, according to the police interviewed, is their relationship with and access to their communities – a feature of their practice which the PSNI does *not* want to disturb. However, the same police officers also made the point that the rules have changed. The community can no longer police themselves and telephone the PSNI only when it suits them or when they are 'allowed' to by other social control agents in the community. This, the police acknowledge, is a major mind shift for the community, but one which needs to take place. This need for ownership of justice by the police is also felt at the community level:

> I feel that the police realise that CRJI is a good conduit to the community, that we can help them quite a lot in resolving things in the community. We can deal with things better sometimes than they can do, and they realise that. It is like a relationship that is evolving on a constant basis, and it is a working relationship, it is about building that relationship and getting over those barriers that were there. And we say to the police that we are not there to work for them, we are there to work with the issues that affect the community, and *help* the community to deal with those issues.[27]

Trust was highlighted by CRJI workers, PSNI officers, and senior executives of Probation and the Housing Executive alike as the key to the development and future praxis of any partnership between CRJI and statutory agencies. However, establishing community trust in the police will not be an easy undertaking, and perhaps some police take a simplistic view of the Nationalist community, considering the history of policing in Northern Ireland:

We are talking about 30 years of conflict here, and this is an area which has been severely affected by the Troubles, and this is an area where there is no trust in the police, where they are afraid of the police, where their experience of the police is having their door knocked in, you know, in the past. And we need to be careful about how we talk to people ... how we introduce people to the fact that certain things need to be reported to the police ... it is difficult.[28]

These developments signify a considerable challenge for both police and the community. In an interview with two senior PSNI officers, one of whom had been involved in developments around community restorative justice since the beginning, the term 'it is a challenge' was mentioned many times. They mentioned that some individual police officers would be very reluctant to work with CRJI and Alternatives because of the backgrounds of practitioners and volunteers. However, it was obvious that these two officers genuinely wanted these partnerships to work, while simultaneously recognising the many challenges ahead.

One of the many difficulties with these partnerships, as highlighted by a senior police officer, was the building of relationships that were not there in the past. This is completely new, and, hence, it will take some time to get it right. Yet he felt that this was time well invested since, if the police get it wrong, the resulting loss of trust may be very difficult to repair. In this regard, the manager of CRJI commented:

And I think it is in everybody's best interest, that if we work together we can get to a resolution. And I think that – and this is a term I don't really like using – but we have a *window* here of an opportunity, where we can have the possibility of having a unique experience. I am not always sure that it is possible – different days like – but today I think it is possible. That this relationship with the cops has something that could make us world-leading in this ... where you have a structured community willing to engage in a partnership with the police who are willing to serve them. ... What seems to have happened is that individuals in both organisations have contact at a human level and have started to build trust. And on one level I am encouraging that, because of their experiences as human beings, that is reflected back into both organisations. Because relationships in those organisations are like relationships anywhere else, those things will rub off and there is a ripple effect within the organisations.[29]

This 'window of opportunity' is also recognised by the police. In the interview with the two senior PSNI officers, they noted that the changes that had taken place in relation to the dynamic between CRJI and the police were 'monumental' and 'huge', and further that there has 'been a sea change in Nationalist and Republican areas led by Sinn Féin. There was always an expectation that this change would take place, even though the road there has been rocky, and finally the change happened'. For the first time, both organisations were working towards the same goal as opposed to defending their respective positions and the status quo.[30]

The police have been the most progressive organisation among the statutory bodies, which is nothing short of remarkable within the transitional context, particularly when one considers the volatile history between the police and Nationalist communities. However, this does not mean that all members of the PSNI view these developments positively; instead, these views are a reflection of strong leadership from certain individuals. In this respect, the PSNI is reflective of CRJI, in that these developments would not have taken place without the moral, political and practical leadership of a few committed individuals. However, just as CRJI had difficulty in selling their new concept to the community, so have these individual police officers had difficulty in selling it to the rest of their organisation. The manager of CRJI was very aware of this situation:

> I think that there are individuals within the cops, and there are obviously those who know what we do and are fine with that. But I think that they have a hard time selling what we do to the rest of the organisation. For example, if Sergeant A or Constable B who is working with us, goes down to Cookstown or the Antrim coast or wherever, somewhere where they have never heard about restorative justice, and they are saying [to their police colleagues] that they need to be working with the community, then they look at Sergeant A and Constable B as if they had just sprouted another head![31]

A further obstacle to partnership is the problem of the police and the Nationalist community having very little knowledge about each other. Up until very recently, the means by which the police communicated important information was limited to posters on the outside walls of the police stations in the area, and the main way of accessing information on day-to-day issues in the Nationalist community was by reading the opinion pages in the local newspaper.[32] This lack of experience of the 'Other' constitutes another obstacle that needs to be traversed for the relationship between the police and the community to continue to improve:

> I think it is a completely new learning curve for them [the police] too. Because now they have to be involved in civil policing, whereas in the past it was political policing.[33]

On the other hand, since people in these communities have little experience of civil policing, it was mentioned by one CRJI caseworker that the picture community members have of 'ordinary' policing comes from television shows such as *The Bill* or American shows such as *CSI* or *Law and Order*. Consequently, people have unreasonably high expectations of what the police can do, and the community is quick to point its finger when something is not carried out according to its expectations. One senior PSNI officer gave the hypothetical example of someone reporting a burglary, telling the police that 'so and so did it'. This might be enough for the informal system, but not for the criminal justice system, which requires sufficient evidence to arrest and prosecute. This lack of knowledge within the community as to how the police actually operate was problematic, but the same interviewee agreed that CRJI could potentially help facilitate the transfer of such knowledge since it has access to the community in ways that the police do not.

Consequently, CRJI is providing leadership within the community about how to work with the police, but it is also providing the police with important knowledge and information about how to work with the community:

> We are leading the way on this. And also ... it is not just about giving the police information about stuff, but it is about *educating* them about the nuances within the community. Things that would make it OK for them to do certain things, and *not* to do others, whereas they would see very little of that, because they don't know. We are essentially paving the way for their acceptability, which was always the role that we envisaged, from years ago, because we knew it was going to happen. But they are only prepared, and we are only prepared to be dealing with them – and to be fair to the cops, they have accepted that so

far – if that engagement is based on equality. They are not the superiors in terms of knowledge about criminal justice issues. The community also has knowledge, maybe *different* knowledge, but perspectives that are complementary.[34]

Police responses to community crime and conflict in the past were often heavy-handed, and arrived in the shape of armoured jeeps with helicopter support. This would arguably antagonise most people in 'normal' communities, but in an area where the police are actively constructed as the enemy and hence 'fair game' for attack by bricks or firebombs, the consequence was often a full-scale riot. Now, at least on occasion, the police can phone ahead to a CRJI office to say that they are coming in, and CRJI caseworkers can then help to keep the situation calm once the police arrive at the location. Importantly, communities are not passive recipients of top-down partnership initiatives, and Northern Ireland certainly has a long-standing history of strong community action as resistance. Hence, formal partnerships are the product of negotiation between two parties where power is not located solely with one of the organisations. Such exchanges help to slowly build trust and understanding between police and community on a case-by-case basis.

The heterogeneity of the Nationalist community and the different degrees of willingness and readiness to cooperate with each other from both a CRJI and a police perspective have resulted in some areas being more progressive than others. In one area in West Belfast in particular, this has been the case, thanks to the leadership displayed by both the CRJI coordinator and the senior constable for the area. On one occasion, the CRJI coordinator had been walking along the street where a policeman was sitting in an armoured jeep. The coordinator, who had the senior constable's phone number, had phoned him and asked, 'Is that you sitting in the jeep? Why don't you come out and say hello?' – and so the police officer did. Then, in front of a large group of youths, they shook hands and had a chat. This story was also recounted in an interview with the chief executive of the Housing Executive who mentioned that this was a groundbreaking event: a former IRA volunteer publicly shaking hands with a senior police officer. Through such actions, a very powerful message is sent out to the community about the acceptability of policing:

And he [the senior constable] is coming in to the office in plain clothes on his day off. And that is showing a degree of trust. That is unheard of. That has to have an impact.[35]

The impact of such public displays of cooperation, even camaraderie, between former enemies should not be underestimated, and they make up one part of the broader community education effort by CRJI and the police at this stage of the transition. As one interviewee asserted:

And we just can't sit back as if we were still in the '70s and '80s and deal with them the way we did then. We got to be mindful of that feeling. It is our job to get in there and get people civil policing.[36]

This is a tall order indeed that the projects have set for themselves. Community education is a practice which all CRJI practitioners engage in on almost a daily basis. However, such work is far from easy:

One of the first times I was trying to engage with a group and discuss these issues was with Relatives for Justice. Probably one of the most difficult groups, because they all had people who were murdered by the cops. And there were about 25 people in the room, and there was this guy from Tyrone [rural county in Northern Ireland] and his two brothers had been ambushed by the cops and murdered. And he was saying, 'Never! This should not take place.' He did not know anyone, he said, who would *ever* have any dealings with the PSNI. And I said, 'I accept what you are saying, but tell me this: are you saying that there are no sex offenders in Tyrone? Ever?' 'Well, of course there are sex offenders in Tyrone,' he said. 'Well,' I said 'Imagine if a sex offender raped and killed the girl who lived in the farm next to you, and you saw him coming out of that house. What would you do?' 'Aha, but I don't mean that,' he said.[37]

This is community education in practice, where CRJI coordinators are trying to move this mind shift forward, by challenging people's views about the police in transitional Northern Ireland. Such a change will not happen solely through mediation or casework, but also through advocacy:

You go back to when that type of thing happened in the areas, people would have went to an armed organisation, give them the information and let them deal with it. And you can walk away and forget about the problem. And again, it is all about that mindset and breaking down those barriers, and CRJI has a very big involvement in that. CRJI is filling that void, and they have taken it and run with it so to speak. And I think they are now playing a big part in the re-education of our community and how we deal with them types of situations, and also taking away the old taboos about 'You are touting' or 'You should not be going to the police.'[38]

The significance of the leadership provided by ex-political prisoners and former combatants is central here, and such leadership is now moving into a new phase, towards acceptability of the police. As mentioned by one CRJI coordinator, himself an ex-prisoner:

You see how ex-prisoners carry the community's opinion, and what they feel or think towards a certain issue. Here, policing would come to mind in relation to Northern Ireland. There are people who have been involved in the conflict, who have been in jail, people who have been at the coal face of what went on here for 30-odd years. They are now sitting in clubs, pubs, halls, whatever, and are saying, 'This is what we should be doing, this is what we have to do.' And people respond to that, because maybe this is a person who has been involved in the conflict, who is maybe an ex-combatant, who has been here for quite some time. And they are taking those first steps and they are approaching the police and are seen speaking to the police, and people are realising that this is not just 'you go ahead and do it yourselves', but that they are leading the way in that respect as well. Because if they [ex-prisoners and former combatants] are not seen to be doing it, then people would just sit back and say, 'Right, that's just fine, just tell us what to do and we will do it.' It is quite unique that them people are lifting up the ball and running with it there.[39]

This arguably moves far beyond what most restorative justice initiatives engage with and exemplifies the potential of restorative justice in transition, of justice activism that transforms the political, social, cultural and political environment in which it works. The challenge now is the interface between community restorative justice and the criminal justice system, where informal bottom-up meets formal top-down. Some of the key issues in this debate in the near future will most likely be in relation to a common definition of restorative justice, reciprocal education and understandings of different working ethoses, clear guidelines for practice, and common tools for success and evaluation. Issues of trust and mutual respect are core values of this exercise in partnership building, within a process of wider community and policing legitimisation. The future, however, is uncertain.

In this context in which peace has apparently been brokered between the formal justice system and community restorative justice, they will now face a different challenge, albeit one which is familiar to many other community-based justice projects with strong ties to the state. As prominent writers within the informal justice tradition such as Cain (1985), Matthews (1988) and Fitzpatrick (1992) have argued, such is the hegemonic power and will to dominate of the justice system that it can 'swallow up' community-based programmes, professionalise them, and reconfigure them into the image of the state to such an extent that they ultimately lose their specific community focus and legitimacy. Staff at CRJI and Alternatives are acutely aware of this possibility:

> There is a saying: 'be careful what you wish for, it might become true.' And certainly we all crave some sort of stability and that can only come financially from the formal system. But if that is at a cost, then it might be too great a cost. I think it should be, on our terms to a certain extent, that we won't sign up to anything formal without keeping the community onboard. If we jump in feet first to do what the formal system wants, and then be seen as just another agent of the formal system, we will lose all that community-based stuff. ... Because in the areas we work in, it's because of a lack of proper policing in the past which means the community would use us in the first place. And I would not want to lose that. If working with the formal system means that people will see us as an extension of it and it would be like going to the probation or whatever, then it might be a pyrrhic victory. And that would be a shame.[40]

One of the challenges of community–police partnerships is to maintain a focus on the issues that matter most for the community, an area of concern for many restorative justice initiatives (Boyes-Watson 1999, 2004; Dzur and Olson 2004). This is also recognised by the Criminal Justice Inspectorate, which has gained considerable first-hand knowledge of the projects throughout their inspections:

> The future will depend very much on the political situation, and as long as it continues to stabilise, this should continue to

develop. I think that the main challenge is that when CRJI gets funded, that they continue as a community organisation, that they don't lose that ethos, because that would be devastating to their whole endeavour.[41]

It is too early to say with any certainty if such will be the fate of these projects in the near future, and the projects themselves are acutely aware of the need to hold onto their distinct community identity in this new dispensation. There is certainly pressure from some directions to continue the process of bringing these 'unruly' restorative projects under further state control. A PSNI superintendent noted that 'when CRJI is no longer needed, we have succeeded [in establishing trust in the police in the community]'.[42] This comment arguably reflects the opinion held by some groups within statutory agencies that community restorative justice is a feature of the transition, and a 'normalisation' of criminal justice in Northern Ireland equates to the demise of these projects, and the continued presence of 'regulatory capture' as a long-term strategy.

Notes

1 Policing in Northern Ireland has been covered by several authors: for some excellent accounts, see Ellison and Smyth 2000; Ellison and Mulcahy 2001; Mulcahy 2006.
2 Interview, CRJI caseworker, 22 January 2008.
3 The Report of the Independent Commission on Policing, known generally as the Patten Report (1999), titled *A New Beginning*, was the result of an extensive consultation process in Northern Ireland in the wake of the Belfast Agreement of 1998. It laid out the framework for a reformed police force and included 175 recommendations as to how this would be achieved. The commission was headed by Chris Patten, a former Minister of State for Northern Ireland and the last British governor of Hong Kong, where he oversaw the transfer of power from Britain to China.
4 Interview with support worker at Shankill Alternatives, 19 May 2005.
5 Interview, 27 May 2005.
6 It also reflects a difference in research access, and the second stage of data collection, which took place in December 2007 and January 2008 focused explicitly on CRJI and the relevant statutory organisations.
7 Interview with CRJI coordinator, 18 January 2008.
8 Interview CRJI caseworker, 22 January 2008.
9 Interview, 18 January 2008.
10 Interview, 18 January 2008.

11 Interview with CRJI coordinator, 15 January 2008.

12 Interview, 11 January 2008.

13 Interview with CRJI coordinator, 18 January 2008.

14 'Threats Aimed at Justice Scheme', *BBC News*, 30 October 2008.

15 See, for example: 'Bombs and Death Threats: Dissidents Step Up Efforts to Derail Power-Sharing', *Guardian*, 28 July 2008; 'Dissident Northern Ireland Republican Threat "Higher Than from Islamic extremists"', *The Belfast Telegraph*, 30 July 2008; '80–100 "Active Dissident Members"', *BBC News*, 13 August 2008; 'Dissident Republicans in Rocket Attack on Police in Northern Ireland', *Guardian* 18 August 2008; '"Dissidents" Threaten to Kill 5 Local Youths', *Andersonstown News*, 20 August 2008; 'Civilians Targeted by Dissident Republicans', *Belfast Telegraph*, 27 October 2008; 'The Afterlife of the IRA: The Dissident Groups Bent on Shattering the Peace in Northern Ireland', *The Independent*, 8 November 2008.

16 '"Very Real Threats" Lead to 2-Hour Police Delay', *The Irish News*, 17 November 2008.

17 Interview, 14 January 2008.

18 Copies of case files held by author. Any personal details regarding clients, such as name and address, have been removed to maintain confidentiality.

19 Interview with CRJI manager, 18 January 2008.

20 Interview with CRJI manager, 18 January 2008.

21 Interview with CRJI caseworker, 11 January 2008.

22 Interview with CRJI caseworker, 15 January 2008.

23 This is not as much of a problem in Loyalist areas, and Alternatives do not have to make referrals on people's behalf in the same manner.

24 Interview, 11 January 2008.

25 Interview, 15 January 2008.

26 Interview with PSNI chief inspector, 12 January 2006.

27 Interview with CRJI coordinator, 15 January 2008.

28 Interview with CRJI coordinator, 11 January 2008.

29 Interview, 18 January 2008.

30 Interview, 14 January 2008.

31 Interview, 18 January 2008.

32 Interview with PSNI officer, 14 January 2008.

33 Interview with CRJI coordinator, 15 January 2008.

34 Interview with CRJI manager, 18 January 2008.

35 Interview with CRJI manager, 18 January 2008.

36 Interview with CRJI coordinator, 15 January 2008.

37 Interview with CRJI manager, 18 January 2008.

38 Interview, 15 January 2008.

39 Interview, 15 January 2008.

40 Interview with Alternatives caseworker, 27 May 2005.

41 Interview with Criminal Justice Inspectorate, 14 January 2008.

42 Interview, 9 January 2008.

Conclusion

Rethinking restorative justice

Several unique themes emanate from the practice of community restorative justice within the transitional context. While these themes emerged in the particular context of Northern Ireland's journey from conflict to peace, a number of them can be generalised to other transitional and indeed settled societies. For example, it is important to note that these now thriving community restorative justice projects did not emerge as part of a grand peacemaking plan. In particular, restorative justice did not form part of the initial community discussions around a non-violent alternative to paramilitary punishment violence (Winston 1997; McEvoy and Mika 2001). Indeed, it was pure coincidence that key individuals were found in each community who could provide a framework of restorative justice for their practice. Without these individuals, who brought with them a strong commitment to non-violence and restorative justice, these unique efforts at peacemaking may not have been established in their current form, which has proven successful in these endeavours far beyond what was originally imagined.

Furthermore, the concept of restorative justice within community practice remains fluid, dynamic and responsive to community needs. This means that the practice of these projects is needs-based and holistic in nature in that they aim to address the underlying reasons for conflict and antisocial behaviour within their communities. Their practice does not stringently adhere to one specific model of restorative justice, but rather the needs of any particular participants dictate what type of intervention is most suitable. The follow-up of cases, particularly by Alternatives in relation to both young people and victims, is an important feature of such a holistic approach. Practitioners and volunteers clearly recognise that a single conference or mediation will not transform a young person's life, nor will it substantially reduce a victim's fear of crime and further victimisation. Hence, the time and effort spent on follow-up in relation to all participants are important (Stuart and Pranis 2006) in challenging long-standing and embedded cultures of violence within Northern Ireland. This needs-based approach, coupled with the initial focus on paramilitary punishment attacks, has resulted in a widened scope of practice. The result is restorative justice work that deals with serious violence, and engages with long-standing and complex conflicts between families and neighbours; participants who present a multitude of problems such as addiction to alcohol, prescription medication and illegal drugs; and efforts of community empowerment and capacity building.

Importantly, the Northern Irish experience teaches us that 'community' is not necessarily a peaceful place but can be characterised by violence-supporting norms and values that contain strong opposition to the state. In such circumstances, a top-down approach to crime prevention partnerships may not only fail, but may actually increase alienation and tension between the state and the community in question. Moreover, many places in Northern Ireland already have 'strong' communities with high levels of social capital and collective efficacy. However, rather than being seen as a resource, 'community' is often constructed as a threat and something to be suppressed, and the various state actors within Northern Ireland have clearly vocalised reactions that range from mild unease to open hostility to any kind of organised community action in relation to justice matters. Such reactions are understandable in light of the protracted conflict, which has left deep scars at all levels of society, but they are nonetheless unhelpful during this time of transition.

These projects are distinctive in that they have developed completely independently of the state, and in practice have existed for 10 years outside any formal partnership. This position has arguably allowed them to develop organically, and to meet the needs of victims, offenders and communities during a time of considerable social change. The projects represent a truly bottom-up approach to the challenges faced by the transitional society in relation to crime management and prevention. Moreover, the independent nature of these projects is one reason why they have had greater opportunities to aim at transformative justice in their practice, where they can affect broader community structures, including both the organised and the disorganised community, in developing new norms regarding conflict resolution and approaches to harm. By utilising existing social networks (Sampson *et al.* 1997; Putnam 2000; Bazemore and Schiff 2001) with which they are intimately familiar, and tapping into the power and information existing within the community, they are arguably more effective than the formal criminal justice system in this regard. The reach of the criminal justice system is severely limited owing to the fraught relationship between state and community that arose as a consequence of the violent conflict (McEvoy and Mika 2001, 2002).

CRJI and Alternatives have attempted, and arguably succeeded, in building bridges between formerly estranged communities and the state through community empowerment and capacity building, by organic approaches to partnership, and by simply providing an invaluable resource for the criminal justice system within hard-to-reach areas in certain communities in Northern Ireland. A working partnership between community restorative justice on both sides of the communal divide and statutory agencies is important for the future practice of these projects. However, there is a very real risk that such a partnership could be forged at the expense of community ownership (Crawford 1999a, b; Hughes 2006). Within this context, it is important to aim for partnerships that are based on communal objectives, the formation of community support and the enhancement of community resources.

The styles of leadership displayed by former combatants and ex-political prisoners have been central to these developments. Key individuals who display political, military and moral styles of leadership are central to the educative aspects of community restorative justice in the transitional context (McEvoy and Eriksson 2006). One consequence of these three styles of leadership is the opportunity to challenge and change embedded cultures of violence within Republican and Loyalist communities. It has been argued that community restorative justice can indeed make an important contribution in challenging a culture of violence relating to practices of punishment violence, both for individual victims of attacks and for the larger structures of paramilitary organisations. CRJI and Alternatives were established to provide a non-violent alternative to paramilitary punishment violence, explicitly targeting the endemic and violent behaviour within their communities emanating from paramilitary organisations (Auld *et al.* 1997; Winston 1997). The structure of their practice works effectively within the hierarchal, organised, military structures of the Provisional IRA and the UVF, but less so in relation to the disorganised community, which lacks the structure of the paramilitary groups, and, importantly, lacks effective leadership.

However, even if the practices of the disorganised community cannot be challenged as effectively as those of the organised community, the work of restorative justice projects can raise the threshold of punitive attitudes in the community, consequently lessening calls for punishment violence and vigilante-type actions. The effects can be seen in relation to participants in a restorative justice process, the views of volunteers, and wider community structures. Furthermore, by addressing the situation in which many youths find themselves, a situation characterised by disadvantage and marginalisation, another maintaining factor of a culture of violence is affected (Steenkamp 2005). Hence, the values embedded in social networks that help to sustain a culture of violence in the transitional phase can arguably be challenged and even changed, through bottom-up restorative justice initiatives. At least that is the experience from the Northern Irish context.

It is important to re-emphasise that in these communities there already existed extensive community networks and, particularly in Nationalist areas, a strong tradition of self-help. Hence, some of the core structures for a successful informal justice initiative were already in place, as may not be the case elsewhere. It is clear that in many other communities this level of social capital and collective efficacy does not exist, and even within Northern Ireland there is a difference between Loyalist and Republican communities. This is perhaps one reason why the remit and practice of Alternatives has been less extensive than that of CRJI, in that the supporting community structures existed to a higher degree in the latter areas. It is arguably a reflection of the construction of each community, not of the quality of work carried out by the staff and volunteers in the different projects.

There are certainly lessons to be drawn from the findings of this book which can have implications for the wider restorative justice literature and practice. Three key issues in particular stand out: the process of restorative justice, the role of volunteers, and the inherent flexibility of restorative justice that makes it suitable to extend much of its current focus to encompass serious incidents of violence and criminality. In relation to the first point, the research has consistently highlighted the importance of the restorative justice *process* as a key component of practice. Importantly, the process should ideally be guided by certain key values, such as inclusiveness, reparation, personalism, empowerment and reintegration to ensure good practice; however, the emphasis need not be on the *outcome* per se, but rather on the process that precedes it. Practitioners and volunteers described the process as their safety net: principles of practice which they could rely on when facilitating discussions around highly emotive issues and serious incidents of communal or interpersonal conflict. Such lessons would surely be of relevance to many current developments of restorative justice practices in relation to adult offenders and more serious incidents of violence and criminality within the formal justice system as well.

Secondly, the key role played by a relatively large number of committed volunteers has been crucial to the success of these projects. It was also noted, however, that this situation could possibly change with the formation of a formal partnership with the criminal justice system. The issue for other restorative justice initiatives is twofold. Firstly, without a core group of volunteers who are representative of the community in which both offenders and victims live, and who are perceived by participants to be so, the impact of restorative projects will arguably be less extensive. Secondly, it is also possible that the longevity of the project will be undermined without this group of committed people, a problem which has been highlighted in previous writings on the topic (see Crawford and Newburn 2003; Roche 2003; Dzur and Olson 2004). Finally, restorative justice can be well suited to deal with serious incidents of interpersonal and communal violence, and is sufficiently flexible to be adapted to different cultural, social, historical and political environments. In dealing with such issues, however, the design of the original model, the quality of the staff and volunteers engaged with the model, and continuing monitoring and evaluation are crucial components.

It is likely that the additional difficulties encountered by crime prevention and control in the transitional society can have important implications for criminological research in other contexts as well: for ordinary, stable democracies, particularly high-crime communities in such contexts; and for post-conflict societies elsewhere (Roberts and McMillan 2003; McEvoy 2007). Obviously, the issue of former combatants and ex-political prisoners is not directly relevant to most stable democracies, but former 'ordinary' prisoners who have 'made good' (Maruna 2001), particularly in high-crime areas, may very well play an invaluable role in local efforts to challenge cultures of violence and promote community capacity building.

The arguments in this book strongly support the view that restorative justice should be seen as more than a simple technique for preventing recidivism and increasing participant satisfaction. It is a fundamentally different way of thinking about and dealing with conflicts. This includes conflicts that have their basis in either criminal behaviour or civil disputes, but also more deep-running and pervasive forms of conflict that have their roots in politics, religion and/or ethnicity. It has been argued that the way restorative justice is being implemented in an overwhelming majority of practices does not amount to viewing criminal behaviour through a 'new lens' (Zehr 1990). Instead, it involves a mere tinkering with the criminal justice system that minimises its transformative potential. One possible reason for this is that most people take the language, values and structures of the existing criminal justice system for granted and then try to adapt restorative justice techniques and responses to the dominant system (Johnstone 2002). Restorative practices that are intimately linked or integrated within the formal criminal justice system in this way are also condemned to dealing with minor crimes and certain types of offenders, predominantly juveniles, and often exclude active community participation, with a consequent existence on the fringes of the criminal justice system. This, it can be argued, diminishes the potentially transformative aspects of restorative justice in relation to wider societal change and to the underlying structural injustices that often are the root causes of crime and broader conflicts (Pepinsky and Quinney 1991).

Sullivan and Tifft (1998) note that if restorative justice is to be achieved, efforts cannot be confined to conventionally defined acts of harm and injustice. Rather, it is necessary to address the social structural conditions that reproduce harm, inequality and violence. I would argue that this is what community restorative justice in Northern Ireland is trying to achieve, by not only addressing the offending and victimisation of individuals, but by actively working to deal with the underlying causes of such outcomes. They challenge long-standing structural hierarchies within the community by providing non-violent alternatives to paramilitary systems of punishment and by educating individuals and the larger community in non-violent and inclusive conflict management and resolution.

Restorative justice can be a vehicle for transformative justice in situations where the processes of restorative justice are actively used not only to transform the relationship between participants (McDonald and Moore 2001), but also to change the structural circumstances that gave rise to the conflict in the first place. For many, such a view of restorative justice may seem too idealistic at best and unworkable at worst, but I think that one of the key lessons from Northern Ireland is that transformative justice is indeed possible. This is because good restorative justice practice has the potential of taking into account the political, social and economic factors that underlie and sustain criminal and antisocial behaviour in the transitional society. Moreover, the forward-looking philosophy and practice of restorative justice provides a useful focal point of intervention (Braithwaite 1989). Such a forward-looking approach can allow for the focus of conflict resolution practices in the transitional society to be on the maintaining factors of a culture of violence and the subsequent criminality and antisocial behaviour, instead of only on the causes of the violent conflict per se. I would argue that the experiences of community restorative practices within Northern Ireland contribute strongly to broader debates within restorative justice elsewhere, particularly in attempting to determine the extent to which the framework may be applied to far more serious instances of violence and criminality, rather than its traditionally narrow focus on juvenile and minor crimes.

The case studies, interviews and observations conducted for this research clearly indicate that working within a restorative framework in the aftermath of decades of punitive retribution and armed struggle has changed people's perceptions of 'conflict' — be it personal, communal or on a national scale. This includes the root causes of conflict, its different expressions, and views on how to resolve it. For many of the people who have been on the front line of the armed struggle for decades, as part of a paramilitary organisation or as part of the wider community heavily affected by the conflict, a personal transformation has taken place. The threat directed towards these individuals from dissident or other paramilitary organisations should be seen as an indicator of how far these practitioners and volunteers have moved away from the retributive mindset so evident during the many decades of armed conflict in Northern Ireland.

Related to this is the debate within the literature over whether restorative justice and transformative justice are the same, or whether they should be treated as distinct concepts (Harris 2006). Based on the Northern Ireland experience, I would argue that they are different, but that restorative justice which is ambitious enough in scope can facilitate the space needed for transformative justice to occur. By ambitious, I do not refer to the scope of the restorative initiative per se, in that one does not have to aim for national reconciliation to be deemed ambitious. Instead, I refer to the personal and emotional space provided for individual participants that allows for sufficient empowerment to transcend previously held views, about oneself, one's neighbours, one's community, and indeed one's relationship with the state. That is ambitious, and it is possible. In particular, it is possible when the restorative process is based on the needs of participants, free from the retributive and legalistic framework inevitably imposed when functioning within the formal criminal justice system. It is possible when led by individuals with a strong personal commitment to the betterment of their community and who possess the skills, legitimacy and moral authority to work towards such transformations.

Much criticism has been directed towards community restorative justice in Northern Ireland – a great deal of which has been outlined in this book – and towards informal justice alternatives more generally: about the risks of self-declared community 'leaders' claiming to speak for the whole community under the guise of legitimate restorative practice while engaged in oppressive and hegemonic activities against the very community they are claiming to 'help'. This can indeed be a serious concern and one about which we should never be complacent. However, communities are not hidden places, and restorative justice projects in Republican and Loyalist areas in Northern Ireland have arguably been subjected to more oversight, inspection and debate than any other justice organisation in the jurisdiction, the only exception being the police. Importantly, the community-based restorative projects have had to fight for their legitimacy every step of the way, both in the eyes of the community and of the state.

This has resulted in a process of legitimisation to which state-based restorative justice programmes do not have to be subjected. The fact that the latter are created and run by the criminal justice system itself directly confers legitimacy on them (Beetham 1991), such that they do not have to prove that they 'work' beyond increasing participant satisfaction and perhaps reducing recidivism. This is not to say that there are not many extraordinary people working within state-based restorative justice programmes around the world, attempting to counterbalance the increased calls for punishment and retribution. Rather, my argument is that the dangers of informal justice are in some instances exaggerated, and, moreover, that state-based processes rarely provide the space within which transformative justice can take place, constrained as they are by the very system within which they work.

It is possible that transitional societies provide greater space – both politically and socially – for transformative restorative justice to take root and flourish. Perhaps when the expressions and locations of social control are more or less forced to be renegotiated, informal justice that can transform the historical, political and social sphere within which it exists can actually work. Indeed, by aiming for such transformations, a platform is provided and a voice given to previously alienated individuals and communities, for former enemies to become 'friends' within a framework of restorative justice.

However, what the future holds for these projects, as partnerships with the police and statutory organisations become formalised and the projects begin to rely on state funding, is shrouded in uncertainty. The accreditation of the projects and their adherence to the Protocols designed to regulate relations between the state and community restorative justice projects do not mean that disputes over justice ownership are magically resolved in Northern Ireland. Rather, they arguably provide an agreed framework within which such disputes can be addressed.

Bridge-building between the state and strong but historically estranged communities requires a concurrent emphasis on organic and bottom-up styles of partnerships, a willingness from the state in particular to cede some ownership and control, and a commitment on all sides to the development of real partnerships based upon trust and mutual respect (McEvoy and Eriksson 2008). This is a major undertaking for everyone involved, and the question marks are many. Will they be able to maintain the strong community legitimacy and credibility on which their existence relies? Will they continue to challenge conflict resolution behaviour at both the community and state levels, and maintain their unique transformative potential? Will they emerge from the transition as a leading example of shared ownership of justice and their betterment of their communities at the forefront? No doubt these questions will be the subject of future publications on the topic, but for now it can be stated that a full 10 years after they began, these developments herald the potential for a real organic partnership developing on the ground between Republican/Loyalist communities, the police, and other elements of the formal justice system.

On the basis of such conclusions, I would reassert the argument from Chapter 1, that criminology in general, and restorative justice in particular, can be useful frameworks around which to construct indigenous initiatives of conflict resolution. This is because good restorative practice has the potential of taking into account the political, social and economic factors that underlie and sustain criminal and antisocial behaviour in the transitional society. A criminological approach offers multidisciplinary lines of enquiry and methodological approaches that arguably make it well suited to take into account not only the many interrelated issues regarding victims, offenders and communities, but also the highly politicised context that often signifies transition. Moreover, critical criminological enquiries in such contexts contain the potential of transformative and peacemaking research, evaluation and application (Braithwaite 2002b; McEvoy 2003; McEvoy and Newburn 2003). Such a focus arguably contributes to an emerging criminology within post-conflict societies, by stretching the criminological imagination beyond much current application towards making a significant contribution to the many challenges faced by transitional societies around the world.

Appendix A

Paramilitary groups in Northern Ireland

The role and function of the different paramilitary groups in Northern Ireland has been, and remains, prominent in any discussion of informal justice and social control in many working-class communities. Considering the number of different groups and their real or inferred relationship with community restorative justice schemes in both communities, a brief description here of these organisations is helpful in understanding the sometimes prominent and complex role they occupy in everyday life in the Republican and Loyalist communities under investigation. Outside observers tend to focus on the Provisional IRA, but in fact there are eight different paramilitary organisations operating in Northern Ireland.

Republican organisations

(a) **Provisional Irish Republican Army (IRA).** Up until its statement of 28 July 2005 and subsequent decommissioning on 26 September that same year, the Provisional IRA remained a centralised and relatively disciplined organisation that engaged in violence, organised crime, recruitment and training (English 2003). The General Army Council was the IRA's supreme decision-making authority, which in turn selected the Provisional Army Council (PAC). For day-to-day purposes, authority was vested in the PAC, which, as well as directing policy and making major tactical decisions, appointed the Chief of Staff. Under the Chief of Staff is the General Headquarters, which consists of a number of individual departments, including Education and Communication, Engineering, Finance, Intelligence, Operations, Publicity, Quartermaster General, Security and Training. The so-called Civil Administration was responsible for the complaints system which utilised punishment violence. The Provisional IRA was a well-funded organisation deriving substantial income from smuggling and other criminal activities, and from overseas contributions particularly from the USA (Taylor 1997; O'Doherty 1998). The Independent Monitoring Commission (IMC) reported in November 2008 that the IRA is committed to an exclusively political path and has completely disbanded all military departments including the Army Council. It is no longer perceived as a threat.

(b) **The Official IRA (OIRA),** also known locally as 'the stickies', split from the provisional IRA after the latter declared a ceasefire in the early 1970s. Although in 1982 it formed a political party – the Workers Party, which later became Democratic Left and ultimately merged with the Labour Party in the Irish Republic – the Official IRA never decommissioned its weapons. It has engaged in sporadic acts of violence including feuds with other Republican groupings, occasional punishment shootings and attacks, and armed robberies, but has largely abstained from violent attacks, apart from involvement in some feuds, such as those with the Provisional IRA in 1975 (English 2003).

(c) **Continuity IRA (CIRA).** The CIRA was the military wing of Republican Sinn Féin, which split from Sinn Féin in the mid-1980s over the decision by the Adams/McGuinness leadership to recognise the legitimacy of the Dublin Parliament (Dáil Éireann) and to take up any seats there if elected. Although the CIRA has been sporadically active in, for example, incendiary attacks on hotels and retail premises in the border areas, it is also a small and heavily infiltrated organisation. It, too, has been involved in occasional acts of punishment violence in parts of Belfast and Derry (Neumann 2002). According to the twentieth report of the IMC published in November 2008, the CIRA remains a very serious threat in Northern Ireland. The organisation is attempting to enhance its capabilities through recruitment, training, the acquisition and manufacturing of weapons, and raising funds. It continues to plan and take part in a range of serious criminal activity, including drug dealing, robbery, extortion, fuel laundering, smuggling and 'tiger kidnappings' of whole families as hostages. In particular, the CIRA focuses its attacks on members of the PSNI.

(d) **The Real IRA (RIRA)** emerged in late 1997 after a split from the Provisional IRA by members who were opposed to the 1997 ceasefire, the Belfast Agreement, and the potential decommission of Republican weapons (Neumann 2002). This organisation was responsible for the Omagh bomb in August 1998, which killed 29 civilians and two unborn children. It is a small organisation with limited capacity for sustained violence. It has also been deeply infiltrated by the security services on both sides of the border. The Real IRA has been responsible for some punishment attacks, but mainly in relation to feuds within its own organisation or between different Republican splinter groups. Its members have also engaged in bombings and attacks on police and security forces (English 2003). In 2008, the RIRA followed a similar trajectory to that of the CIRA, by increasing its capabilities through recruitment and training of new members. The organisation is also engaged in similar criminal activities, including attacks on the PSNI, and remains a serious threat in Northern Ireland.

(e) **The Irish National Liberation Army (INLA)** emerged in late 1974 as a breakaway faction from the so-called Official IRA (Neumann 2002), and it became the military wing of a radical left-wing political party, the Irish Republican Socialist Party. Its initial core members were disaffected members of the Official IRA and the Provisional IRA following the 1972 ceasefire. The INLA 'gained a reputation for hard-left politics and ruthless violence' (English 2003: 177). The organisation declared a ceasefire on 22 August 1998, but, according to the IMC, and based on interview data, the INLA was still active in 2004–6 in relation to punishment violence and distribution of drugs, particularly in North Belfast. According to the IMC, the INLA remained a threat in 2008 both south and north of the border. Albeit less active than the CIRA and the RIRA, the INLA is involved in drug dealing, extortion, robbery and smuggling. There is less evidence, however, of recruitment and training of new members.

Loyalist organisations

(a) **The Ulster Defence Association (UDA)** has its origins in the vigilante groups that were formed in Protestant working-class areas in Northern Ireland at the beginning of the Troubles in the early 1970s. At the time, its membership was estimated to be around 30,000. It is the largest of the Loyalist paramilitary groups and became a proscribed organisation in 1992, but continues to recruit and train members. It is organised into six brigades, each under the command of a 'brigadier' and they all undertake paramilitary activities (Bruce 1992; Taylor 1999; McAuley 2004). According to the IMC, and this is also backed up by the interview data, the UDA remains active in organised crime including drugs and intimidation, especially of business people. It has also mounted sectarian attacks and been involved in practices of punishment violence and some high-profile feuds, particularly with the UVF in 2000. In 2008, the IMC reported that a split had occurred in the UDA, and the mainstream part of the organisation is distinguished by a leadership trying to disband the organisation's military force and instead engage in community activity. The breakaway faction, however, mainly located in south-east Antrim, has not shown the same type of restraint and continues to be involved in criminality and violence.

(b) **The Ulster Volunteer Force (UVF)** emerged in the 1960s. Although smaller than the UDA, it has been involved in political violence and sectarian killings throughout the conflict and is generally considered to be the better organised of the Loyalist groupings (Nelson 1984; Cusack and McDonald 1997; Taylor 1999). The Red Hand Commando is generally seen to be a cover name for some of the more violent UVF operations. The UVF was involved in a serious feud with the LVF during the summer of 2005, resulting in four murders and nine attempted murders. The UVF is also the only Loyalist paramilitary organisation that openly supports community restorative justice work in Loyalist areas. In May 2007, its leaders announced that they are transforming into a non-military organisation and are putting their weapons 'beyond use'. In 2008, the IMC reported that the UVF is continuing along the path set out in the 2007 statement by further decreasing its size, and is no longer involved in predatory or violent terrorist activities. There are some members, however, who seem reluctant to follow this new order, and the remaining leadership of the UVF is seen as vital in bringing about the change needed.

(c) **The Loyalist Volunteer Force (LVF)** was formed in 1996 by former members of the mid-Ulster brigade of the UVF, including the high-profile Billy Wright. These members had been expelled from the UVF following a disagreement with the leadership over the UVF's response to the resumption at that time of Provisional IRA violence. Its membership is quite small, and it is centred on Portadown with some support in Belfast and Antrim. In the past, it has played a prominent role in the annual Orange parade in Drumcree. The LVF has no political representation, and it declared a ceasefire in 1998, which the group used to get its prisoners released under the Belfast Agreement. It continued to be involved in violent activities, even though such actions were primarily aimed at other Loyalist paramilitaries. In 2001, the government declared that the organisation's ceasefire was no longer recognised due to high-profile involvement in violent activities. Following the feud with the UVF in 2005, the organisation announced that it was standing down (Stevenson 1996; Cusack and McDonald 1997; Taylor 1999). The IMC has reported that the LVF continues to be involved in organised crime and drug trafficking. In 2008, the IMC assessed the LVF to be a small organisation without any political role. It consists of a loose association of people who use the name of the organisation for criminal purposes. Crimes by members are committed mainly for personal gain, not for the advancement of the organisation.

Appendix B

Timeline for key events and government documents relating to community restorative justice in Northern Ireland

Date	Event/publication
1994	**First ceasefire**. In this year the IRA declared a 'complete cessation of military' operation. One month later, the Combined Loyalist Military Command (representing the UDA, UVF and Red Hand Commando – a small offshoot of the UVF) made a similar ceasefire declaration: 'policing activities', i.e. punishment violence and exclusions, were to be abandoned. The ceasefire was called off in February 1996 because of dissatisfaction with government negotiations.
1996	**Tom Winston began research** on an alternative to punishment violence in the Shankill area of West Belfast.
1997	**Second IRA ceasefire**
December 1997	Following dialogue between the IRA and four community activists (Jim Auld, Brian Gormally, Kieran McEvoy and Mike Ritchie), the *Blue Book* **was published,** suggest community-based restorative justice projects as an alternative to punishment violence.
1998	**A funding proposal was drafted** by the *Blue Book* authors and submitted to Atlantic Philanthropies. Jim Auld was appointed Director of CRJI, and four CRJI pilot projects were opened, three in Belfast and one in Derry.
1998	**Greater Shankill Alternatives** opened after dialogue between Tom Winston, the UVF and other key stakeholders. The organisation recruited Debbie Watters, an experienced restorative justice practitioner, as one of its first employees.
1998	**Good Friday Agreement signed**

1999	**CRJI projects were established** in Upper Springfield, Twinbrook, Brandywell and North Belfast.
June 1999	**NIO published the first** *Protocol on Restorative Justice.*
2000	**CRJI and NIA restorative justice umbrella groups established**
March 2000	*Criminal Justice Review* **was published.** The Review was a result of the Good Friday Agreement and was tasked with reviewing the operation of all branches of the criminal justice system. It was carried out by civil servants with a number of prominent criminal justice specialists. It mentioned community restorative justice only in passing, and clearly demonstrated a lack of understanding of the operations of the projects, and a fear of community ownership of justice: 'Community-based schemes which have no or only tenuous links with the formal criminal justice system will by definition not lie at the heart of mainstream approaches. ... We do not therefore see these as central ... but, in view of the interest in them and their existence in parts of Northern Ireland, we address the issues that they raise at the end of this chapter' (Criminal Justice Review 2000: para 9.57). The Review concluded that while community-based schemes may have a role to play in dealing with low-level crimes, they should receive referrals only from a statutory criminal justice agency.
2002	**Andersonstown CRJI project established**
2003	**Alternatives established projects** in Kilcooley, and East and North Belfast.
July 2004	**Second Report by the Justice Oversight Commissioner** The Criminal Justice Inspectorate, with Lord Clyde as Oversight Commissioner, was established following Recommendation 263 in the *Criminal Justice Review*. It was tasked with monitoring and reporting the progress of the implementations following the review. Lord Clyde, in his publications, has been consistently positive and supportive of community restorative justice. The Second Report stated in relation to CRJI and Alternatives:

> Essentially the purpose of both sets of bodies is to provide a service of mediation within the community, to resolve the problems which arise out of minor offensive behaviour with a view to restoring harmony in the community and to divert people, particularly young people, away from the temptations of criminal conduct. They also seek to reintegrate offenders with their own community. They are not and do not seek to be an

alternative to the criminal justice system. They should become complementary to it. (p. 101)

Furthermore:

It is now necessary to take steps to find a way in which the existing organisations can be interlinked, so far at least as regards to the activities which fall within the scope of the recommendations, with the criminal justice system, to their mutual benefit. The failure to have achieved guidelines or some statement of common principles by now is at the least disappointing and a real effort should now be made through discussion and negotiation to work towards a universally acceptable solution. ... The development of these community restorative justice schemes which was recommended by the Review and has been accepted by the Government is a matter of considerable importance and should be pursued in an active, forward-looking, co-operative, sensitive and open-minded spirit. (p. 102)

January 2005 **Third Report by the Justice Oversight Commissioner**

In this report, Lord Clyde made note of the positive contributions made by CRJI and Alternatives, and further stated:

The implementation of this recommendation remains one of unacceptable delay. Reference should be made to the comments made in the Second Report. Discussions and negotiation on the draft guidelines will be the next important step forward.

It is unfortunate that the name 'restorative justice' is liable to be misunderstood. It is certainly desirable that efforts be made to achieve greater understanding on the part of the public about the substances and the advantages of restorative justice and in particular community restorative justice. But that is only one element behind the difficulties which presently exist. Among other factors the political situation and an element of mistrust may also be contributing to the slow rate of progress. The problem may require to be resolved by movements at all levels. All those involved may need to be flexible in their approach and ready to move forward. (p. 105)

June 2005 **Fourth Report by the Justice Oversight Commissioner**

Some progress had been made when this report was published, but Lord Clyde continued to emphasise the important contribution made by the projects, and he was somewhat alone in doing so among his colleagues:

> After some delay, some very positive initiatives have been taken in the progressing of Recommendation 168 (community restorative justice) and I hope that the momentum now achieved in that regard will be maintained and that positive practical developments may be achieved over the next period of the oversight work. (p. 13)

In fact, it took almost two more years before one of the projects, NIA, was able to sign up to the Protocols, which was not due to any hesitation on their side. Lord Clyde further stated:

> CRJI and NIA have been continuing to work with cases of low-level crime in their respective areas in addition to their other work but have reported an increasing concern at the poor level of progress which was being made towards the implementation of this recommendation. Continued delay in progress risks the loss of the available experience which the many volunteers engaged in this work have built up over the years. (p. 102)

July 2005

IRA decommission. See link below for full statement from the IRA.

http://news.bbc.co.uk/1/hi/events/northern_ireland/latest_news/85905.stm

October 2005

Seventh Report by the IMC

The Independent Monitoring Commission (the IMC) was established on 7 January 2004. Its purpose was to 'help promote the establishment of a stable and inclusive devolved government in a peaceful Northern Ireland' (IMC home page). It is made up of four independent members whose tasks are threefold: to report to the government on paramilitary activity, to report on the normalisation of security measures in Northern Ireland, and to investigate claims that assembly parties or local ministers are not living up to the standards required of them.

The various IMC reports (15 altogether) have also made several statements on community restorative justice, particularly in relation to perceived links to active paramilitary organisations, claims of community oppression and control (claims made mainly by the SDLP), and the possible contribution to tackling crime and antisocial behaviour in their local communities. The information used by the IMC is received from a range of sources and includes political parties, government officials, the police, a range of community groups, churches, charities, pressure groups and other organisations, businesses, lawyers, journalists, academics, victims, private citizens, and former combatants.

December 2005   *Consultation on Draft Guidelines for Community-Based Restorative Justice Schemes* **published by the NIO**

January 2006   **Fifth Report by the Justice Oversight Commissioner**
Here Lord Clyde stated:

> I should also mention under this heading the important Recommendation 168 (Community Restorative Justice) which has been slowly progressing and which I very much hope may see a positive advance in the near future. (p. 13)

February 2006   **Eighth Report by the IMC**
In this report, the IMC began by repeating and reconfirming their comments from the previous report in regards to the positive influence the schemes had in their communities and the need for safeguards and inspection. It then turned to some allegations that had been communicated to them since the last report. These accounts had two main features:

> First, that there have been some instances of people known for their involvement in community restorative justice schemes, and sometimes apparently speaking in the name of such schemes, who have tried to exert improper pressure on individuals, whether victims, alleged offenders, or members of their families. Those who have exerted this pressure are sometimes known for their paramilitary connections. As reported to us, this pressure is seen by those on whom it is exerted as intended to secure the disposal of the crime without recourse to the criminal justice system, including police, for example by requiring the alleged offender to move to another location or refrain from visiting certain places in the future. While the allegations put to us may not always have involved actual violence against victims and offenders they have sometimes referred to what has been described as an 'undercurrent of threat' – and threat has been sufficient. The second feature of the accounts has been the type and seriousness of the offences, which fall well outside the scope of ordinary restorative justice schemes.

March 2006   **Ninth Report by the IMC**
This report did not mention community restorative justice at all; nor did the following six reports.

June 2006	**Sixth Report by the Justice Oversight Commissioner**
	In this report, Lord Clyde largely rehearsed old ground, and again made negative comments regarding the slow progress of the Protocols:
	The delays in pursuit of this recommendation and the failure to consider support for activities undertaken by the current schemes outside the scope of Recommendation 168 risks the future existence of some at least of the schemes and the resulting vacuum may be a source of additional problems in the future both for communities which they serve and for the government. Progress remains a matter of some sensitivity and difficulty and the recommendations must await future implementations. (p. 139)
July 2006	*Draft Protocol for Community-Based Restorative Justice Schemes* **published by the NIO**
September 2006	*A Protocol for Community-Based Restorative Justice Schemes: Consultation and Equality Impact Assessment* **published by the NIO**
January 2007	**Sinn Féin endorsed the PSNI**
	The motion before the Sinn Féin Ard Fheis empowered the party's executive to:
	Support the Police Service of Northern Ireland (PSNI) and the criminal justice system; Hold the police and criminal justice systems north and south fully to account, both democratically and legally, on the basis of fairness and impartiality and objectivity. Authorise our elected representatives to participate in local policing structures in the interests of justice, the quality of life for the community and to secure policing with the community as the core function of the PSNI. And actively encouraging everyone in the community to co-operate fully with the police services in tackling crime in all areas and actively supporting all the criminal justice institutions.
	See Ard Fheis Motion Motion passed by the Sinn Féin Ard Fheis – 28 January 2007, http://www.sinnfeinonline.com/policies (last visited 7 March 2007).
2007	*Northern Ireland Affairs Committee: First Special Report: Draft Protocols for Community-Based Restorative Justice Schemes: Government Response to the Committee's First Report on Session 2006–7*
February 2007	**Final** *Protocol for Community-Based Restorative Justice Schemes* **published by the NIO**
April 2007	**Sinn Féin and the DUP formed power-sharing executive**
2007	**Criminal Justice Inspectorate published report on**

	Alternatives, recommending that the projects receive accreditation.
May 2007	**The UVF announced** that it was transforming into a non-military organisation and was putting its weapons 'beyond use'.
August 2007	**Alternatives accredited by the Northern Ireland Office**
October 2007	**Criminal Justice Inspectorate published a pre-inspection report** on CRJI with a view to accreditation.
June 2008	**Criminal Justice Inspectorate published report** after its final inspection of CRJI, recommending accreditation.
31 July 2008	**CRJI accredited by the Northern Ireland Office,** and was now in a position to seek funding from the state for its continued practice.

References

Abel, R. (ed.) (1982a) *The Politics of Informal Justice* (vol. 1, *The American Experience*). New York: Academic Press.

Abel, R. (ed.) (1982b) *The Politics of Informal Justice* (vol. 2, *Comparative Studies*). New York: Academic Press

Abrahams, R. (1998) *Vigilante Citizens: Vigilantism and the State*. Cambridge: Polity Press.

Abrahams, R. (2002) 'What's in a Name? Some Thoughts and the Vocabulary of Vigilantism and Related Forms of "Informal Criminal Justice"', in D. Feenan (ed.), *Informal Criminal Justice*. Aldershot: Ashgate, 25–40.

Achilles, M. (2004) 'Will Restorative Justice Live up to Its Promise to Victims?', in H. Zehr and B. Toews (eds), *Critical Issues in Restorative Justice*. Monsey, NY and Cullompton: Criminal Justice Press/Willan Publishing, 65–74.

Achilles, M. and Zehr, H. (2001) 'Restorative Justice for Crime Victims: The Promise, the Challenge', in G. Bazemore and M. Schiff (eds), *Restorative Community Justice: Repairing Harm and Transforming Communities*. Cincinnati, OH: Anderson 47–62.

Ahmed, E., Harris, N., Braithwaite, J. and Braithwaite, V. (2001) *Shame Management Through Reintegration*. Cambridge: Cambridge University Press.

Anderson, B. ([1983] revised edn 1991) *Imagined Communities: Reflections on the Origin and Spread of Nationalism*. London/New York: Verso.

Annan, K. (2004) 'Learning the Lessons of Peace Building', Tip O'Neill Lecture, Magee Campus, University of Ulster, Northern Ireland, 18 October.

Ashworth, A. (2002) 'Responsibilities, Rights and Restorative Justice', *British Journal of Criminology*, 43 (3): 578–595.

Auld, J., Gormally, B., McEvoy, K. and Ritchie, M. (1997) *Designing a System of Restorative Justice in Northern Ireland*. Belfast: The Authors.

Babo-Soares, D. (2004) 'Nahe Biti: The Philosophy and Process of Grassroots Reconciliation (and Justice) in East Timor', *Asia Pacific Journal of Anthropology*, 5 (1): 15–33.

Barton, C. (2000) 'Empowerment and Retribution in Criminal Justice' in H. Strang and J. Braithwaite (eds), *Restorative Justice: From Theory to Practice*. Aldershot: Ashgate Dartmouth, 55–76.

Barton, C. (2003) *Restorative Justice: The Empowerment Model*. Sydney: Hawkins Press.

Bauman, Z. (2001) *Community: Seeking Safety in an Insecure World*. Oxford: Blackwell.

Bazemore, G. (2001) 'Young People, Trouble, and Crime: Restorative Justice as a Normative Theory of Informal Social Control and Social Support', *Youth and Society*, 33 (2): 199–226.

Bazemore, G. and Schiff, M. (eds) (2001) *Restorative Community Justice: Repairing Harm and Transforming Communities*. Cincinnati, OH: Anderson.

Bazemore, G. and Umbreit, M.S. (2003) 'A Comparison of Four Restorative Conferencing Models', in G. Johnstone (ed.), *A Restorative Justice Reader: Texts, Sources, Context*. Cullompton: Willan Publishing, 225–244.

Bazemore, G. and Walgrave, L. (1999) 'Restorative Juvenile Justice: In Search of Fundamentals and an Outline of Systematic Reform', in G. Bazemore and L. Walgrave (eds), *Restorative Juvenile Justice: Repairing the Harm of Youth Crime*. Monsey, NY: Criminal Justice Press, 45–74.

Beetham, D. (1991) *The Legitimation of Power*. London: Macmillan.

Belfast Agreement (1998) 'The Agreement Reached in Multi-Party Negotiations'. Belfast: Northern Ireland Office.

Bell, C. (1996) 'Alternative Justice in Ireland', in N. Dawson, D. Greer and P. Ingram (eds), *One Hundred and Fifty Years of Irish Law*. Legal Publications, Northern Ireland: Sweet and Maxwell.

Belloni, R. (2001) 'Civil Society and Peace Building in Bosnia and Herzegovina', *Journal of Peace Research*, 38 (2): 163–180.

Blagg, H. (2001) 'Aboriginal Youth and Restorative Justice: Critical Notes from the Australian Frontier', in A. Morris and G. Maxwell (eds), *Restorative Justice for Juveniles: Conferencing, Mediation and Circles*. Oxford: Hart Publishing, 227–242.

Bolton, S. (2006) 'Crime Prevention in the Community: the Case of Neighborhood Watch', *Criminal Justice Matters*, 64: 40–41.

Borer, T.A. (2003) 'A Taxonomy of Victims and Perpetrators: Human Rights and Reconciliation in South Africa', *Human Rights Quarterly*, 25 (4): 1088–1116.

Bourgois, P. (2001) 'The Power of Violence in War and Peace: Post-Cold War Lessons from El Salvador', *Ethnography*, 2 (1): 5–34.

Boutellier, H. (1997) 'Right to the Community: Neighbourhood Justice in the Netherlands', *European Journal of Criminal Policy and Research*, 4 (95): 43–52.

Boutellier, H. (2001) 'Hans Boutellier, Crime and Criminal Justice in the Postmodern Age: A Review of Hans Boutellier's "crime and morality"', *Crime, Law and Social Change*, 35 (4): 360–362.

Bowyer Bell, J. (1993) *The Irish Troubles: A Generation of Violence*. Dublin: Gill and Macmillan.

Boyes-Watson, C. (1999) 'In the Belly of the Beast? Exploring the Dilemmas of State-Sponsored Restorative Justice', *Contemporary Justice Review*, 2 (4): 261–281.

Boyes-Watson, C. (2004) 'What Are the Implications of the Growing State Involvement in Restorative Justice?', in H. Zehr and B. Toews (eds), *Critical Issues in Restorative Justice*. Monsey, NY and Cullompton: Criminal Justice Press/Willan Publishing, 215–226.

Braithwaite, J. (1989) *Crime, Shame and Reintegration*. Cambridge: Cambridge University Press.

Braithwaite, J. (1999) 'Restorative Justice: Assessing Optimistic and Pessimistic Accounts', *Crime and Justice: A Review of Research*, 25: 1–127.

Braithwaite, J. (2002a) *Restorative Justice and Responsive Regulation*. Oxford: Oxford University Press.

Braithwaite, J. (2002b) 'Setting Standards for Restorative Justice', *British Journal of Criminology*, 42 (3): 563–577.

Braithwaite, J. and Daly, K. (1994) 'Masculinities, Violence and Communitarian Control', in T. Newburn and E. Stanko (eds), *Just Boys Doing Business?* London: Routledge, 189–213.

Braithwaite, J. and Mugford, S. (1994) 'Conditions of Successful Reintegration Ceremonies', *British Journal of Criminology*, 34: 139–171.

Braithwaite, J. and Strang, H. (eds) (2001) *Restorative Justice and Civil Society*. Cambridge: Cambridge University Press.

Brewer, J. D., Lockhart, B. and Rodgers, P. (1998) 'Informal Social Control and Crime Management in Belfast', *The British Journal of Sociology*, 49 (4): 570–85.

Brewer, J. D., Lockhart, B. and Rodgers, P. (1999) 'Crime in Ireland 1945-95', in A. Heath, R. Breen and P. Whelan (eds), *Ireland North and South: Perspectives from the Social Sciences*. Oxford: Oxford University Press.

Bruce, S. (1992) *The Red Hand: Protestant Paramilitaries in Northern Ireland*. Oxford: Oxford University Press.

Bruce, S. (1993) 'Loyalists in Northern Ireland: Further Thoughts on "Pro-State Terror"', *Terrorism and Political Violence*, 5 (4): 252–265.

Burman, S. and Scharf, W. (1990) 'Creating People's Justice: Street Committees and People's Courts in a South African City', *Law and Society Review*, 24 (3): 693–744.

Bursik, R. and Grasmick, H. (1993) *Neighbourhood and Crime: The Dimension of Effective Community Control*. Lexington, MA: Lexington Books.

Burton, F. (1978) *The Politics of Legitimacy: Struggles in a Belfast Community*. London: Routledge and Kegan Paul.

Cain, M. (1985) 'Beyond Informal Justice', *Contemporary Crisis*, 9: 335–373.

Campbell, C., Devlin, R., O'Mahony, D., Doak, J., Jackson, J., Corrigan, T. and McEvoy, K. (2005) *Evaluation of the Northern Ireland Youth Conference Service*. Belfast: Northern Ireland Office.

Candio, P. and Bleiker, R. (2001) 'Peace Building in East Timor', *Pacific Review*, 14 (1): 63–84.

Cartwright, J. and Jenneker, M. (2005) 'Governing Security: A Working Model in South Africa – The Peace Committee', in A New Decade of Criminal Justice in South Africa – Consolidating Transformation? Cape Town: Centre for the Study of Violence and Reconciliation. Unpublished proceeding, Criminal Justice Conference, Pretoria South Africa.

Cartwright, J., Jenneker, M. and Shearing, C. (2004) 'Local Capacity Governance in South Africa: A Model for Peaceful Coexistence', Paper originally presented at the 'In Search for Security' conference in Montreal hosted by the Law Commission of Canada.

Chayes, A.H. and Chayes, A. (1998) 'Mobilizing International and Regional Organizations for Managing Ethnic Conflict', in E. Weiner (ed.), *The Handbook of Interethnic Coexistence*. New York: Continuum, 280–309.

Cherif Bassiouni, M. (ed.) (2002) *Post-Conflict Justice*. Ardsley, NY: Transnational Publishers.

Christie, N. (1977) 'Conflict as Property', *British Journal of Criminology*, 17: 1–26.

Clear, T. and Karp, D. (1999) *The Community Justice Ideal: Preventing Crime and Achieving Justice*. Boulder, CO: Westview Press.

Cochrane, A. (1986) 'Community Politics and Democracy', in D. Held and C. Pollitt (eds), *New Forms of Democracy*. London: Sage.

Cohen, A.P. (1985) *The Symbolic Construction of Community*. London: Routledge.

Cohen, A.P. (1987) *Whalsay: Symbol, Segment and Boundary in a Shetland Island Community*. Manchester: Manchester University Press.

Cohen, D. and Nesbitt, R. (1994) 'Self-Protection and the Culture of Honor: Explaining Southern Violence', *Personality and Social Psychology Bulletin*, 20 (5): 551–567.

Cohen, S. (1996) 'Crime and Politics: Spot the Difference', *British Journal of Sociology*, 47 (1): 1–21.

Conway, P. (1997) 'A Response to Paramilitary Policing in Northern Ireland', *Critical Criminology: An International Journal*, 8 (1): 109–121.

Corrado, R.R., Cohen, I.M. and Odgers, C. (2003) 'Multi-Problem Violent Youth: A Challenge for the Restorative Justice Paradigm', in E. Weitekamp and H.J. Kerner (eds), *Restorative Justice in Context: International Practices and Directives*. Cullompton: Willan Publishing, 1–22.

Cottino, A. (1999) 'Sicilian Cultures of Violence: The Interconnections Between Organized Crime and Local Society', *Crime, Law and Social Change*, 32 (2): 103–113.

Coulter, C. (1999) *Contemporary Northern Ireland Society: An Introduction*. London: Pluto Press.

Crawford, A. (1994) 'Appeals to Community and Crime Prevention', *Crime, Law and Social Change*, 22 (2): 97–126.

Crawford, A. (1999a) *The Local Governance of Crime: Appeals to Community and Partnerships*. Oxford: Oxford University Press.

Crawford, A. (1999b) 'Questioning Appeals to Community Within Crime Prevention and Control', *European Journal on Criminal Policy and Research*, 7: 509–530.

Crawford, A. (2001) 'Joined-up but Fragmented: Contradiction, Ambiguity and Ambivalence at the Heart of New Labour's "Third Way"' in R. Matthews and J. Pitts (eds), *Crime, Disorder and Community Safety: A New Agenda?* London: Routledge.

Crawford, A. (2003) 'In the Hands of the Public?', in G. Johnstone (ed.), *A Restorative Justice Reader: Texts, Sources, Context*. Cullompton: Willan Publishing, 312–319.

Crawford, A. (2006) '"Fixing Broken Promises?" Neighbourhood Wardens and Social Capital', *Urban Studies*, 43 (5/6): 957–976.

Crawford, A. and Clear, T. (2001) 'Community Justice: Transforming Communities Through Restorative Justice?' in G. Bazemore and M. Schiff (eds), *Restorative Community Justice: Repairing Harm and Transforming Communities*. Cincinnati, OH: Anderson, 127–149.

Crawford, A. and Clear, T. (2003) 'Community Justice: Transforming Communities Through Restorative Justice?', in E. McLaughlin, G. Fergusson, G. Hughes and L. Westmarland (eds), *Restorative Justice: Critical Issues*. London: Sage, 215–229.

Crawford, A. and Newburn, T. (2003) *Youth Offending and Restorative Justice: Implementing Reform in Youth Justice*. Cullompton: Willan Publishing.

Criminal Justice Inspectorate (2007) *Northern Ireland Alternatives: Report of an Inspection with a View to Accreditation Under the Government's Protocol for Community Based Restorative Justice*. Belfast: Criminal Justice Inspectorate Northern Ireland.

Criminal Justice Review (2000) *Review of the Criminal Justice System in Northern Ireland*, Belfast: Stationary Office.

Crocker, D.A. (1998) 'Transitional Justice and International Civil Society: Toward a Normative Framework', *Constellations Volume*, 5 (4): 492–517.

Crow, G. and Allan, G.A. (1994) *Community Life: An Introduction to Local Social Relations*. London: Harvester Wheatsheaf.

Cunneen, C. (2002) 'Restorative Justice and the Politics of Decolonization', in E. Weitekamp and H.J. Kerner (eds), *Restorative Justice: Theoretical Foundations*. Cullompton and Portland, OR: Willan Publishing, 32–49.

Cunneen, C. (2003) 'Thinking Critically About Restorative Justice', in E. McLaughlin, R. Fergusson, G. Hughes and L. Westmarland (eds), *Restorative Justice: Critical Issues*. London: Sage/Open University, 182–194.

Cunneen, C. (2004) 'What Are the Implications of Restorative Justice's Use of Indigenous Traditions?', in H. Zehr and B. Toews (eds), *Critical Issues in Restorative Justice*. Monsey, NY and Cullompton: Criminal Justice Press/ Willan Publishing, 337–340.

Cunningham, M. (2001) *British Government Policy in Northern Ireland, 1969-89*. Manchester: Manchester University Press.

Curle, A. (1999) *To Tame the Hydra: Undermining the Culture of Violence*. Charbury: John Carpenter.

Cusack, J. and McDonald, H. (1997) *UVF*. Dublin: Poolbeg.

Daly, K. (2000) 'Revisiting the Relationship Between Retributive and Restorative Justice', in H. Strang and J. Braithwaite (eds) *Restorative Justice: From Philosophy to Practice*. Aldershot: Dartmouth, 33–54.

Daly, K. (2001) 'Conferencing in Australia and New Zealand: Variations, Research Findings and Prospects', in A. Morris and G. Maxwell (eds), *Restorative Justice for Juveniles: Conferencing, Mediation and Circles*. Oxford: Hart, 85–101.

Daly, K. (2002) 'Restorative Justice: The Real Story', *Punishment and Society*, 4 (1): 55–79.

Daly, K. (2003) 'Mind the Gap: Restorative Justice in Theory and Practice', in A. von Hirsch, J. Roberts, A.E. Bottoms, K. Roach and M. Schiff (eds), *Restorative Justice and Criminal Justice: Competing or Reconcilable Paradigms?* Oxford: Hart, 219–236.

Daly, K., Venables, M., McKenna, M., Mumford, L. and Christie-Johnston, J. (1998) *South Australia Juvenile Justice Research on Conferencing*. Technical Report no. 1. Project Overview and Research Instruments. Brisbane: Griffith University, School of Criminology and Criminal Justice.

Darby, J. and MacGinty, R. (2000) 'Northern Ireland: Long, Cold Peace', in J. Darby and R. MacGinty (eds), *The Management of the Peace Process*. London: Macmillan, 61–106.

Dickinson, L.A. (2003) 'The Promise of Hybrid Courts', *American Journal of International Law*, 97 (2): 295–309.

Dignan, J. (2000) *Restorative Justice Options for Northern Ireland: A Comparative Review*. Belfast: HMSO.

Dignan, J. (2005) *Understanding Victims and Restorative Justice*. Maidenhead: Open University Press.

Dixon, B. and van der Spuy, Elrena (2004) *Justice Gained? Crime and Crime Control in South Africa's Transition*. Cullompton: Willan Publishing.

Drumbl, M.A. (2000a) 'Punishment Postgenocide: From Guilt to Shame to "Civis" in Rwanda', *New York University Law Review*, 75 (5): 1221–1326.

Drumbl, M.A. (2000b) 'Retributive Justice and the Rwandan Genocide', *Punishment and Society*, 2 (3): 287–308.

Drumbl, M.A. (2000c) 'Sclerosis: Retributive Justice and the Rwandan Genocide', *Punishment and Society*, 2 (3): 287–308.

Drumbl, M.A. (2002) 'Restorative Justice and Collective Responsibility: Lessons for and from the Rwandan Genocide', *Contemporary Justice Review*, 5 (1): 5–22.

Duff, A.R. (2003) 'Restorative Punishment and Punitive Restoration' in G. Johnstone (ed.), *A Restorative Justice Reader: Texts, Sources, Context*. Cullompton: Willan Publishing, 382–397.

du Toit, P. (2001). *South Africa's Brittle Peace: The Problem of Post-Settlement Violence*. Basingstoke: Palgrave Macmillan.

Dyck, D. (2006) 'Reaching Toward a Structurally Responsive Training and Practice of Restorative Justice', in D. Sullivan and L. Tifft (eds), *The Handbook of Restorative Justice: A Global Perspective*. London: Routledge, 527–545.

Dzur, A.W. and Olson, S.M. (2004) 'The Value of Community Participation in Restorative Justice', *Journal of Social Philosophy*, 35 (1): 91–107.

Eisnaugle, Carrie, J.N. (2003) 'An International "Truth Commission": Utilizing Restorative Justice as an Alternative to Retribution', *Vanderbuilt Journal of Transnational Law*, 36: 209–301.

Ellison, G. and Mulcahy, A. (2001) 'The Policing Question in Northern Ireland', *Policing and Society*, 11 (3–4): 243–258.

Ellison, G. and Smyth, J. (2000) *The Crowned Harp: Policing Northern Ireland*. London: Pluto Press.

Elster, J. (2004) *Closing the Books: Transitional Justice in Historical Perspectives*. Cambridge: Cambridge University Press.

Elster, J. (2006) *Retribution and Reparation in the Transition to Democracy*. Oxford: Oxford University Press.

English, R. (2003) *Armed Struggle: A History of the IRA*. London: Macmillan.

Eriksson, A. (2008) 'Challenging Cultures of Violence Through Community Restorative Justice in Northern Ireland', *Sociology of Crime, Law and Deviance*, 11: 231–260.

Etcheson, C. (2005) *After the Killing Fields: Lessons from the Cambodian Genocide*. Westport, CT: Praeger.

Etzioni, A. (1994) *The Spirit of Community: The Reinvention of American Society*. New York: Touchstone.

Evans-Kent, B. (2002) 'Bringing People Back: Grassroots Approaches to Peace in Bosnia-Herzegovina', *Journal of International Relations and Development*, 5 (3): 294–310.

Evenson, E.M. (2004) 'Truth and Justice in Sierra Leone: Coordination Between Commission and Court', *Columbia Law Review*, 104 (3): 730–767.

Farrow, K. and Prior, D. (2006) '"Togetherness"? Tackling Anti-Social Behaviour Through Community Engagement', *Criminal Justice Matters*, 46: 4–5.

Feenan, D. (2002) 'Justice in Conflict: Paramilitary Punishment in Ireland (North)', *International Journal of the Sociology of Law*, 30: 151–172.

Feenan, D. (2002b) 'Researching Paramilitary Violence in Northern Ireland', *International Journal of Social Research Methodology*, 5 (2): 147–163.

Ferme, M.C. (2001) *The Underneath of Things: Violence, History, and the Eeveryday in Sierra Leone*. Berkeley, CA: University of California Press.

Fitzpatrick, P. (1992) 'The Impossibility of Popular Justice', *Social and Legal Studies*, 1: 199–215.

Foster, J. (1995) 'Informal Social Control and Community Crime Prevention', *British Journal of Criminology*, 35 (4): 563–583.

Foster, J. (2002) '"People Pieces": The Neglected but Essential Elements of Community Crime Prevention', in G. Hughes and A. Edwards (eds), *Crime Control and Community: The New Politics of Public Safety*. Cullompton: Willan Publishing, 167–196.

Froestad, J. and Shearing, C. (2007) 'Conflict Resolution in South Africa: A Case Study', in G. Johnstone and D. Van Ness (eds), *Handbook of Restorative Justice*. Cullompton: Willan Publishing, 534–556.

Gaarder, E. and Presser, L. (2006) 'A Feminist Vision of Justice? The Problems and Possibilities of Restorative Justice for Girls and Women', in D. Sullivan and L. Tifft (eds), *The Handbook of Restorative Justice: A Global Perspective*. London and New York: Routledge, 483–493.

Garland, D. (2001) *The Culture of Control: Crime and Social Order in Contemporary Society*. Chicago, IL: University of Chicago Press.

Gastil, R.D. (1971) 'Homicide and a Regional Culture of Violence', *American Sociological Review*, 36 (3): 412–427.

Geary, R., McEvoy, K. and Morison, J. (2000) 'Lives Less Ordinary: Crime, Communities and Policing in Northern Ireland', *Irish Journal of Sociology*, 10: 49–74.

Goldstone, R.J. (1999) 'Justice as a Tool for Peace-Making: Truth Commissions and International Criminal Tribunals', *International Law and Politics*, 28: 485.

Govier, T. and Verwoerd, W. (2004) 'How Not to Polarize "Victims" and "Perpetrators"', *Peace Review*, 16 (3): 371–377.

Grabosky, P.N. (1995) 'Fear of Crime and Fear Reduction Strategies', Trends and Issues in Crime and Criminal Justice, no. 44. Australian Institute of Criminology.

Graham, B. (1998) 'Contested Images of Place Among Protestants in Northern Ireland', *Political Geography*, 17 (2): 129–144.

Gready, P. (2005) 'Analysis: Reconceptualising Transitional Justice; Embedded and Distanced Justice', *Conflict, Security and Development*, 5 (1): 3–21.

Groff, L. and Smoker, P. (1996) 'Creating Global/Local Cultures of Peace', in UNESCO (ed.), *From a Culture of Violence to a Culture of Peace*. Paris: UNESCO Publishing, 103–128.

Hagan, F.E. (1997) *Political Crime: Ideology and Criminality*. Boston: Allyn and Bacon.

Hamber, B. (1999) 'Have no Doubt There is Fear in the Land: An Exploration of Continuing Cycles of Violence in South Africa', *South African Journal of Child and Adolescent Mental Health*, 12 (1): 5–18.

Hamber, B. (2002) '"Ere their story die": Truth, Justice and Reconciliation in South Africa', *Race and Class*, 44 (2): 61–79.

Hamill, H. (2002) 'Victims of Paramilitary Punishments Attacks in Belfast', in C. Hoyle, R. Young and Centre for Criminological Research, University of Oxford (eds), *New Visions of Crime Victims*, Oxford and Portland, OR: Hart Publishing, pp. 49–70.

Harper, E. (2005) 'Delivering Justice in the Wake of Mass Violence: New Approaches to Transitional Justice', *Journal of Conflict and Security Law*, 10: 149.

Harris, K.M. (2006) 'Transformative Justice: The Transformation of Restorative Justice', in D. Sullivan and L. Tifft (eds), *The Handbook of Restorative Justice: A Global Perspective*. London and New York: Routledge, 555–566.

Hayes, B.C. and McAllister, I. (2001) 'Sowing Dragon's Teeth: Public Support for Political Violence and Paramilitarism in Northern Ireland', *Political Studies*, 49: 901–922.

Hayes, H., Prenzler, T. and Wortely, R. (1998) *Making Amends: Final Evaluation of the Queensland Community Conferencing Pilot*. Griffith University, Australia.

Hayner, P.B. (1994) 'Fifteen Truth Commissions – 1974 to 1994: A Comparative Study', *Human Rights Quarterly*, 16 (4): 597–655.

Hayner, P.B. (2001) *Unspeakable Truths: Facing the Challenge of Truth Commissions*. London: Routledge.

Hezlet, A.R. (1972) *The 'B' Specials: A History of the Ulster Special Constabulary*. London: Tom Stacey.

Higgins, J. and Martin, O. (2003) *Violence and Young People's Security*. Partnership Organisation, Hague Appeal for Peace.

Higgins, K. and McElrath, K. (2000) 'The Trouble with Peace: The Ceasefires and Their Impact on Drug Use Among Youth in Northern Ireland', *Youth and Society*, 32 (1): 29–59.

Hillyard, P. (1985) 'Popular Justice in Northern Ireland: Continuities and Change', in S. Stitzer and A.T. Scull (eds), *Research in Law, Deviance and Social Control*, London: Jai Press, 247–267.

Hillyard, P. (2001) 'Political Crime', in E. McLaughlin and J. Muncie (eds), *The Sage Dictionary of Criminology*. London: Sage, 211–212.

Hoggett, P. (ed.) (1997) *Contested Communities: Experiences, Struggles, Policies*. Bristol: Policy Press.

Holter, A.C., Martin, J. and Enright, R.D. (2006) 'Restoring Justice Through Forgiveness: The Case of Children in Northern Ireland', in D. Sullivan and L. Tifft (eds), *The Handbook of Restorative Justice: A Global Perspective*. London and New York: Routledge, 311–320.

Hope, T. and Foster, J. (1992) 'Conflicting Forces Changing the Dynamics of Crime and Community on "Problem" Estates', *British Journal of Criminology*, 32 (4): 488–503.

Hope, T. and Sparks, R. (2000) *Crime, Risk and Insecurity: Law and Order in Everyday Life and Political Discourse*. London and New York: Routledge.

Hudson, J. and Galaway, B. (eds) (1996) *Restorative Justice: International Perspectives*. Monsey, NY: Criminal Justice Press.

Hughes, G. (1998) *Understanding Crime Prevention: Social Control, Risk and Late Modernity*. Buckingham: Open University Press.

Hughes, G. (2006) *The Politics of Crime and Community*. London: Palgrave Macmillan.

Hughes, G. and Edwards, A. (eds) (2002) *Crime Control and Community: The New Politics of Public Safety*. Cullompton: Willan Publishing.

Humphrey, M. (2004) 'International Intervention, Justice and National Reconciliation: The Role of the ICTY and ICTR in Bosnia and Rwanda', *Journal of Human Rights*, 2 (4): 495–505.

Jantzi, V. (2004) 'What is the Role of the State in Restorative Justice?' in H. Zehr and B. Toews (eds), *Critical Issues in Restorative Justice*. Monsey, NY and Cullompton: Criminal Justice Press/Willan Publishing, 189–202.

Jarman, N. (2004) 'From War to Peace? Changing Patterns of Violence in Northern Ireland, 1990–2003', *Terrorism and Political Violence*, 16 (3): 420–438.

Johnston, L. (1996) 'What Is Vigilantism?', *British Journal of Criminology*, 36 (2): 220–236.

Johnstone, G. (2002) *Restorative Justice: Ideas, Values, Debates*. Cullompton: Willan Publishing.

Johnstone, G. and Van Ness, D. (eds) (2007) *Handbook of Restorative Justice*. Cullompton: Willan Publishing.

Justice Oversight Commissioner (JOC) (2005) 'Third Report of the Justice Oversight Commissioner'. Belfast: JOC.

Justice Oversight Commissioner (JOC) (2004) 'Second Report of the Justice Oversight Commissioner'. Belfast: JOC.

Kaminski, M., Nalepa, M. and O'Neill, B. (2006) 'Normative and Strategic Aspects of Transitional Justice', *Journal of Conflict Resolution*, 50 (3): 295–302.

Katzenstein, S. (2003) 'Hybrid Tribunals: Searching for Justice in East Timor', *Harvard Human Rights Journal*, 16: 245–278.

Kelman, H.C. (1990) 'Applying a Human Needs Perspective to the Practice of Conflict Resolution: The Israeli-Palestinian Case', in J.W. Burton (ed.), *Conflict: Human Needs Theory*. New York: St. Martin's Press, 283–300.

Kennedy, L. (1995) 'Nightmares Within Nightmares: Paramilitary Repression Within Working-Class Communities', in L. Kennedy (ed.), *Crime and Punishment in West Belfast*. Belfast: Summer School, West Belfast, 67–80.

Knight, M. and Ozerdam, A. (2004) 'Guns, Camps and Cash: Disarmament, Demobilization and Reinsertion of Former Combatants in Transitions from War to Peace', *Journal of Peace Research*, 41 (45): 499–516.

Knox, C. (2002) 'See No Evil Hear No Evil: Insidious Paramilitary Violence in Northern Ireland', *British Journal of Criminology*, 42 (1): 164–185.

Knox, C. and Monaghan, R. (2002) *Informal Justice in Divided Societies: Northern Ireland and South Africa*. Palgrave: Macmillian.

Kotsonouris, M. (1994) *Retreat from Revolution: The Dail Courts, 1920–24*. Dublin: Irish Academic Press.

Kynoch, G. (2005) 'Crime, Conflict and Politics in Transition-Era South Africa', *African Affairs*, 104 (416): 493–514.

Lebow, R.N. (1976) 'Vigilantism in Northern Ireland', in H.J. Rosenbaum and P.C. Sederberg (eds), *Vigilante Politics*. Philadelphia: University of Pennsylvania Press, 234–260.

Leebaw, B. (2001) 'Restorative Justice for Political Transitions: Lessons from the South African Truth and Reconciliation Commission', *Contemporary Justice Review*, 4 (3–4): 267–289.

Leisenring, A. (2006) 'Confronting "Victim" Discourses: The Identity Work of Battered Women', *Symbolic Interaction*, 29 (3): 307–330.

Levrant, S., Cullen, F.T., Fulton, B. and Wozniak, J.F. (1999) 'Reconsidering Restorative Justice: The Corruption of Benevolence Revisited?', *Crime and Delinquency*, 45 (1): 3–27.

Little, D. (1999) 'A Different Kind of Justice: Dealing with Human Rights Violations in Transitional Societies', *Ethics and International Affairs*, 13: 65.

Llewellyn, J. (2007) 'Truth Commissions and Restorative Justice', in G. Johnstone and D. Van Ness (eds), *Handbook of Restorative Justice*, Cullompton: Willan Publishing, 351–370.

Llewellyn, J. and Howse, R. (1999) 'Institutions for Restorative Justice: The South African Truth and Reconciliation Commission', *University of Toronto Law Review*, 49: 355–388.

MacGarry, J. and O'Leary, B. (1995) *Explaining Northern Ireland: Broken Images*. Oxford: Blackwell.

MacGarry, J. and O'Leary, B. (2004) *The Northern Ireland Conflict: Consociational Engagement*. Oxford: Oxford University Press.

MacGinty, R. (2000) 'Hate Crimes in Deeply Divided Societies: The Case of Northern Ireland', *New Political Science*, 22 (1): 49–60.

MacGinty, R. and Darby, J. (2002) *Guns and Government: The Management of the Northern Ireland Peace Process*. London: Palgrave Macmillan.

Maguire, K. (1993) 'Fraud, Extortion and Racketeering: The Black Economy in Northern Ireland', *Crime, Law and Social Change*, 20 (4): 273–292.

Maguire, M. (2002) 'Crime Statistics: The "Data Explosion" and Its Implications', in M. Maguire, R. Morgan and R. Reiner (eds), *The Oxford Handbook of Criminology* (3rd edn). Oxford: Oxford University Press, 322–375.

Mallinder, L. (2008) *Amnesty, Human Rights and Political Transitions: Bridging the Peace and Justice Divide*. Oxford: Hart Publishing.

Mani, R. (2002) *Beyond Retribution: Seeking Justice in the Shadows of War*. Malden, MA: Polity Press.

Marshall, T.F. (1988) 'Informal Justice: the British Experience', in R. Matthews (ed.), *Informal Justice?* London: Sage, 150–177.

Marshall, T.F. (1996) 'The Evolution of Restorative Justice in Britain', *European Journal on Criminal Policy and Research*, 4 (4): 21–43.

Marshall, T.F. (1998) 'Out of Court: More or Less Justice?', in R. Matthews (ed.), *Informal Justice?* London: Sage, 25–50.

Maruan, S. (2001) *Making Good: How Ex-Convicts Reform and Rebuild Their lives*, Washington, DC: American Psychological Association Books.

Matthews, R. (ed.) (1988) *Informal Justice?* London: Sage.

Maxwell, G. and Hayes, H. (2006) 'Restorative Justice Developments in the Pacific Region: A Comprehensive Survery', *Contemporary Justice Review*, 9 (2): 27–54.

Maxwell, G., Morris, A. and Hayes, H. (2006) 'Conferencing and Restorative Justice', in D. Sullivan and L. Tifft (eds), *The Handbook of Restorative Justice: A Global Perspective*. London and New York: Routledge, 91–107.

McAuley, J.W. (2004) 'Peace and Progress? Political and Social Change Among Young Loyalists in Northern Ireland', *Journal of Social Issues*, 60 (3): 541–562.

McCold, P. (1996) 'Restorative Justice and the Role of the Community', in B.J. Galaway and B.J. Hudson (eds), *Restorative Justice: International Perspectives*. Monsey, NY: Criminal Justice Press, 85–102.

McCold, P. (2000) 'Toward a Holistic Vision of Restorative Juvenile Justice: A Reply to the Maximalist Model', *Contemporary Justice Review*, 3 (4): 357–414.

McCold, P. (2004) 'What Is the Role of Community in Restorative Justice Theory and Practice?', in H. Zehr and B. Toews (eds), *Critical Issues in Restorative Justice*. Monsey, NY and Cullompton: Criminal Justice Press/Willan Publishing, 155–172.

McCold, P. and Wachtel, T. (1998) 'Community Is Not a Place: A New Look at Community Justice Initiatives', *Contemporary Justice Review*, 1 (1): 71–85.

McCold, P. and Wachtel, T. (2003) 'Community Is Not a Place: A New Look at Community Justice Initiatives', in G. Johnstone (ed.), *A Restorative Justice Reader: Texts, Sources, Context*. Cullompton: Willan Publishing, 294–302.

McDonald, J. and Moore, D. (2001) 'Community Conferencing as a Special Case of Conflict Transformation, in J. Braithwaite and H. Strang (eds), *Restorative Justice and Civil Society*. Cambridge: Cambridge University Press, 130–148.

McEvoy, K. (2003) 'Beyond the Metaphor: Political Violence, Human Rights, and "New" Peacemaking Criminology', *Theoretical Criminology*, 7 (3): 319–346.

McEvoy, K. (2007) 'Beyond Legalism: Towards a Thicker Version of Transitional Justice', *Journal of Law and Society*, 34 (4): 411–440.

McEvoy, K. and Ellison, G. (2003) 'Criminological Discoursed in Northern Ireland: Conflict and Conflict Resolution', in K. McEvoy and T. Newburn (eds), *Criminology, Conflict Resolution and Restorative Justice*. London: Palgrave Macmillan, 45–82.

McEvoy, K. and Eriksson, A. (2006) 'Restorative Justice in Transition: Ownership, Leadership and "Bottom-up" Human Rights', in D. Sullivan and L. Tifft (eds), *The Handbook of Restorative Justice: Global Perspectives*. London: Routledge, 321–336.

McEvoy, K. and Eriksson, A. (2008) 'Who Owns Justice? Community, State and the Northern Ireland Transition', in J. Shapland (ed.), *Justice, Community and Civil Society: A Contested Terrain*. Cullompton: Willan Publishing.

McEvoy, K., Gormally, B. and Mika, H. (2002) 'Conflict, Crime Control and the "Re"-Construction of State/Community Relations in Northern Ireland', in G. Hughes, E. McLaughlin and J. Muncie (eds), *Crime Prevention and Community*. Buckingham: Open University Press, 182–212.

McEvoy, K., McConnachie, K. and Jamieson, R. (2007) 'Political Imprisonment and the "War on Terror"', in Y. Jewkes (ed.), *Handbook on Imprisonment*. Cullompton: Willan, 293–323.

McEvoy, K. and McGregor, L. (eds) (2008) *Transitional Justice from Below: Grassroots Activism and the Struggle for Change*. Oxford and Portland, OR: Hart Publishing.

McEvoy, K. and Mika, H. (2001) 'Punishment, Politics and Praxis: Restorative Justice and Non-Violent Alternatives to Paramilitary Punishment', *Policing and Society*, 11 (1): 359–382.

McEvoy, K. and Mika, H. (2002) 'Restorative Justice and the Critique of Informalism in Northern Ireland', *British Journal of Criminology*, 43 (3): 534–563.

215

McEvoy, K. and Newburn, T. (eds) (2003) *Criminology, Conflict Resolution and Restorative Justice*. Basingstoke and New York: Palgrave Macmillan.

McEvoy, K., Shirlow, P. and McElrath, K. (2004) 'Resistance, Transition and Exclusion: Politically Motivated Ex-Prisoners and Conflict Transformation in Northern Ireland', *Terrorism and Political Violence*, 16 (3): 646–670.

McKay, S. (2005) *Northern Protestants: An Unsettled People* (2nd edn). Belfast: Blackstaff Press.

Merry, S.E. and Milner, N.A. (1993) *The Possibility of Popular Justice: A Case Study of Community Mediation in the United States*. Ann Arbor, MI: University of Michigan Press.

Mika, H. (2004) 'Unpublished Evaluation of Community Restorative Justice Ireland and Northern Ireland Alternatives' (Author's copy).

Mika, H. (2007) *Community Based Restorative Justice in Northern Ireland: An Evaluation*. Queen's University Belfast: Institute of Criminology and Criminal Justice.

Mika, H. and McEvoy, K. (2001) 'Restorative Justice in Conflict: Paramilitarism, Community and the Construction of Legitimacy in Northern Ireland', *Contemporary Justice Review*, 3 (4): 291–319.

Minow, M. (1998) *Between Vengeance and Forgiveness: Facing History after Genocide and Mass Violence*. Boston: Beacon Press.

Mitchell, C. (2003) 'Protestant Identification and Political Change in Northern Ireland', *Ethnic and Racial Studies*, 26 (4): 612–631.

Monaghan, R. (2002) 'The Return of "Captain Moonlight': Informal Justice in Northern Ireland', *Studies in Conflict and Terrorism*, 25: 41–56.

Monaghan, R. (2004) '"An Imperfect Peace": Paramilitary "Punishments" in Northern Ireland', *Terrorism and Political Violence*, 16 (3): 439–461.

Monaghan, R. (2008) 'Community-Based Restorative Justice in Northern Ireland and South Africa', *International Criminal Justice Review*, 18 (1): 83–105.

Moore, D. and O'Connell, T. (1994) 'Family Conferencing in Wagga Wagga: A Communitarian Model of Justice', in C. Adler and J. Wundesitz (eds), *Family Conferencing and Juvenile Justice: The Way Forward or Misplaced Optimism?* Canberra: Australian Institute of Criminology.

Moore, D. and Forsythe, L. (1995) *A New Approach to Juvenile Justice: An Evaluation of Family Conferencing in Wagga Wagga*. New South Wales: Centre for Rural Social Research, Charles Stuart University.

Morison, J. and Geary, R. (1993) 'Studying Crime and Conflict: The Northern Ireland Example', *Northern Ireland Legal Quarterly*, 44 (1): 65.

Morris, A. and Maxwell, G. (1993) 'Juvenile Justice in New Zealand: A New Paradigm', *Australian and New Zealand Journal of Criminology*, 26 (1): 72–90.

Morris, R. (2000) *Stories of Transformative Justice*. Canada: Canadian Scholars Press.

Morrissey, M. and Pease, K. (1982) 'The Black Criminal Justice System in West Belfast', *Howard Journal*, 21 (Spring): 159–166.

Mulcahy, A. (2006) *Policing Northern Ireland: Conflict, Legitimacy and Reform*. Cullompton: Willan Publishing.

Muncie, J. (2001) 'Official criminal statistics', in E. McLaughlin and J. Muncie (eds), *The Sage Dictionary of Criminology*. London: Sage Publications, 194–197.

Munck, R. (1984) 'Repression, Insurgency and Popular Justice: The Irish Case', *Crime and Social Justice*, 21/22: 81–94.

Munck, R. (1988) 'The Lads and the Hoods: Alternative Justice in an Irish Context', in M. Tomlison, T. Varley and C. McCullagh (eds), *Whose Law and Order?* Belfast: Sociological Association of Ireland, 41–53.

Napoleon, V. (2004) 'By Whom, and by What Processes, Is Restorative Justice Defined, and What Bias Might This Introduce?', in H. Zehr and B. Toews (eds), *Critical Issues in Restorative Justice*, Monsey, NY and Cullompton: Criminal Justice Press/Willan Publishing, 33–46.

Nelken, D. (1985) 'Community Involvement in Crime Control', *Current Legal Problems*, 38: 239–267.

Nelson, S. (1984) *Ulster's Uncertain Defenders: Protestant Political, Paramilitary and Community Groups and the Northern Ireland Conflict*. Belfast: Appletree.

Neuffer, E. (2002) *The Key to My Neighbor: Seeking Justice in Bosnia and Rwanda*. London: Bloomsbury.

Neumann, R.P. (2002) 'The Imperfect Peace: Explaining Paramilitary Violence in Northern Ireland', *Low Intensity Conflict and Law Enforcement*, 11 (1): 116–138.

Nina, D. (1993) 'Community Justice in a Volatile South Africa: Containing Community Conflict, Clermont, Natal', *Social Justice*, 20 (3–4): 129–42.

Nolan, P.C. and McCoy, G. (1996) 'The Changing Pattern of Paramilitary Punishment in Northern Ireland', *Injury*, 27: 405–406.

Nolan, P.C., McPherson, J., McKeown, R., Diaz, H. and Wilson, D. (2000) 'The Price of Peace: The Personal and Financial Cost of Paramilitary Punishment in Northern Ireland', *Injury*, 31: 41–45.

Nowrojee, B. (2005) *'Your Justice Is Too Slow': Will the ICTR Fail Rwanda's Rape Victims?* Geneva: United Nations Research Institute for Social Development.

O'Doherty, M. (1998) *The Trouble with Guns: Republican Strategy and the Provisional IRA*. Belfast: Blackstaff.

O'Mahony, D., Chapman, T. and Doak, J. (2002) *Restorative Cautioning: A Study of Police Based Restorative Cautioning Pilots in Northern Ireland*. Northern Ireland Statistics and Research Agency.

O'Mahony, D., Geary, R., McEvoy, K. and Morison, J. (2000) *Crime, Community and Locale: The Northern Ireland Communities Crime Survey*. Aldershot: Ashgate.

Pankhurst, D. (1999) 'Issues of Justice and Reconciliation in Complex Political Emergencies: Conceptualising Reconciliation, Justice and Peace', *Third World Quarterly*, 20 (1): 239–255.

Patten Report (1999) *A New Beginning: Policing in Northern Ireland.* Belfast: HMSO.

Pavlich, G. (2001) 'The Force of Community', in H. Strang and J. Braithwaite (eds), *Restorative Justice and Civil Society.* Cambridge: Cambridge University Press, 56–68.

Pavlich, G. (2004) 'What Are the Dangers as Well as the Promises of Community Involvement?', in H. Zehr and B. Toews (eds), *Critical Issues in Restorative Justice.* Monsey, NY and Cullompton: Criminal Justice Press/ Willan Publishing, 173–183.

Pavlich, G. (2005) *Governing Paradoxes of Restorative Justice.* London: Glasshouse Press.

Pelikan, C. and Trenczek, T. (2006) 'Victim-Offender Mediation and Restorative Justice: The European Landscape', in D. Sullivan and L. Tifft (eds), *The Handbook of Restorative Justice: A Global Perspective.* Routledge, 63–90.

Pepinsky, H.E. and Quinney, R. (eds) (1991) *Criminology as Peacemaking.* Bloomington and Indianapolis, IN: Indiana University Press.

Pranis, K. (2004) 'The Practice and Efficacy of Restorative Justice', *Journal of Religion and Spirituality in Social Work,* 23 (1–2): 133–157.

Putnam, R.D. (2000) *Bowling Alone: The Collapse and Revival of American Community.* Carmichael, CA: Touchstone Books.

Rigby, A. (2001) *Justice and Reconciliation: After the Violence.* Boulder, CO: Lynne Rienner.

Roach, K. (2000) 'Changing Punishment at the Turn of the Century: Restorative Justice on the Rise', *Canadian Journal of Criminology,* 42 (3): 249–280.

Roberts, P. (2003) 'Restoration and Retribution in International Criminal Justice: An Exploratory Analysis', in A. von Hirsch (ed.), *Restorative Justice: Competing or Reconcilable Paradigms?* Oxford: Hart Publishing, 115–134.

Roberts, P. and McMillan, N. (2003) 'For Criminology in International Criminal Justice', *Journal of International Criminal Justice,* 1 (2): 315–338.

Roche, D. (2001) 'The Evolving Definition of Restorative Justice', *Contemporary Justice Review,* 4 (3–4): 341–354.

Roche, D. (2002) 'Restorative Justice and the Regulatory State in South African Townships', *British Journal of Criminology,* 42 (3): 514–533.

Roche, D. (2003) *Accountability in Restorative Justice.* Oxford: Oxford University Press.

Rosenbaum, H.J. and Sederberg, P.C. (eds) (1976) *Vigilante Politics.* Philadelphia: University of Pennsylvania Press.

Ruane, J. and Todd, J. (1996) *The Dynamics of Conflict in Northern Ireland: Power, Conflict and Emancipation.* Cambridge: Cambridge University Press.

Rupesinghe, K. and Rubio, M. (eds) (1994) *The Culture of Violence.* New York: United Nations University Press.

Ruth-Heffelbower, D. (2000) 'Indonesia: Restorative Justice for Healing a Divided Society'. Paper presented at the April 2000 'Just Peace?' conference in Auckland, New Zealand.

Sampson, R.J. (1987) 'Personal Violence by Strangers: An Extension and Test of the Opportunity Model of Predatory Victimization', *Journal of Law and Criminology*, 78 (2): 327–356.

Sampson, R.J. and Groves, B.W. (1989) 'Community Structure and Crime: Testing Social-Disorganization Theory', *American Journal of Sociology*, 94 (4): 774–802.

Schabas, W.A. (2004) *An Introduction to the International Criminal Court*. Cambridge: Cambridge University Press.

Seigel, R.L. (1998) 'Transitional Justice: A Decade of Debate and Experience', *Human Rights Quarterly*, 20: 431–454.

Sharpe, S. (2004) 'How Large Should the Restorative Justice "Tent" Be?', in H. Zehr and B. Toews (eds), *Critical Issues in Restorative Justice*. Monsey, NY and Cullompton: Criminal Justice Press/Willan Publishing, 17–32.

Shearing, C. (2001) 'Local Capacity Policing', in J. Sarkin (ed.), *Policing, Crime and Justice*. Brussels: Maklu, 191–197.

Shearing, C., Cartwright, J. and Jenneker, M. (2006) 'A Grass Root Governance Model: South African Peace Committees', in V. Luker, S. Dinnen and A. Patience (eds), *Law, Order and HIV/AIDS in Papua New Guinea*. Canberra: Pandanus.

Shirlow, P. and Murtagh, B. (2006) *Belfast: Segregation, Violence and the City*. London: Pluto.

Silke, A. (1998a) 'The Lords of Discipline: The Methods and Motives of Paramilitary Vigilantism in Northern Ireland', *Low Intensity Conflict and Law Enforcement*, 7 (2): 121–156.

Silke, A. (1998b) 'In Defense of the Realm: Financing Loyalist Terrorism in Northern Ireland – Part One: Extortion and Blackmail', *Studies in Conflict and Terrorism*, 21: 331–361.

Silke, A. (1999) 'Rebel's Dilemma: The Changing Relationship Between the IRA, Sinn Fein and Paramilitary Vigilantism in Northern Ireland', *Terrorism and Political Violence*, 11 (Spring): 55–93.

Silke, A. (2000a) 'Drinks, Drugs and Rock 'n' Roll: Financing Loyalist Terrorism in Northern Ireland – Part Two', *Studies in Conflict and Terrorism*, 23: 107–127.

Silke, A. (2000b) 'The Impact of Paramilitary Vigilantism on Victims and Communities in Northern Ireland', *International Journal of Human Rights*, 4, (1): 1–24.

Silke, A. and Taylor, M. (2000) 'War Without End: Comparing IRA and Loyalist Vigilantism in Northern Ireland', *Howard Journal*, 39 (3): 249–266.

Simpson, G. (1993) 'Women and Children in Violent South African Townships', in M. Motshekya and E. Delport (eds), *Women and Children's Rights in a Violent South Africa*. Pretoria West: Institute for Public Interest, Law and Research, 3–13.

Skelton, A. (2002) 'Restorative Justice as a Framework for Juvenile Justice Reform: A South African Perspective', *British Journal of Criminology*, 42: 496–513.

Skogan, W.C. (1986) 'Fear of Crime and Neighbourhood Change', *Crime and Justice*, 8: 203–229.

Sluka, J.A. (1989) *Hearts and Minds, Water and Fish: Support for the IRA and INLA in a Northern Irish Ghetto*. London: JAI Press.

Sluka, J.A. (1990) 'Participant Observation in Violent Social Contexts', *Human Organization*, 49: 114–126.

Smyth, M. (1998) 'Remembering in Northern Ireland: Victims, Perpetrators and Hierarchies of Pain and Responsibility', in B. Hamber (ed.), *Past Imperfect: Dealing with the Past in Northern Ireland and Societies in Transition*. Derry/Londonderry: INCORE, University of Ulster, 31–49.

Sparks, R., Bottoms, A. and Hay, W. (1996) *Prisons and the Problem of Order*. Oxford: Clarendon Press.

Staub, E. (1989) *The Roots of Evil: The Origins of Genocide and Other Group Violence*. New York: Cambridge University Press.

Staub, E. (1996) 'The Cultural-Societal Roots of Violence: The Examples of Genocidal Violence and of Contemporary Youth Violence in the United States', *American Psychologist*, 51: 117–132.

Staub, E. (1999) 'The Origins and Prevention of Genocide, Mass Killing and Other Collective Violence', *Peace and Conflict: Journal of Peace Psychology*, 5: 303–337.

Staub, E. (2003) 'Notes on Cultures of Violence, Cultures of Caring and Peace, and the Fulfillment of Basic Human Needs', *Political Psychology*, 24 (1): 1–21.

Steenkamp, C. (2005) 'The Legacy of War: Conceptualising a "Culture of Violence" to Explain Violence After Peace Accords', *The Round Table*, 94 (379): 253–267.

Stevenson, J. (1996) *We Wrecked the Place: Contemplating and End to the Northern Ireland Troubles*. New York: The Free Press.

Strang, H. (1995) 'Replacing Courts with Conferences', *Policing*, 11 (3): 39–78.

Strang, H. (2002) *Repair or Revenge? Victims and Restorative Justice*. Oxford: Clarendon Press.

Strang, H. (2004) 'Is Restorative Justice Imposing Its Own Agenda on Victims?', in H. Zehr and B. Toews (eds), *Critical Issues in Restorative Justice*. Monsey, NY and Cullompton: Criminal Justice Press/Willan Publishing, 95–106.

Strang, H., Barnes, G., Braithwaite, J. and Sherman, L. (1999) *Experiments in Restorative Policing: A Progress Report on the Canberra Reintegrative Shaming Experiments*. Canberra: Australian National University.

Strang, H. and Braithwaite, J. (eds) (2001) *Restorative Justice and Civil Society*. Cambridge: Cambridge University Press.

Stuart, B. and Pranis, K. (2006) 'Peacemaking Circles: Reflections on Principal Features and Primary Outcomes', in D. Sullivan and L. Tifft (eds), *The Handbook of Restorative Justice: A Global Perspective*. London: Routledge, 121–133.

Sudbury, J. (ed.) (2005) *Global Lockdown: Race, Gender and the Prison-Industrial Complex*. New York and London: Routledge.

Sullivan, D. and Tifft, L. (2001) *Healing the Foundations of Our Everyday Lives*. Monsey, NY: Willow Tree Press.

Sullivan, D. and Tifft, L. (2004) 'What Are The Implications of Restorative Justice for Society and Our Lives?', in H. Zehr and B. Toews (eds), *Critical Issues in Restorative Justice*. Monsey, NY and Cullompton: Criminal Justice Press/Willan Publishing, 387–395.

Sullivan, D. and Tifft, L. (eds) (2006) *The Handbook of Restorative Justice: Global Perspectives*. London and New York: Routledge.

Sunshine, J. and Tyler, T.R. (2003) 'The Role of Procedural Justice and Legitimacy in Shaping Public Support for Policing', *Law and Society Review*, 37 (3): 513–547.

Sykes, G.M. and Matza, D. (1957) 'Techniques of Neutralization: A Theory of Delinquency', *American Sociological Review*, 22: 664–670.

Taylor, P. (1997) *Provos: The IRA and Sinn Fein: The Book of the BBC TV Series*. London: Bloomsbury.

Taylor, P. (1999) *Loyalists*. London: Bloomsbury.

Teitel, R. (1997) 'Transitional Jurisprudence: The Role of Law in Political Transformations', *Yale Law Journal*, 106: 2009–2082.

Teitel, R. (2000) *Transitional Justice*. Oxford: Oxford University Press.

Teitel, R. (2003) 'Transitional Justice Genealogy', *Harvard Human Rights Journal*, 16: 69-94.

Teitel, R. (2003b) 'Transitional Justice in a New Era', *Fordham International Law Journal*, 26 (4): 893–906.

Theidon, K. (2006) 'Justice in Transition: The Micropolitics of Reconciliation in Postwar Peru', *Journal of Conflict Resolution*, 60 (3): 433–457.

Thigpen, M., Keiser, G. and Barajas, E. (eds) (1996) *Community Justice: Striving for Safe, Secure, and Just Communities*. US Department of Justice, National Institute of Correction.

Thompson, W. and Mulholland, B. (1995) 'Paramilitary Punishments and Young People in West Belfast', in L. Kennedy (ed.), *Crime and Punishment in West Belfast*. Belfast, West Belfast: Summer School.

Toews, B. and Katounas, J. (2004) 'Have Offender Needs and Perspectives Been Adequately Incorporated into Restorative Justice?', in H. Zehr and B. Toews (eds), *Critical Issues in Restorative Justice*. Monsey, NY and Cullompton: Criminal Justice Press/Willan Publishing, 107–118.

Tombs, S. and Hillyard, P. (2004) 'Towards a Political Economy of Harm: States, Corporations and the Production of Inequality', in P. Hillyard, C. Pantazis, S. Tombs and D. Gordon (eds), *Beyond Criminology: Taking Harm Seriously*. Black Point, Nova Scotia: Fernwood Publishing, 30–54.

Tonge, J. (1998) *Northern Ireland: Conflict and Change*. London: Prentice Hall.

Torpey, J. (ed.) (2003) *Politics and the Past: On Repairing Historical Injustices*. Oxford: Rowman and Littlefield.

Touval, D. and Zartman, W. (1985) *International Mediation in Theory and Practice*. Monsey, NY: Willow Tree Press.

Tutu, D. (1999) *No Future Without Forgiveness*. New York: Random House.
Tyler, T.R. (1990) *Why People Obey the Law*. New Haven, CT and London: Yale University Press.

Umbreit, M.S. (1995) 'Holding Juvenile Offenders Accountable: A Restorative Justice Perspective', *Juvenile and Family Court Journal*, 46 (2): 31–42.
Umbreit, M.S. (2000) *Guidelines for Victim–Sensitive Victim-Offender Mediation: Restorative Justice Through Dialogue*. St. Paul, MN: Centre for Restorative Justice and Peacemaking, School of Social Work, University of Minnesota.
Uvin, P. and Mironko, C. (2003) 'Western and Local Approaches to Justice in Rwanda', *Global Government*, 9: 219–231.

Van Ness, D. (1993) 'New Wine and Old Wineskins: Four Challenges of Restorative Justice', *Criminal Law Forum*, 4 (2): 251–276.
Van Ness, D., Morris, A. and Maxwell, G. (2001) 'Introducing Restorative Justice', in A. Morris and G. Maxwell (eds), *Restorative Justice for Juveniles: Conferencing, Mediation and Circles*. Oxford: Hart Publishing, 3–12.
Van Ness, D. and Strong, K. (1997) *Restoring Justice*. Cincinnati, OH: Anderson.
Van Ness, D. and Strong, K. (2002) *Restoring Justice* (2nd edn). Cincinnati, OH: Anderson Publishing.
Van Tongeren, P. (ed.) (2005) *People Building Peace II: Successful Stories of Civil Society*. London: Lynne Rienner.
Van Zyl, P. (1999) 'Dilemmas of Transitional Justice: The Case of South Africa's Truth and Reconciliation Commission', *Journal of International Affairs*, 52:
Verwimp, P. and Verpoorten, M. (2004) 'What Are All the Soldiers Going to Do? Demobilisation, Reintegration and Employment in Rwanda', *Conflict, Security and Development*, 4 (1): 39–57.
Villa Vincencio, C. (1999) 'A Different Kind of Justice: The South African Truth and Reconciliation Commission', *Contemporary Justice Review*, 1: 407–429.
Villa Vincencio, C. (2006) 'Transitional Justice, Restoration, and Prosecution', in D. Sullivan and L. Tifft (eds), *The Handbook of Restorative Justice: A Global Perspective*. London and New York: Routledge, 387–400.
Vogelman, L. and Lewis, S. (1993) 'Gang Rape and the Culture of Violence in South Africa', *Der Überblick*, 2: 39–42.
von Hirsch, A. and Ashworth, A. (eds) (2000) *Principled Sentencing: Readings on Theory and Policy* (2nd edn). Oxford: Hart Publishing.
von Hirsch, A., Bottoms, A.E., Burney, E. and Wikstrom, P. (1999) *Criminal Deterrence and Sentence Severity: An Analysis of Recent Research*. Oxford: Hart Publishing.

Wachtel, T. and McCold, P. (2000) 'Restorative Justice in Everyday Life', in J. Braithwaite and H. Strang (eds), *Restorative Justice and Civil Society*. Cambridge: Cambridge University Press, 117–125.
Waldorf, L. (2006) 'Rwanda's Failing Experiment in Restorative Justice', in D. Sullivan and L. Tifft (eds), *The Handbook of Restorative Justice: A Global Perspective*. London and New York: Routledge, 422–434.

Walgrave, L. (1995) 'Restorative Justice for Juveniles: Just a Technique or a Fully Fledged Alternative?', *Howard Journal*, 34 (3): 228–249.

Walgrave, L. (1998) *Restorative Justice for Juveniles: Potentials, Risks, and Problems for Research*. Leuven: Leuven University Press.

Walgrave, L. (2000) 'How Can a Maximalist Approach to Restorative Justice Remain? Or Can a Purist Model of Restorative Justice Become Maximalist?', *Contemporary Justice Review*, 3 (4): 415–432.

Walgrave, L. (2003) 'Restorative Justice for Juveniles: Just a Technique or a Fully Fledged Alternative?', in G. Johnstone (ed.), *A Restorative Justice Reader: Texts, Sources, Context*. Cullompton: Willan Publishing, 255–269.

Walgrave, L. (2007) 'Integrating Criminal Justice and Restorative Justice', in G. Johnstone and D. Van Ness (eds), *Handbook of Restorative Justice*. Cullompton: Willan Publishing, 559–579.

Weitekamp, E. and Kerner, H.J. (eds) (2002) *Restorative Justice: Theoretical Foundations*. Cullompton: Willan Publishing.

Whyte, J. (1991) *Interpreting Northern Ireland*. Oxford: Clarendon Press.

Wilmott, P. (1987) *Policing and the Community*. London: Policy Studies Institute.

Wilson, J.Q. and Kelling, G.L. (1982) 'Broken Windows: The Police and Neighborhood Safety', *Atlantic Monthly*, 249: 29–38.

Wilson, R.A. (2001) *The Politics of Truth and Reconciliation in South Africa: Legitimizing the Post-Apartheid State*. Cambridge: Cambridge University Press.

Winston, T. (1997) 'Alternatives to Punishment Beatings and Shootings in a Loyalist Community in Belfast', *Critical Criminology: An International Journal*, 8 (1): 122–128.

Wright, J. and Bryett, K. (2001) *Policing and Conflict in Northern Ireland*. New York: Palgrave Macmillan.

Zehr, H. (1990) *Changing Lenses: A New Focus for Crime and Justice*. Scottsdale, PA: Herald Press.

Zehr, H. and Mika, H. (1998) 'Fundamental Concepts of Restorative Justice', *Contemporary Justice Review*, 1 (1): 47–55.

Zehr, H. and Mika, H. (2003) 'Fundamental Concepts of Restorative Justice', in E. McLaughlin, R. Fergusson, G. Hughes and L. Westmarland (eds), *Restorative Justice: Critical Issues*. London: Sage, 40–43.

Zehr, H. and Toews, B. (eds) (2004) *Critical Issues in Restorative Justice*. Monsey, NY and Cullompton: Criminal Justice Press/Willan Publishing.

Index

Abel, R. 12, 34
Abrahams, R. 49, 50, 51
Accountability in Restorative Justice 4
Achilles, M. 9
Ahmed, E. 1, 8
Alternatives
  background 52, 59–60
  bottom-up approach 76, 141
  change of perception of 73–6
  community development
    initiatives 104–5
  community-state relations 143–8
  consultation process 65–6
  cooperation with police 97, 163,
    167–79
  differences among projects 80
  establishment of 65–8
  ex-prisoners and 129–31, 132–3
  holistic approach 182–3
  Justice Oversight Reports 198–200
  opposition to 134
  personal experiences of 100–1
  preventative work 101–3
  procedure 98–9
  recommendation for government
    accreditation 154, 204
  reducing punishment violence 96
  referrals 96
  remit of practice 68–9, 96–7, 114,
    185

role of armed groups and 112–13
state funding 119, 151
suspicions of motives of 70–3
training 124
victim intervention 103–4
volunteers 123, 124–5, 127–9
youth work 96, 97–101
amnesties 19
Anderson, B. 13
Anglo-Irish Agreement 44
Anglo-Saxon legal powers 35
Annan, Kofi 129
anti-social behaviour
  alternative ways of addressing 42
  community responsibilities in
    relation to 14
  focus of Alternatives work 99,
    100, 102–3
  reason for punishment attacks 37,
    39, 40, 45
  reduced community reliance on
    paramilitaries 118
  vigilante actions 49
Ashworth, A. 3, 10, 23
Auld, J. 24, 35, 36, 39, 42, 60, 65, 81,
  86, 91, 116, 133, 158n

'B Specials' 50, 57n
Babo-Soares, D. 134
Barton, C. 2, 7, 127

Base 2 90–1
Bauman, Z. 12, 29
Bazemore, G. 3, 7, 14, 16, 17, 20, 23,
    134, 144, 184
Beetham, D. 164, 189
Bell, C. 35, 36, 37, 40, 91, 148
Belloni, R. 18
Blagg, H. 27
Bleiker, R. 28
Blue Book 60–1, 116, 157, 197
Bolton, S. 51, 52
Borer, T.A. 9
bottom-up approach 20, 28, 47, 48,
    112, 178, 183, 185
  to Alternatives 76, 141
  bridge building and community
      partnerships 141–8, 190
  to CRJI 61, 141
Bourgois, P. 107
Boutellier, H. 18
Bowyer Bell, J. 44
Boyes-Watson, C. 147, 179
Braithwaite, J. 1, 3, 4, 5, 6, 7, 8, 9,
    12, 13, 15, 23, 77, 91, 100, 125, 139,
    146, 188, 191
Brehon law 35
Brewer, J. D. 20, 30
bridge building, state and community
    28, 140
  from above 148–58
  from below 141–8, 184, 190
'broken windows' thesis 29
Bruce, S. 37, 41, 43, 44, 68, 195
Bryett, K. 161
Burman, S. 35
Bursik, R. 20, 29
Burton, F. 39, 41

Cain, M. 49, 179
Campbell, C. 9, 17
Candio, P. 28
Cartwright, J. 18, 24, 25, 110, 119,
    140, 160
Chayes, A. 17
Chayes, A.H. 17
Cherif Bassiouni, M. 32n
Chivers, Kit 144, 154, 158n
Christie, N. 1, 4, 8

Christmas reintegration 92–3
Citizen Defence Committees 39
Clear, T. 13, 14, 31, 109, 148
Cochrane, A. 13
Cohen, A.P. 12, 13, 30
Cohen, D. 107
Cohen, S. 96
Colin, West Belfast 83–4, 87
community
  contested concept of 11–16, 28,
      54–5
  in the transitional society 29–32
  practices of conflict resolution
      114–19
  reactions to restorative justice
      70–7
  state-community partnerships
      139–58
Community Charter 61–5, 117
community crime 176
  control and prevention 20, 28, 29,
      149, 183
community education 64, 74, 125,
    127, 133, 177
Community Peace Programme 25
'community policing' 161, 164
community practices of conflict
    resolution 114–19
Community Restorative Justice
    Ireland (CRJI)
  background 52, 59–65
  case studies 86–9
  change in perception of 73–7
  community-state relations 141–7
  cooperation with police 70, 135,
      167–80
  differences among projects 80
  dissatisfaction with 134
  draft Community Charter 61–3
  endorsement of Republican
      movement 68, 69
  establishment of 59–60
  ex-prisoners and 129–31, 132–3
  existing community networks and
      185
  Justice Oversight Reports 199–200
  outcomes 85–6
  pilot projects 197

process 82–5
recommendation for government
    accreditation 154–6
referrals to 81–2
reintegration work 91–5
remit of practice 69–70, 81, 114
role of armed groups and 112–14
state funding 119, 151, 204
statistics for 2007 83–5
suspicions of motives of 70–3
training 124
volunteers 123, 124–9
community service 7, 100, 115, 120n
Community Watch 51–3, 70, 81
compensation 19, 85
conferencing 82–3, 95 see also family
    group conferencing
conflict resolution, practices of in the
    community 114–19
Continuity IRA (CIRA) 134, 193
Conway, P. 36, 39, 41, 43, 44, 68,
    158n
Corrado, R.R. 1
Cottino, A. 107
Crawford, A. 9, 12, 13, 14, 18, 20,
    23, 29, 31, 43, 51, 52, 109, 128, 129,
    139, 146, 184, 186
crime
    alternative ways of addressing 42
    community responsibilities in
        relation to 14
    control and prevention of 11, 49,
        50, 107, 171, 183, 186
    informal social control 29–30
    lack of consensus on definition
        11, 170–1
    personal/community injury 4, 11
    reason for punishment attacks 37,
        39, 40, 45
    reduced community reliance on
        paramilitaries 118
    rising levels of organised 22
    vigilante actions 49
crime rates, during Northern Ireland
    conflict 30
Criminal Justice Review 150, 198
criminology, emergence of 21–4,
    190–1

CRJI see Community Restorative
    Justice Ireland
Crocker, D.A. 18, 19
culture of violence 22, 34, 48, 105,
    106–14
    leadership in a 123–37
    learned through socialisation
        108
    in Northern Ireland 107–14
    sustaining factors 110, 118
    young people 110–11
Cunneen, C. 12, 27
Cunningham, M. 140
Curle, A. 107
Cusack, J. 43, 44, 68, 137n, 195, 196

Dáil Courts 36, 39, 55n
Daly, K. 1, 2, 8, 9, 13, 85
Darby, J. 106, 107, 110
death threats 38, 134, 167–8
Dickinson, L.A. 19
Dignan, J. 9, 12, 71, 130
disorganised community 33, 34, 48,
    183–4, 185 see also vigilantism
Dixon, B. 22
Draft Guidelines for the Regulation of
    Community-based Restorative Justice
    Schemes 151
drugs 68, 100–101, 102, 111–12, 183,
    194
Drumbl, M.A. 18, 19, 26, 27, 119
Duff, A.R. 10
du Toit, P. 106, 110
Dyck, D. 27
Dzur, A.W. 144, 146, 148, 179, 186

Edwards, A. 23, 34
Eisnaugle, Carrie, J.N. 16, 24, 25
Ellison, G. 30, 161, 162, 180n
Elster, J. 9, 19
embedded justice 26
empowerment 16n, 23, 89, 94–5, 97,
    188
    community 146, 183, 184
    as value of restorative justice
        interventions 4, 7–8, 112, 186
    of volunteers in community
        restorative justice 124, 127

Eriksson, A. 76, 81, 123, 129, 131, 133, 137n, 140, 150, 157, 161, 184, 190
'establishment violence' 50
Etcheson, C. 18, 19
Etzioni, A. 18
Evans-Kent, B. 18
Evenson, E.M. 19, 20
exclusion/exclusionary practices 6, 7, 11, 86, 89–90, 94, 100
    community characteristics of 12, 30–1
    method of punishment violence 37, 40, 56n
ex-political prisoners, as leaders 70, 72, 106, 127, 128, 129–31, 136–7
    cause of strained relations with statutory agencies 146, 150
    concerns over suitability 152, 153
    direct dialogue with paramilitary groups 81
    moving towards acceptance of police 178
    status of 135, 184
    styles of leadership 131–5

face-to-face meetings 82, 100
family group conferencing 3, 5, 80
    see also conferencing
Farrow, K. 51, 52
Feenan, D. 35, 37, 40, 41, 56, 89, 91, 148, 170
Ferme, M.C. 106
Fitzpatrick, P. 179
follow up, of cases 80, 87, 182–3
former combatants, as leaders 70, 72, 106, 128, 129–31, 136–7, 157
    cause of strained relations with statutory agencies 146, 150
    concerns over suitability 152, 153
    direct dialogue with paramilitary groups 81
    moving towards acceptance of police 178
    styles of leadership 131–5, 184
Foster, J. 13, 20, 30,
Froestad, J. 24, 25, 28, 119

Gaarder, E. 8
gacaca system 24, 26–7
Galaway, B. 11
Garland, D. 20, 23
Gastil, R.D. 107
Geary, R. 30
Gillespie, Judith 168
Goldstone, R.J. 19, 20
Good Friday Agreement 40, 44, 47, 52, 57n, 120n, 153, 198
Govier, T. 9
Grabosky, P.N. 105
Graham, B. 44
Grasmick, H. 20, 29
grass-roots approaches 20, 24, 25, 26, 28, 61, 70, 74, 76, 82, 106, 112, 119, 128, 141
Gready, P. 18, 20, 26, 27
Groff, L. 108
Groves, B.W. 29

Hagan, F.E. 55
Hamber, B. 25, 107
Hamill, H. 37, 57n, 116
harm 11
    difficulty defining 11, 170–1
    repairing 1, 7, 8, 10, 23, 85
Harper, E. 19
Harris, K.M. 188
Hayes, B.C. 106, 162
Hayes, H. 1, 8
Hayner, P.B. 24, 32n
Hezlet, A.R. 57n
Higgins, J. 110, 111
Hillyard, P. 43, 55n
Hoggett, P. 54, 161
'hoods' 42, 45, 116, 117, 132, 136
Hope, T. 20, 30
Howse, R. 12, 28
Hudson, J. 11
Hughes, G. 13, 23, 29, 34, 139, 184
human rights abuses 17, 18, 22
Humphrey, M. 19, 20
hybrid tribunals 19

IMPACT project 68, 80
informal justice 33–55
    historical overview 34–6

in transitional societies 31
paramilitary justice 36–48
vigilantism 48–55
informal social control 29–30, 32,
33–4, 39, 53, 90, 109, 113, 114, 147
contest over ownership of 70
continuing use of violence for
107, 108
International Criminal Court (ICC)
19
International Criminal Tribunal for
Rwanda (ICTR) 19, 26
International Criminal Tribunal for
the Former Yugoslavia (ICTY) 19
International Monitoring Commission
149
intimidation 53, 78n, 89, 90, 195
IRA
acceptability of police 164–5, 176
ceasefires 39, 197
change in communitty perception
of 42
community policing by 39
Continuity IRA (CIRA) 134, 193
Dáil Courts 36
decommissioning of 201
disbandment of Provisional 168
hunger strikes 55n
informal justice 39–40, 41
non-violent approach 51–2, 53–4
Official IRA (OIRA) 193
organised communities 29–30,
33–4
Provisional described 192–3
punishment violence by 37–8, 45,
46, 56n
Real IRA (RIRA) 134, 194
support for CJRI 69, 72–3
Irish National Liberation Army
(INLA) 194
Irish War of Independence 36

Jantzi, V. 147
Jarman, N. 32, 37, 41, 89, 91, 107,
109, 110
Jenneker, M. 18, 24, 25
Johnston, L. 49, 50
Johnstone, G. 2, 3, 4, 6, 8, 14, 17, 187

Justice and Community Development
160

Kaminski, M. 19
Karp, D. 148
Katounas, J. 10
Katzenstein, S. 19
Kennedy, L. 56
Kerner, H.J. 4
Knight, M. 134
Knox, C. 44, 46, 48, 81, 106, 107, 115,
129, 149, 152
Kotsonouris, M. 36
Kynoch, G. 106

labelling of participants 9, 89, 125
Lebow, R.N. 50
Leebaw, B. 16, 24, 25, 136
Leisenring, A. 16
Levrant, S. 128
Lewis, S. 106
Little, D. 18, 19
Llewellyn, J. 12, 24, 28
Loyalist communities
punishment violence in 43–5
vigilante action in 53
Loyalist Volunteer Force (LVF) 195–6
lustration 19

MacGarry, J. 31, 162
MacGinty, R. 106, 107, 110
macro-communities 15
Maguire, Harry 159n
Maguire, M. 46, 57n
Mallinder, L. 18, 19
Mani, R. 19, 22, 129, 140, 160
Marshall, T.F. 5, 14, 123
Martin, O. 110
Matthews, R. 12, 179
Matza, D. 125
Maxwell, G. 3, 4, 82
McAllister, I. 106, 162
McAuley, J.W. 108, 195
McCold, P. 4, 13, 14, 15, 25, 85, 128
McCoy, G. 40
McDonald, H. 43, 44, 68, 137n, 195,
196
McDonald, J. 187

McElrath, K. 111
McEvoy, K. 8, 18, 19, 20, 21, 22, 23,
  24, 30, 32n, 35, 37, 42, 44, 47, 48,
  55n, 59, 60, 61, 64, 65, 68, 69, 72,
  74, 76, 77n, 81, 89, 91, 96, 110, 112,
  123, 129, 131, 133, 136, 137n, 140,
  148, 150, 157, 161, 182, 184, 186,
  190, 191, 197
McGregor, L. 18, 20, 23, 32n
McKay, S. 44
McMillan, N. 20, 21, 22, 110, 186
Merry, S.E. 126, 148
micro-communities 15
Mika, H. 8, 9, 24, 35, 37, 42, 44, 47,
  48, 59, 60, 61, 64, 65, 68, 69, 74,
  81, 85, 89, 91, 94, 96, 104, 105, 112,
  114, 120n, 123, 134, 148, 150, 161,
  182, 184
military leadership 132–4
Milner, N.A. 126, 148
Minow, M. 16, 18, 24
Mironko, C. 26, 27
Mitchell, C. 162
Monaghan, R. 35, 36, 37, 39, 40, 44,
  45, 46, 48, 65, 81, 89, 106, 107, 111,
  115, 129, 149
Moore, D. 82, 187
moral leadership and community
  building 134–7
Morison, J. 30
Morris, A. 3
Morrissey, M. 39, 40, 41, 65
Mugford, S. 3, 4, 91, 100
Mulcahy, A. 18, 158, 161, 180n
Mulholland, B. 39, 40, 41, 45, 56n
multi-agency approach 48
Muncie, J. 57n
Munck, R. 37, 39, 40, 41, 45
Murtagh, B. 30, 31, 32, 44, 108

Napoleon, V. 25
neighbour disputes 53, 83, 85, 86,
  156
Nelken, D. 11
Nelson, S. 195
Nesbitt, R. 107
Neuffer, E. 28
Newburn, T. 9, 22, 110, 128, 186, 191

Neumann, R.P. 9, 22, 110, 128, 186,
  191
Nina, D. 19
Nolan, P.C. 40, 56n
Northern Ireland Alternatives (NIA)
  see Alternatives
Northern Ireland Housing Executive
  89, 90–1, 144–5, 147
Northern Ireland Office (NIO) 151,
  160, 204
Northern Ireland Select Committee
  149
Nowrojee, B. 17, 26, 27, 28

O'Connell, T. 82
O'Doherty, M. 193
offenders in restorative justice 10–11
Official IRA (OIRA) 193
O'Leary, B. 31, 137, 162
Olson, S.M. 144, 146, 148, 179, 186
O'Mahony, D. 17, 30
Opportunity Youth 101, 120n
organised community 33–4, 41,
  183–4, 185 see also punishment
  violence
Ozerdam, A. 134

Pankhurst, D. 27
paramilitary groups 192–6
  changing attitudes within 53–4,
    113, 115
  link to drug trade 111
  young people joining 110–12, 168
paramilitary justice see punishment
  violence
participation 5, 85
  community 28, 146, 187
  voluntary nature of 89
Patten Report 57n, 162–3, 180n
Pavlich, G. 2, 8, 9, 10–11, 12, 14, 16n,
  18, 71, 129
peace walls 31, 32n, 108
Pease, K. 39, 40, 41, 65
Pelikan, C. 123
People's Courts 39
Pepinsky, H.E. 187
personalism 4, 186
persuasion, process of 133–4

Peru 24, 26
police
    beginning of community-police
        partnerships 168–80
    building relationships with CRJI
        and Alternatives 135, 144
    dissident threats to 167–8
    legitimacy of 162–8
    loyalist relationship with 43–4,
        97, 163
    republican relationship with 143,
        156, 164–6, 167–8
    role in origins of informal justice
        36–7
    Sinn Féin's endorsement of PSNI
        144, 148, 162, 164, 165
    statistics of violence 45–7, 53
    synonymous with violence 161
political leadership 131–2
political parties
    concern over suitability of staff
        153
    misgivings about community
        restorative justice 70n, 150, 151
Pranis, K. 7, 9, 14, 16n, 60, 61, 80,
    183
Presser, L. 8
Prior, D. 51, 52
Protocols 157, 160, 190, 200, 202,
    203
    bureaucratic nature of 169
    formulation and publication of
        151–2
    key areas of concern 152
    key features of revised 152–4
    recommendation for accreditation
        154
    several attempts to draft 149–50
    what constitutes a crime 170
Protocol for Community-Based
    Restorative Justice Schemes 151,
    154, 203
Provisional IRA see IRA
'Provo police stations' 39
Public Prosecution Service (PPS) 152,
    169–70
punishment violence 36–48, 55n,
    56n, 96, 116, 197

extent of in Northern Ireland
    45–8
methods of 37
newspaper reports 37–8
origins of 36–7
practices in Loyalist communities
    43–5
practices in Republican
    communities 39–42
reasons for 37
statistics 45–8
Putnam, R.D. 134, 146, 184

Quinney, R. 187

Real IRA (RIRA) 134, 194
reintegration 4, 6–7, 19, 22, 35, 45,
    85, 89–95, 100 see also Christmas
    reintegration
reparation 4, 5–6, 7, 35, 85, 112
Republican communities
    Community Restorative Justice
        Ireland (CRJI) 60–4
    punishment violence in 39–42
restoration 6, 9
restorative justice
    community reactions to 70–7
    contested community 11–16
    definition 1–3
    establishment of in Northern
        Ireland 59–68
    implementation of in transitional
        societies 24–32
    offenders in 9–10
    paramilitaries and 68–70
    practice of 80–119
    values and goals of 3–8
    victims in 8–9
Rigby, A. 18
ripple effect 74, 77, 112, 118, 126,
    132, 133
Ritchie, M. 197
Roach, K. 1
Roberts, P. 20, 21, 22, 26, 110, 119,
    186
Roche, D. 1, 2, 3, 4, 5, 6, 8, 14, 17,
    18, 19, 24, 25, 28, 82, 119, 124, 128,
    186

Rosenbaum, H.J. 49, 50, 57n
Royal Ulster Constabulary (RUC) 39, 57n, 161, 162
Ruane, J. 31, 162
Rubio, M. 107
Rupesinghe, K. 107
Ruth-Heffelbower, D. 17
Rwanda genocide 24, 26, 27

Safer Neighbourhood Schemes 51–3, 70, 155, 171
Sampson, R.J. 29, 184
Schabas, W.A. 19, 20
Scharf, W. 35
Schiff, M. 23, 134, 144, 184
SDLP, concerns over community restorative justice 71, 78n, 151–2, 154
secret societies 35
Sederberg, P.C. 49, 50, 57n
self-help, tradition of 142, 185
Shankill 32n, 65, 67, 73, 78n, 80
Sharpe, S. 4
Shearing, C. 18, 24, 25, 28, 110, 119
Shining Path rebellion 26
Shirlow, P. 30, 31, 32n, 44, 108
shuttle mediation 82, 95
Silke, A. 41, 43, 46, 56n, 111, 129
Simpson, G. 110
Sinn Féin 55n, 71, 134, 144, 151, 152, 174, 193, 203
    endorsement of PSNI 148, 162, 164, 165
    establishment of Dáil Courts 36, 55n
    establishment of 'Provo police stations' 39
Skelton, A. 24
Skogan, W.C. 105
Sluka, J.A. 28, 162
Smoker, P. 108
Smyth, J. 161, 162, 180n
Smyth, M. 9
South Africa 24–5, 27
Sparks, R. 20, 23, 164
state-community trust 139–50
    bridge building from above 148–58

bridge building from below 141–8
statutory agencies
    cooperation complicated 146–7
    and ex-prisoners 130, 131, 135, 146, 153
    informal partnerships with community restorative justice projects 73–4
    less complicated relationship with Alternatives 145, 163
    misgivings about community restorative justice 150
    suspicion of by communities 48, 142–3
    suspicion of community schemes by 150–1
    utilised by CRJI and Alternatives 144
Staub, E. 107
Steenkamp, C. 22, 34, 106, 107, 108, 109, 110, 185
Stevenson, J. 196
Strang, H. 1, 5, 7, 8, 9, 13, 17, 104
Strong, K. 4, 5, 6
Stuart, B. 16n, 80, 183
Sullivan, D. 1, 4, 5, 149, 187
Sunshine, J. 7, 164
Sykes, G.M. 125

Taylor, M. 46
Taylor, P. 43, 193, 195, 196
Teitel, R. 16, 18, 24
The Symbolic Construction of Community 11
Theidon, K. 26
Thigpen, M. 74
Thompson, W. 39, 40, 41, 45, 56n
Tifft, L. 1, 4, 5, 149, 187
Todd, J. 31, 162
Toews, B. 10, 147
Tombs, S. 11
top-down approaches 18, 20, 25, 27, 47, 61, 183
    bridge building and community partnerships 148–58
Torpey, J. 18
Touval, D. 4

transformative justice 105, 119, 146,
  183, 187–8, 189
transitional justice
  approaches to 18–21
  definition of 18
  emergence of criminology 21–4
transitional societies
  community in 29–32
  culture of violence in 105, 110
  implementation of restorative
    justice principles in 24–8
Trenczek, T. 123
trials and prosecutions 19
truth commissions 19–20, 32n
Truth and Reconciliation Commission
  (TRC) 19, 25
Tutu, D. 1, 8
Tyler, T.R. 7, 164

Ulster Defence Association (UDA)
  29, 37, 48, 66, 78n, 194–5
Ulster Volunteer Force (UVF)
  description of 195
  ex-combatants and Alternatives
    132–3
  non-violent approach 51–2, 54
  organised communities 33–4
  punishment attacks 37
  referrals to Alternatives 96
  response to Alternatives 66, 68,
    69, 71, 78n
  weapons beyond use 121n, 204
  youth work 97–8, 100–1
Umbreit, M.S. 1, 3, 4, 17
Uvin, P. 26, 27

van der Spuy, Elrena 22
Van Ness, D. 1, 2, 3, 4, 5, 6, 17, 82
Van Tongeren, P. 18
Van Zyl, P. 25
Verpoorten, M. 134
Verwimp, P. 134

Verwoerd, W. 9
victim–offender mediation 3, 5, 80,
  83, 99, 103, 120n
victims
  and community development
    work 103–5
  in restorative justice 8–9
vigilantism 31, 33, 48–55
  defining 49–51
  in Northern Ireland 51–5
Villa Vincencio, C. 18, 24, 28
violence see cultures of violence
Vogelman, L. 106
volunteers see Alternatives;
  Community Restorative Justice
  Ireland (CRJI)
von Hirsch, A. 23

Wachtel, T. 13, 128
Waldorf, L. 24, 26, 27, 119
Walgrave, L. 1, 2, 3, 7, 8, 16n, 85,
  149
Watters, Debbie 67, 159n, 198
Weitekamp, E. 4
Whyte, J. 77n
Wilmott, P. 13
Wilson, J.Q. 29
Wilson, R.A. 25
Winston, T. 24, 37, 43, 65, 67, 68, 69,
  77n, 96, 111, 130, 133, 159n, 182,
  184, 197, 198
women, punishment violence against
  41
Wright, Billy 195
Wright, J. 161

Youth Initiative 84
Youth Justice Agency 98, 100, 120n
youth-related disputes 83, 85

Zartman, W. 4
Zehr, H. 1, 2, 5, 9, 85, 147, 187